Ollie Walls
910 Jac...
Pe...
73077

Please read and return.

IN THIS LAND

I Have Planted Thee

IN THIS LAND

The story of the first 25 years of
Southern Baptist missions in Alaska

by
Naomi Ruth Hunke

ALASKA BAPTIST CONVENTION
Anchorage, Alaska

IN THIS LAND

Library of Congress catalog card number: 75-142782
Printed in the United States of America

Acknowledgments

To the Alaska Baptist Convention for use of back issues of the *Alaska Baptist Messenger*, Minutes of the Executive Board, Minutes of the Executive Committee, and Minutes of the annual convention sessions

To the Woman's Missionary Union of the Alaska Baptist Convention for resource and state missions materials

To the Southern Baptist Convention Home Mission Board for use of pictures and articles from *Home Missions*

To Richard A. Miller for use of his fifteen year history of Southern Baptists in Alaska

To Louise Yarbrough for the history of Woman's Missionary Union in Alaska

To Mabel Cary for use of Orland Cary's files and his notes on Tom Willock

To Mrs. Wilma Jenkins for use of Hilda Krause's letters

To Mr. and Mrs. L. A. Watson, Dr. and Mrs. J. T. Spurlin, and Dr. and Mrs. Felton Griffin for tapes and materials

To Mr. Marion Dunham, Mrs. Opal Miller, Mrs. Dee Johnson, Miss Valeria Sherard, and Miss Judy Rice for tapes

To the pastors and church clerks who helped compile material and to all who helped type the manuscript

And to my husband, E. W. Hunke, Jr., executive secretary of the Alaska Baptist Convention, for picture layout and constant encouragement and help, I acknowledge my sincere appreciation.

Naomi Ruth Hunke
May 1970

"Yea, I will rejoice over them to do them good, and I will plant them in this land assuredly with my whole heart and with my whole soul."

JEREMIAH 32:41

Contents

Introduction

Trying to finish writing this history in time to leave for the 1970 Southern Baptist Convention in Denver gave me nightmares. My most recent one went like this:

My husband and I were already at Denver doing a bit of conventioneering in the hallway when a preacher in a big hat and boots walked up and spoke to us.

"Preacher," he said, "where yaw'l from?"

Now, Alaska is the only thing in the world that can make a Texan humble, so instead of saying "Texas," as he ordinarily would have done, my husband replied, "Alaska."

"Well, I pastor down in Texas. Greatest state in the union. You can take all of New England and throw in Mississippi too, and they'll fit into just a little corner of Texas," the big-hatted one announced.

"Pardon me, Preacher," my husband interrupted, trying to save the Texas brother from embarrassing himself, "I said I'm from Alaska, more than twice the size of Texas, one-fifth the size of the whole United States. Why, man, we've got five thousand glaciers and icefields in Alaska, more than all the rest of the inhabited world put together. That makes twenty thousand square miles of ice; one of our glaciers, the Malaspina, is larger than the state of Rhode Island."

The Texan gave him a stare that looked as if it came straight off one of those glaciers, and continued, "As I was saying, you can't think of a thing Texas hasn't got. We've got four hundred miles of coastline . . ."

"Four hundred miles!" My husband roared with laughter while I tried to find an exhibit to hide behind. "Alaska has 33,904 miles of coastline—more than all the rest of the United States coastline combined. Did you know Juneau is further from Pt. Barrow than .

Seattle is from Mexico and further from Dutch Harbor than San Francisco is from New York City? And, I'll tell you something else; Semisopochnoi Island in the Aleutians is the farthest eastern point in the United States because it stretches across the one-hundred eightieth meridian, and at the same time Amatignak Island is the farthest west point in the United States because it lies just twenty miles this side of the one-hundred eightieth meridian. Besides that, we have two oceans, one sea, and so many straits, fiords, gulfs, and bays that no one has ever bothered to count them, together with seven million acres of fresh water lakes . . ."

"Let me tell you about our mountains," the Texan tried to continue. "There's El Capitan in the Guadalupes, nine thousand feet high. That's thousands of feet higher than anything down South."

"Fellow," Bill Hunke returned, "that's just a little foothill. If you want a real he-man's mountain, take Mount McKinley. That old ermine shouldered gal is 20,320 feet high; that makes her about 11,280 feet higher than anything you've got down in—what's the name of that place?"

"And," the Texan went on, unabashed, "there's the old Rio Grande. What a river!"

"Think of the Yukon. It's two thousand miles long, and nobody ever jumped across any part of it. And did you know our continental shelf spans over 550,000 square miles, and from it Alaska could produce six billion pounds of fish a year. Then too, Alaska is the air crossroads of the world. We have flights to the Orient and over the North Pole to Europe. Brigadier General Billy Mitchell said in 1935 that he believed he who held Alaska would hold the world because he thought it was the most important strategic place in all the world."

That Texas preacher was beginning to get green around the gills, but the poor soul couldn't seem to hush his mouth. "We've got oil and gas and gold and silver and lead in Texas," he went on.

"Alaska has all those, and *our* oil reserve is believed to be the largest in the world, and we have the only tin deposit in the United States and some of the largest iron and copper deposits, besides platinum, sulphur, tungsten, coal, antimony, pellacium, pitchblend, mercury, and one of the largest ammonia and urea plants on the West Coast . . ."

"And there isn't anything we can't grow in Texas. Did you ever see a Texas watermelon?"

"Yes," Bill responded, "about half the size of a Matanuska cabbage. Richest land in the world, that Matanuska Valley. They raise peas and lettuce there that are so tender even a dirty look will bruise them."

"But what we're really known for," the Texan came back, "is our men. It takes real men to live in Texas. Did you ever hear of those Blue Northers that rip down through our Panhandle?"

"Why, those are just baby Williwaws we send down there for scrimmage," was the scornful return. "We let them get up to a hundred miles per hour down there before they come back up to Alaska and work out on real men. We're still young enough to give 'em a good rassle. Our median age is just 23.3 years old, and there's room to work up a real blow in Alaska because we have two square miles for every person up there."

When he paused for breath, Texas muttered something about wondering how Alaska ever got in the union anyhow, which just set Bill Hunke off again.

"You should have been there when Alaska was voted in. In Fairbanks they dyed the Chena River gold and floated a fifty foot gold star suspended by giant balloons overhead. People all over the state laughed and cried, shouted and shook hands with strangers in the streets; church bells pealed, sirens screamed, and in Anchorage a fifty-ton bonfire blazed. When we got in, the federal government held 99.8% of our land. As Secretary of the Interior, Wally Hickel has charge of ten times as much of Alaska today as he had as Governor of the state . . ."

The Texas boots had already slinked away with the owner mumbling something about loudmouths and braggarts. I came out of hiding and was shaking my former Texan husband's coat tail, when I awoke to find the bed shaking with another of our little run-of-the-mill earthquakes. "Thank goodness he didn't get started telling how many earthquakes we have, the Northern Lights, and the great hunting and fishing, and how cold it gets, and how much fun our legislature had this year playing around with a $900,000,000 oil lease bonanza, and a million other things," I thought rather grimly. "And there's our miraculous Baptist history he could have gotten wound up on." But that's where I came in.

1

". . . The Door of Faith . . ."

Acts 14:27

Alaska, "Great Land," full of wonder and splendor, fitting reflection of God's majesty, when I gaze into your star-studded skies
or attempt to comprehend your vast distances, I can but con-
template with amazement my Creator's concern for me, his choosing
me to carry on his creative activity.

When Miss Hilda Krause first came to Juneau in 1934, she paid
no attention to the gulls that seemed to be flying cover for the
sandpipers on the beach, even when they made sudden swoops to
snatch a fish from a careless tern, leaving the bird complaining
angrily. Neither did she notice the whistling wind tugging at her
hair, whipping it as though it would yank it out by the roots.

Instead, she eagerly lifted her eyes from the sparkling sapphire
waters of the Inland Passage dotted with green-forested islands
and gazed at the steep-flanked mountains that stood probing the
sky, threatening to crowd the town into the bay. Then she looked
steadfastly at the scattering of small houses clustered around the
steep road up from the wharf and dotting the hillsides beyond.
Those near the shore were built on piles to stand clear of the
tides; a plank sidewalk ran on pilings above the rutted, muddy
road into town.

As she stood grappling with the Taku wind, she thanked God
that he had put into her hands gifts to relay to the needy natives
of Juneau and into her heart the knowledge that though he had
entrusted her with tasks beyond her capabilities, he also would
supply the strength to enable her to carry out his purpose.

Once the name "Alaska" had conjured up a scene of perpetual
ice and snow and waste, but that was before the Home Mission
Society of the Northern Baptist Convention had appointed her to
serve as missionary at their orphanage on Kodiak Island. Permanent

Baptist work began in Alaska when the W. F. Roscoes came to Kodiak in 1886 and built the orphanage. Through the years an average of about seventy native children were served by the orphanage, with only two or three missionaries caring for all their needs. Miss Krause worked at the orphanage from 1923 until 1932, finally leaving for three reasons: ministry to the physical needs of the children did not leave enough time for ministry to their spiritual needs; doctrinal disagreements with the Northern Baptists; and the invitation of friends in Juneau who felt there should be a Baptist church there in spite of its being outside the area allotted to Baptists.

"I trusted in the Lord to take care of me," wrote Miss Krause. The Territorial Department of Public Health paid her to work at the Bethel Beach Home for needy children during her first years of service in Juneau, then in 1938 the department asked her to move into town and open a nursing home for tubercular children. She found a suitable house on Distin Avenue. As soon as it was furnished, a group of children arrived from Ketchikan and the home kept filled to capacity. Miss Krause called the home the Baptist Nursing Home and used it as a Baptist mission station, supporting it herself from the money she received from care of the children. She conducted daily Bible lessons in addition to regular Sunday school classes and worship services, and many times during 1941 the house was crowded out.

A number of the children and young people accepted Christ through her ministry. They prayed for a minister to come who could baptize them. One girl, May Davis, when she was well enough to return to Haines to live with relatives, came to Miss Krause crying because she did not want to leave Juneau without being baptized. Miss Krause wrote, "Rev. Personeus baptized her in the Gastineau Channel opposite the green house, and like the eunuch, she then went on her way rejoicing." A fourteen-year-old boy named David wrote a letter to the editor of the *Baptist Herald*, telling about the children praying for a pastor who could baptize them and a "real" Baptist church for them to belong to. The letter was published in the *Baptist Herald*, causing many letters to come from people who promised to join the group in their prayers.

One outstanding conversion was that of Alice, a Tlinget Indian girl. She was brought to the mission as a last resort before being imprisoned. Miss Krause wrote, "Alice was filthy, foul-mouthed, thieving, non-cooperative, and an altogether unlovely nine-year-old who had known no home except in immoral dives." After scrubbing and de-lousing her, Miss Krause set about persuading Alice to go to school. Under protest, she was escorted to and from school by some of the older children. Twice she ran away from school and was brought back to the mission by the police.

Weeks and finally months passed with no change in Alice. She sat frozen-faced and unresponsive during the daily Bible study periods. The other children were kind and patient with her, sharing their Bibles and song books in an attempt to arouse her interest, but Alice always thrust them rudely away. When they knelt to pray, she sat woodenly in her chair, unmoved by their prayers for her. The only thing about her that gave anyone pleasure was her ravenous appetite. Everyone watched in a kind of furtive awe as she ate three platefuls of food in the time it took the others to finish one.

Very few days passed without her bringing home items which she declared the teacher or some mysterious friend had given her, items which Miss Krause dutifully returned. She seemed to be a hopeless case and only the children's faith kept Miss Krause from giving up in despair and calling the authorities to come for her. Then one day while they were kneeling for their daily prayers, they were shocked to see Alice fall to her knees crying loudly and pitifully, "O Lord, save my miserable soul." The others stayed on their knees while Alice went on crying and gulping out her confession of sins, asking the Lord to keep her from lying and stealing and cursing any more.

A different Alice arose from her knees, one with a smile on her face for the first time. The joy in her heart was shining through the tears in her eyes as she ran from one to another of the children, hugging their necks and saying over and over, "Now I'm a Christian too. I'm just like everyone else."

A few days later Miss Krause met Alice's teacher on the street, and the first thing she asked was, "What in the world has happened to Alice? She has suddenly become such a good, cooperative, and studious child. I can't understand how it could ever happen."

Miss Krause replied that Alice had been born again, and explained how it came about. Mrs. Paul immediately exclaimed, "Well, if that's what made such a difference in a child like Alice, I wish it would happen to all the pupils in my room!"

Another child that Miss Krause called a real trophy of God's grace was eight-year-old Ellen. One day the group was visited by a representative of the Home Mission Society's headquarters in New York. After being introduced to the lady, Ellen astonished her by asking, "Are you saved?" When she received an affirmative answer, Ellen still persisted, "Do you really love the Lord Jesus?" When the lady assured her that she loved the Lord, Ellen very solemnly stated, "I was afraid maybe you didn't know how to be saved because I've never seen you at our meetings."

Another time, Ellen's unsaved father visited her in the home. She rose from her bed and got her father to kneel down beside his chair while she prayed and then pleaded for him to quit being wicked and be "born again too." Both of them wept, but he did not make a commitment to the Lord, promising instead that he would "some day." She continued to pray and live in hope of his surrender to the Lord. Meanwhile, Ellen herself kept growing spiritually. She finished high school and went away to a university in the States to prepare for a medical career.

In July 1941 the first Southern Baptist worker arrived in Juneau. Miss Frances Black had attended Southern seminary, worked in mission stations in Georgia, directed a Goodwill Center among Italians in Florida, and served many years at a children's home in Union Mills, North Carolina. She had reared two girls from the home. One of the girls had married a Mr. Frank Allen and moved to Juneau, taking Miss Black's "grandson," Frankie, with her, so when Mrs. Allen wrote back to Miss Black's home town of Fulton, Missouri, telling her of the needs of the native children of Juneau, Miss Black came. To her, nothing was so heartbreaking as the needs of little children, nothing so poignant as their cry for help; she believed that daily love for children was as necessary as daily bread, so she came to Juneau by faith, wanting to work with children and also hoping to be the means of beginning Southern Baptist work in Alaska.

She began working at the Arketa Children's Home out on the highway. Three months later a Missionary Baptist couple, Mr. and Mrs. W. P. Griffin, came from Arkansas and began holding Baptist services in their home on Gastineau Avenue. Miss Black moved in with them and began helping teach Bible studies. When Miss Krause fell on the icy street in January 1942 and had to remain in the hospital with a broken back for five months, Miss Black took charge of the nursing home and continued the worship services there.

After Miss Krause's release from the hospital, the two ladies decided to pool their resources and rent a house at 218 Main Street for a mission, with Mr. Griffin preaching the Sunday services. Miss Black moved into the rear apartment, then later Miss Krause moved into an upstairs room. The worship services were constantly well attended; Wednesday night adult Bible classes were added to the daily classes for children. In January 1943 Miss Black started a goodwill center downstairs, complete with fulltime week-day activities. She erected a sign, BAPTIST GOODWILL CENTER, and began her barrage of correspondence to the Southern Baptist Convention Home Mission Board for support of Baptist work in Alaska.

In April 1943 the Griffins left Juneau because of Mrs. Griffin's poor health. Two months later Miss Black was called back to her home in Fulton, and Miss Krause again tried to carry on alone. Problems arose at once. She wrote, "Mr. William Youngs, because of his friendship with the Griffins, and his firm conviction that Juneau was Presbyterian territory and Baptists had no right to be here, insisted on taking over the mission for interdenominational work." When she told Miss Black of the problem, Miss Black appealed to Mr. Griffin, then pastor of the Victory Missionary Baptist Church, Saskatoon, Saskatchewan, Canada, and Miss Krause received the following reply:

February 29, 1944

Yesterday I received a letter from Miss Black telling of the bother you were having with Bill Youngs and the lady wanting to use the Baptist Goodwill Center for their services.

I assure you that I heartily endorse your stand in refusing to give them permission to use it for their work, inasmuch as it is by the help of Baptist churches that you are paying the rent on that place, it naturally follows that nothing but Baptist services should be held there.

Baptists have never been interdenominational people, and, in fact, cannot be such. For one to practice such is to cease to be a Baptist . . . .

As for me giving Mr. Youngs permission to have any kind of service there, he certainly is laboring under a false impression. That place was left under the charge of Miss Black and yourself. You as a Baptist are now in full charge of the activities carried on there. . . .

I feel sure Mr. Youngs is aware of my position in this matter of interdenominational work as we have had many discussions on that subject. You may feel perfectly free to show this letter to Mr. Youngs and state this as your ground for refusing to allow the place to be used for any services except Baptist.

Nevertheless, for a year Mr. Youngs conducted the services; in June 1944 Miss Krause wrote, "I *finally* regained control of the mission."

The struggle had drained her strength, forcing her to close the mission temporarily and go to Seattle to recuperate for six weeks. In September 1944 Miss Black met her in Seattle, and together they returned to Juneau and reopened their beloved Baptist mission, again conducting daily Bible studies, Sunday school and worship services, and goodwill center activities, still without support. That month they received word that Northern Baptists were definitely making plans to send a pastor, Rev. Benke, of Alberta, Canada; he was to arrive in the spring of 1945. In the meantime they were to send him monthly reports of the progress of their work.

Miss Black, however, was determined that Southern Baptists should take the work. She continued her flow of letters to Dr. J. B. Lawrence of the Home Mission Board, writing, "I wish I were just beginning my life instead of being almost as old as President Roosevelt . . . a young couple would have so many chances to preach and work here . . . you can see how helpless we two old women are. We can't baptize or hold funerals, to say nothing of the constant preaching."

She wrote to everyone she could think of for help, including Mr. William Petty, pastor of First Baptist Church of Anchorage and editor of the *Alaska Baptist Messenger*. When the *Western Recorder*, the Kentucky Baptist paper, published an article Mr. Petty wrote about Alaska Baptists, Dr. J. T. Spurlin, who was pioneering Southern Baptist work in Michigan, read the article and wrote Mr. Petty about coming to Alaska. Mr. Petty sent him Miss Black's letter of entreaty. Upon reading of the needs in Juneau, Dr. Spurlin presented his desire to go to Alaska to his people at the Antioch Baptist Church of Detroit, Michigan. They voted to give him authority to baptize, receive members, and organize a Southern Baptist church. They also agreed to support him financially, sending their offering through the Kentucky Baptist offices since they belonged to the Grace County Baptist Association of

Kentucky. Dr. Spurlin later stated that he had wondered why the Lord led him to accept the Michigan pastorate when he really didn't want to go up there, but when the church proved willing to send mission money to Alaska, he knew that the Lord's pattern for his life was falling into place.

The ladies in Juneau were concerned with preparing a parsonage for Dr. Spurlin's arrival. Miss Black wrote to Mrs. Armstrong of Fulton, Missouri, who at that time was a member of the executive committee of the Home Mission Board, telling her that they had located a suitable home for sale by one of their group, Mrs. Albert Peterson, for only $6,000. Mrs. Armstrong presented the request to the Board; Dr. Courts Redford also submitted a telegram from Miss Black. The committee agreed that the money would be allotted the Juneau group if Northern Baptists would agree. The Northern Baptist Home Mission Society would not approve money from another Baptist group coming into Alaska, contending that they had immediate plans to establish their churches on the Alaskan mainland. To maintain their integrity and friendly relations with the Northern Baptists, the Home Mission Board refused to allocate the $6,000 to the Juneau group.

Miss Black had the work so heavily laid on her heart that she mortgaged her home in Fulton in order to make it possible for the parsonage to be bought and ready for the Spurlins. The house had two apartments. The lower was rented and the upstairs one redecorated before they arrived.

Mrs. Spurlin admitted that she was not too excited at first about the prospect of coming to Alaska, but after they boarded the *Princess Nora* at Vancouver, British Columbia, and started the trip up the Inside Passage, her excitement increased every time she saw an island of ice slide past or a volcano rear its serrated crater top through a filmy cloud scarf, until she became speechless when she saw her first glacier rearing its two-hundred-foot face in a sheer palisade of glistening white, looking like a frozen cataract transformed to dazzling brilliance by the sunshine. The milky green torrent of glacial streams cutting their way through the ice to join the blue waters of the passage made the family breathless with their beauty.

When the Spurlins arrived in Juneau on August 28, 1945, Miss Black and Miss Krause, together with a group of other women and children, were waiting for them at the end of the gangplank. Dr.

Spurlin rented the American Legion "dugout" for five dollars a Sunday, so the group had services there on Sunday, September 3, 1945. Seventeen people representing four Baptist denominations attended Sunday school, with twenty-seven attending both the morning and evening worship services; the first offering was $47.37. Dr. Spurlin said that the "dugout" was appropriately named because every Sunday morning he had to go down early to dig out all the cigar stubs, cigarette ends, beer cans, whiskey bottles, and other useless impedimenta left from the Saturday night gatherings in the hall.

Dr. Spurlin, who became pastor of Alaska's second Southern Baptist church, came from four generations of Baptist preachers in Kentucky. His great-grandfather, J. E. Spurlin, had organized more Baptist churches in Kentucky during the last century "than anyone else ever got around to doing." He died after preaching a revival at the age of eighty-nine. Though he had to sit down to preach, his voice and faith were strong. The last night he told the congregation, "I'm not sick, but I just don't have any more strength left for this world."

Once when J. T. preached at Princeton, Kentucky, to some who had heard the other three generations of Spurlins preach, he jokingly told them, "You'll probably conclude that the more they come the worse they get." After the message one of the older members seriously concluded, "Son, I believe you told us the truth."

He first saw his future wife at an associational meeting where he was directing the singing and she was the pianist. Saying to himself, "I'm going to have a date with that girl or know the reason why," he rushed across the platform as soon as the benediction ended, met her behind the pulpit, and wasted no time with introductions before asking her for the date. After they became better acquainted, they discovered that L. L. Spurlin, J. T.'s father, had baptized and married her father and mother. Later he married the young couple in the same room, and when J. T. began preaching, he performed his first marriage ceremony there also.

Dr. Spurlin loved the rural area of Kentucky and loved farming. The hardest decision he ever made was to leave his farm and go back to school when he surrendered to preach. He became an evangelistic singer for a time, and once led the singing for a revival preached by Dr. G. W. Ragland. Dr. Ragland served as chairman of the special committee of the Southern Baptist Convention to study the possibility of entering Alaska as a mission field. While pastoring in Missouri, Dr. Spurlin served for six years on that state's mission board. During those years Dr. Courts Redford was president of Southwest Baptist College at Bolivar, and because Spurlin met with the Board, the two men became acquainted. Dr. T. W. Medaris, executive-secretary of Missouri, was a personal friend during that time, and the offering sent from the Antioch church for the work in Juneau came through the Kentucky Baptist office and had Dr. W. C. Boone's signature on the check. When the Southern Baptist Convention officially authorized the acceptance of Alaska as a Home Mission Board field at its 1948 meeting in Memphis, Dr. Boone made the motion for its acceptance and Dr. Medaris seconded it.

When Dr. Robert Baker of Southwestern Seminary, son-in-law of Dr. Fred McCaulley, made a study of the comity agreement, the study resulted in Dr. and Mrs. McCaulley's coming to Alaska to visit the work and report on its needs for the convention. Mrs. McCaulley stayed in Juneau with the Spurlins, who were old friends, while her husband toured the state. The comity agreement was a thorn in the side of Dr. Spurlin. He stated, "Southern Baptists wanted to come to Alaska many years before they did, but they also wanted to maintain their integrity and be a gentleman about it, so they respected the claims of Northern Baptists to the territory. The comity agreement made me an intruder to the churches of Juneau instead of an ally, as I should have been. Our work was stymied for years because of it." After Dr. Spurlin arrived in Juneau, the Northern Baptists relinquished their claims on the Baptist work there. However, their representative, Dr. Lincoln Wadsworth, later on again tried to persuade the church to join his convention, asking over and over why they wouldn't be just as happy as with Southern Baptists. At one point Dr. Spurlin told him that Northern Baptists were losing a church a week, had accepted Alaska in theory but not in fact as their mission responsibility, and finally, "No one in our church is more faithful than Miss Krause. She left the Home Mission Society because of doctrinal differences. We would never break faith with her and Miss Black."

The thing that impressed Mrs. Spurlin most about Alaska was the closeness of the Christian fellowship she found in the church. When the incessant rain in Juneau began to stifle her spirits, Mrs. Wilma Jenkins shared her experience of adjusting by telling that she at first would look out the windows at the rain and cry, but someone told her, "Don't pay any attention to it; get out in it and go on with your business." The Spurlins made good use of the advice and soon were out picking berries, catching king salmon, going duck hunting and doing their church work in the rain just like everybody else.

First Baptist Church of Juneau organized on February 3, 1946, with thirteen charter members, "one more than the Lord had," Dr. Spurlin observed. Four more joined that day, two by baptism. They conducted their first baptismal service the next Sunday at the Seventh Day Adventist Church; Frankie Allen, Miss Frances Black's "grandson," was the first one baptized. Jean Bastian was the other candidate that day. Her husband Bill was in the armed services and was soon transferred to Kotzebue. Upon seeing the need for the gospel in that place, he surrendered to the ministry, went to Midwestern seminary after his release from the service, and now serves as a pastor in Missouri. One of the charter members, Mrs. Albert Peterson, whose home had been purchased for the parsonage, sent to Finland for her church letter. When the letter arrived, she had to translate it into English for the church. It was an official document with the seal of her church affixed to it. The letter told of her conversion and baptism, her activities in the church, her family background, and that she was the 152nd member added to the church.

As soon as the Spurlins came to take the work, Miss Frances Black moved back to her home in Fulton, Missouri, to open up her house as an old folks' nursing home so that she could pay off the mortgage she incurred to make the down payment on the Juneau parsonage. She wanted to be a member of the Juneau church so badly that the first thing she did was to have her letter sent back to Juneau. Her letters to Miss Krause during the next years reflect her love for the Juneau church and her concern about her own membership and offerings:

February 19, 1948
I have been so puzzled to know if I should leave my letter there. I know the covenant says that when we remove we will take our letter. But I told Bro. Harmon and the church here that as they have so much, what little I could give was needed to pay off what was borrowed for the Juneau church and they said that was all right. So as I contribute but very little here, I thought I had as well leave my

letter there. Anyway, I love to belong there. And now that next Sunday's lesson is about "The Fellowship of Christian Believers," and as that dear Juneau church is still my real church. . . . I think each day of each of you who are my closest of all. . . . I hope to keep up the payments due each month and can do it if I keep expenses down here.

April 14, 1948

. . . the Juneau church had a big part in giving Frankie the high ideals that I know will remain all through his life and I know God will have it recorded to the credit of each of you who worked with him there. . . . I am awfully busy with 15 besides myself in the house, but I have to keep this many to meet the monthly payments on the mortgage I put on the house. You know I told the church there I thought of course the people of Missouri would be glad to pay the $15 a month the mortgage called for to get a church building there. I thought the W.M.U. of the state would, but to my surprise our W.M.S. at Christmas 1947 gave $15 and this is every cent that any society has given, so I have had to take in more than this house ever had before and have to run the big coal furnace. . . . I now have all of the amount of the mortgage for the Juneau church paid but $280 so hope to get this off by fall. This is the reason that I have not asked for my letter. I told the church here that I would give my Lottie Moon offering and a little to the cooperative program here, but as I must meet obligations in Juneau, I could not give much.

After thirteen months, the church had an offer to sell the Peterson house for $8,000 and an opportunity to buy another property with two houses, one two-story, the other three-story, for only $10,000. After the transaction was completed, the two-story house was rented, and the three-story house redecorated for church services. Dr. Spurlin relates, "One day while painting the house, I was startled to feel something dripping down my face. Thinking I must have splashed paint, I carefully wiped my brow, only to discover that I was perspiring. That was the first time I ever worked up a sweat in Alaska."

The third floor, "up 234 steps," Mrs. Spurlin recalls, was used for services. The Antioch church sent chairs; it seated fifty-four. The record attendance in the building was fifty-three one Sunday when the North Pacific naval fleet came into the Juneau harbor and the "navy boys" came to church.

"The only fly in the ointment," Dr. Spurlin says, "was that woman on the second floor. She was the stubbornest person I ever saw." Her husband, a prosperous Englishman, had built her the house years before, and she simply refused to move out after it was sold to the church. She stayed on, using the church's water, coal, and electricity, never saying "Thank you," or offering any remuneration except for putting in fifty cents once at a Christmas program. Back in Missouri, Miss Black had her own ideas about how to get the woman out and what to do with the second floor, as revealed in the following letter to Miss Krause:

> August 1947
> . . . I was surprised to hear from you that Dr. Spurlin said they had not been able to get the old woman to move from the second floor of the church. I had told them that it took me from August to April to get an old woman out of the downstairs room I needed here. Before that, Frankie and I were so crowded in a little space upstairs. Dr. Spurlin said "You better come back to Juneau and put the old woman out of the church's third floor and take that." This gave me an idea. If the church would put it in writing and give her a month's notice, she would have to leave. Now when she gets out, would *you* like to live there? Miss Krause, you are too valuable a worker not to be used as far as your strength goes, and I believe that now all that is needed is for you to be sure where God wants you, and since our Father has rewarded the faith of Dr. Spurlin and cared for them, I know this same God will care for you if we believe he will.

One day Mrs. Wilma Jenkins became concerned because she had not seen the old lady around for several days, so she knocked on the door. When she had no response to repeated knocking, she started to push open the door, but found something heavy was preventing the door from opening. Upon peering in and seeing a hand on the floor, she quit pushing and called the police. They found that the woman had been dead two or three days, and also reported that they found almost $5,000 in bills pinned inside her corset. Dr. Spurlin's comment on hearing about the money was, "That money was as safe as the gold at Fort Knox."

Miss Black remained as untiring as ever in her efforts to bring the needs of Alaska to the attention of the Southern Baptist Convention and to encourage Miss Krause to seek the support of a Southern Baptist church to enable her to devote full time to missionary activities. She wrote:

> May 1947
> . . . best of all was meeting Dr. Carpenter who is still interested in Alaska and spoke of writing you, and I want you to know what I

will tell Dr. Spurlin, that is that the first thing Mrs. Una Roberts Lawrence said was that what finally turned the tables with the Board was when they heard from her that I reported last August to her that the Northern Board had written you to work with the Presbyterians for they could not open work there. You see, this finally convinced them it would be all right to enter Alaska.

June 1947

. . . now I will tell you what I heard Mrs. Una Roberts Lawrence (the Southern Baptist mission study leader who writes many of the mission study books) say she told Bro. Felton Griffin at St. Louis: There were some things he would get if he asked the Board, and some he wouldn't. She said orphanages were one he wouldn't get— they felt that the local people should care for that kind of work. Also she told me in Kansas City last August that missionaries employed by the Board could retire at 60 and were required to retire at 65, so as you and I both are nearly retirement age, I fear there would be some hesitation in our being appointed. . . . I suggest that the First Baptist Church of Juneau appoint you officially as their city missionary to do visiting and all else you feel able to do. Then we could let this be known and I will ask and see if enough can't be sent you monthly.

September 1947

. . . I see that I have not made myself clear about your being appointed by the Home Mission Board. . . . What I tried to tell you was that if one is anxious to go to work at once in Alaska, the only way this is possible is for this person to just be sure where God wants him or her and then present his call to this field and let some individual church support him (as Dr. Spurlin did), or some state (as New Mexico sent Bro. Carpenter).

. . . it's just a work of faith. You see, I went there with $300, I believe it was, and never shall forget how that when my teeth had to be pulled and the plate was remodeled, I was asked to care for the cute little ones at Gastineau Hotel and the mother gave me exactly enough for my dental bills. So we want you now to use these last two checks for your eyes since you have some children for other things, and please let us know if these two are enough for the occulist's bill and what your other needs are. Nothing interests women so much as a Christian working with children and since we here can't be doing it ourselves, we are glad to send this to you who are doing it so well, so you may see clearly.

Besides the burden she bore for the Juneau church and Miss Krause's mission activity, Miss Black also dreamed of and planned for a Baptist orphanage for the native waifs who had stirred her heart from the time of her arrival in Alaska. She even had the house picked out to start in, the Hoogstead house on Fifth Street. Miss Krause wrote, "It took endless correspondence with Miss Black that I could not go in with her (to purchase the house) for any purpose. . . . Her heart was so set on that work for Alaska. It was hard for her to give it up."

Her prayers for the proposed orphanage also weighed on Dr. Spurlin's heart. During his vacation in Kentucky in the summer of 1947, he spoke in many churches of the needy children of Juneau and wrote to Miss Black, encouraging her to not give up her high hopes of getting the building:

> July 10, 1947
>
> . . . I have been praying that the Lord would make it possible for us to have a home for the neglected and forsaken natives of Juneau and the Gastineau channel. I have hoped that if it were God's will that he would make it possible for us to do such a work. It seems to me it is the best mission opportunity for Baptists to reach the natives, now that we have a place to bring them for worship and Christian training, and Bible teaching, besides the work we could do for them in the home.

On his way back to Alaska, Dr. Spurlin visited Miss Black in Fulton and spoke to her home church. She later wrote Miss Krause concerning his visit:

> September 1947
>
> . . . One of our women said to me the other day, "Well, how *did* a man like Dr. Spurlin *ever* go to a place like Alaska?" I could answer at once that it was because Mrs. Brockman and others were asking God to send a preacher and because he listened when God called. This encourages me to really believe that if you there and we here will ask God, he will cause Missouri women in some way to arrange for a building to be opened in some place in Alaska (for orphaned native children).

By this time Miss Black knew that Mr. William Petty had resigned the pastorate of First Baptist Church, Anchorage, for the purpose of starting a home for homeless native children there. She also knew that one action of the first session of the Alaska Baptist Convention had to do with beginning such a work as soon as possible. She realized that perhaps the home she envisioned would begin at Anchorage instead of Juneau and her letters more and more reflected her growing concern for the whole territory:

August 1947

. . . we are so glad to get all the information about needs there and I hope that as a missionary from China asked for China, that now since the Baptist work is started at last in Alaska, some Baptist worker may be found in every corner of that big territory. We will always give you thanks and I am sure God will reward you for being the only Baptist in Juneau for so long who stayed true.

In spite of the fact that their daughter Donanell was in bed for seven and a half months with rheumatic fever during their pastorate in Juneau, the Spurlins consider the three years there among the most rewarding of their lives. Dr. Spurlin quips, "We had members from Tallahasee, Florida, to Kotzebue, and gifts came in from everywhere." Shortly after the Spurlins left Juneau, the church was offered $20,000 for the property and two houses. "God gave us $12,000 profit on our investment in three years when we weren't expecting any monetary gain at all," Spurlin recalled.

When Miss Black heard of the profit made on the property sale, she rejoiced. She had mortgaged her home to make the initial investment, and she rejoiced even more that she could still have a part in the work:

December 1949

. . . Surely God's blessings were on the sale of the property and I hope the spiritual blessings now will be just as great. When you get discouraged, you can remember how fortunate I think you are to be there, for after having been there, I will always want to be back. . . . I found that although the principal is paid on the note the church borrowed, still the interest is not, so I have written Bro. Bolton that I can still have a little part in the work until that is paid.

After Miss Krause visited with Miss Black in Fulton one night in October 1949, she wrote this note: "My, how she sacrificed for the Juneau work!"

The bulletin of First Baptist Church, Juneau, for September 1951 carried the following tribute:

Those who remember Miss Frances Black, one of our first members, were saddened to hear the news of her homegoing in Fulton, Missouri.

She came to Juneau to do whatever God had for her to do. Many and varied were the tasks while she was here from July 1941 until June 1943 the first time, and again from September 1944 to August 1946. Among them were teaching school, caring for tubercular chil-

dren in the Baptist Home, starting the Baptist Goodwill Center at
218 Main Street, working in the Sunday school. . . . Her hope and
prayer was that she might return again to Juneau, but God had other
plans for her.

Miss Hilda Krause continued as a faithful member of the church
for many years. On Christmas Day, 1965, she wrote to those on
her "Remembrance List" some thoughts of early Christmases she
remembered in Alaska. The Aleuts and Eskimos follow the old
Julian calendar, so the celebrations she wrote of occurred on January 6, rather than December 25. The following story she related
is my favorite:

> . . . some of the natives had not seen me since my return (from
> furlough) until their Christmas Eve when they went on their "carol-
> ing" tour, twirling a huge star bedecked with multi-colored paper
> flowers, while they *sang* their dirge-like carols from house to house.
> They were not supposed to come to the Mission after they visited
> the other places, but that time their leading Wiseman, Nick Fadaoff,
> did not observe the rule. He needed props to help him stand up
> when they came in; however, with the other dozen carolers, he was
> able to carry their solemn tune.
> In the middle of it, Nick spied me, stopped his twirling and
> pointing his finger at me, he shouted, "I know you *starucha*—the
> mission lady!"
> After that "informative interlude" they all picked up their tune
> where they had left off and kept on caroling for another ten minutes
> or so until our Superintendent appeared with a dishpan full of apples.
> All attention then riveted on the apples, and after each one received
> a polished apple, with many "Merry Christmas" wishes, they vanished
> into the night for more caroling, and the weary mission family got
> off to bed, as for some of us the five o'clock rising time in the morn-
> ing would come before we were ready.
> Around midnight screams outside and pounding on the door
> awakened us. A woman's voice shouted, "I tell mission lady you bite
> off my sweetheart's ear!" The pounding continued until there was
> nothing to do but go out and see what could be done about the
> sweetheart's ear.
> With that multilated organ disinfected, dressed, and taped, they
> were sent on their way with a lecture and prayer for them to let
> the Lord Jesus change their sinful hearts. Little, however, soaked
> into their sodden minds. They were then ordered to go home before
> something worse happened.
> Such debauchery was common during Prohibition days when
> even the Marshal had his own stills hid in the islands and the
> natives made their own *makula*. I learned one Russian word that

evening. An interpreter told me later that *starucha* meant "old woman." Just think how very superannuated I am by this time, thirty-six years later, since Nick thought I was very aged even then.

In December 1968 Mississippi missionary Hollis V. Bryant, one of the seventeen who spent two weeks working in Alaska during the summer of 1968, returned to pastor the First Baptist Church of Juneau. Bryant succeeded Joe Patterson. At the present time, the church's new $130,000 building is nearing completion on Airport Road. The church has been meeting in the Seventh Day Adventist building for five years, since their downtown building was condemned and taken over by the borough. The old building still stands, however, and has been rented by the borough to the Community Art Theater group for $1 a year, while the Baptists have had to pay $10 per service rent for a meeting place.

* * *

The Bible speaks of wars and rumors of wars. The youth of our country face service in the armed forces with mixed emotions, ranging from expectation to despair, but all parents share one feeling—Fear. Where will they be sent? Will they return? Are they adult enough to confront problems in their first venture away from the protection of home and family? Have they learned the right values? Is their faith in God strong enough?

The records of the Historical Society of Hot Springs, Garland County, Arkansas, contain the story of one group of young men who proved they were capable of facing whatever life offered. On June 6, 1941, they were called into service for one year of active duty as "H" Battery of Hot Springs, a part of the 206th Coast Artillery Anti Air Craft Regiment. After training at Ft. Bliss, Texas, they were transferred to Ladd Air Base near Fairbanks, Alaska. There they were housed in makeshift barracks originally used as airplane hangars. Then came December 7, 1941. Their one year of service extended to two, three, and for many, four. The fall of 1943, as the American troops were completing the Aleutian campaign, found several members of the Hot Springs unit in Anchorage. S/Sgt. Eddie Kuntz was one of those, and the story of their work for the Lord in Alaska is told in some yellowed pages and letters treasured by his widow, Zelma Nash Kuntz. Among the papers is an article, "Baptists in Alaska," written by Chaplain Aubrey Halsell and published in the *Southern Baptist Brotherhood Journal* for the spring quarter of 1944. Many Hot Springs residents remembered Halsell as the son-in-law of W. J. Hinsley, then pastor of Second Baptist Church.

Chaplain Halsell wrote, "One Saturday during the Attu invasion I stepped off a troop transport at one of our bases in Alaska. This was my first view of this great country and many were the impressions of my eyes and mind. I beheld the natural beauty—and what a sight! The white-capped waves of the blue Pacific were washing the moss covered rocks of the shoreline. The high mountains were covered with the foliage of the evergreen Alaskan pine trees. A large glacier could be seen in the distant valley between the snowcapped mountains. A train was used to transport our group to an interior base. On this train trip we saw several cabins and also a few little settlements consisting of from three to ten cabins. These cabins were usually vacant and we found out later that such cabins are scattered all over Alaska. Trappers, fishermen, explorers, and miners occupy them for a short time and then move on to other locations. About eleven P.M. we arrived at our destination . . . Anchorage. It was still daylight."

During his student days at Ouachita College in Arkansas, Halsell had vowed that if ever he were in a location without a Baptist church, he would start one. On his first Sunday in Anchorage he drove into town to look for a Baptist church but was told there were no Baptists in Alaska. He wrote to friends saying, "By God's grace this shall not prevail another month." Other Southern Baptist chaplains had felt the same need. John Dodge, who was with a National Guard Unit assigned to Alaska before the war, had discussed the possibility of mission work here, and by November 1941 had sent a survey and map of Alaska with mission needs as he saw them to both the Home Mission Board and Foreign Mission Board, but neither felt able to begin work at that time. Chaplain Alexander Turner, assigned to Fort Ray at Sitka during the early months of the war, conducted religious services in the base theater there. Later he led in remodeling a dining hall to use as a chapel, and from the new chapel he began a daily religious radio broadcast which helped prepare the foundation for Southern Baptist work.

Chaplain Halsell, together with Chaplain Jewell D. Foster, drove around town several days trying to locate a building in which to have revival services. Halsell wrote, "The challenge was thrown at me by my conscience until I could not sleep at night." Upon learning that Axel Niklason, pastor of the Church of the Open Door, was a Baptist, the chaplains made his acquaintance. He had left California in the late thirties to begin mission work in Alaska. Supporting himself by doing carpentry, he built a home with a large room to serve as an assembly, and announced Baptist services. He was informed by other pastors in the city that because Anchorage was Presbyterian territory, he could not have Baptist services. Since he was reaching only a handful of people, Mr. Niklason turned to an interdenominational approach and changed the sign outside his house on Eighth Avenue to "The Church of the Open Door."

Mr. Niklason offered the use of his house for the revival and put up another sign: "Baptist Revival." Halsell wrote, "The main objective of the meeting was that at its conclusion we might organize the first Baptist church in Anchorage." During the services which were held the last two weeks of August 1943, twenty-two professions of faith were recorded. Everyone who attended was asked to fill out an information sheet, the last question being, "Are you willing to cooperate in the organization of a New Testament church in Anchorage to be called 'The First Baptist Church,' affiliated with the mission program of the Southern Baptist Convention, giving your full support in self, service, and substance? (Yes or No)."

Following the revival, at three in the afternoon of September 19, 1943, in Chapel Number Two at Elmendorf Air Force Base, the First Baptist Church was organized with seventeen charter members—twelve enlisted men, three officers, and two civilians. The Second Baptist Church of Hot Springs, Arkansas, the home church of seven of the soldiers, extended a sponsoring arm. Chaplain Halsell moved the organization of the church, S/Sgt. Gaines Parker seconded the motion and everyone present spoke, enthusiastically endorsing the move. After the vote was taken, Captain Carl DeMott led in prayer. Officers elected included: S/Sgt. Leroy James, clerk; S/Sgt. Eddie Kuntz, treasurer; Captain Carl DeMott and S/Sgt. Leroy Jones, deacons; Axel Niklason, Captain Carl DeMott, Major Aubrey Halsell, and S/Sgt. Leroy Jones, trustees; and Chaplain Halsell, moderator. After an offering of $70 was received, Chaplain Halsell preached on "My Church." Following the evening service, three other persons came for membership, including one by baptism.

A letter from Chaplain Halsell, dated September 21, 1943, tells, "Many thrills have come to me recently in this war theater; however, the climax of them all happened during the past three days. The first experience was the realization of a life-time dream. I killed a six foot, eight inch grizzly bear. It was a case of necessity; I had to kill the bear or else enter the pearly gates. The big brute charged my roommate and fortunately I shot just in time to save his life. The bear kept running until I had fired three shots into him. He was so big he could not be picked up by six men. . . . The greatest experience and most lasting one in real value to Christ and His Kingdom was in the organization of the First Baptist Church of Anchorage. The charter members were from Alaska, Alabama, Arkansas, California, Colorado, Mississippi, Michigan, Minnesota, Oklahoma, South Carolina, and Texas."

On September 26, with the temperature at 35 degrees, the church conducted its first baptismal service at Otter Lake. After Chaplain Foster preached, Chaplain Halsell baptized Corporal Herbert Dennis of Pine Bluff, Arkansas. Edmund Smagge, a young man reared in Alaska as a Roman Catholic, upon observing baptism for the first time, made his profession of faith while standing at the lake side. The church voted to receive him, and he was baptized immediately, wearing the wet clothes of the first candidate.

The services of First Baptist Church were held on Sunday afternoons in the base chapel with night services at the home of the Niklasons. The search for suitable property resulted in their locating desirable lots on Sixth Avenue on which stood a burned out residence. The madam of a bawdy house owned the property. When Chaplain Halsell visited her to investigate buying the lots, the woman was drunk and refused to believe he had come on real estate business. Her first price was $6,000, but later she agreed to sell the lots and house for $5,000, with $2,000 down and the balance at $100 per month. When Chaplain Halsell called the church together to act on her offer, they opened their wallets, emptied the contents into the offering plate, and $700 was given toward the down payment. By the next day the soldiers had borrowed enough money from friends to raise the total to a thousand dollars.

When Chaplains Halsell and Foster had discussed with Mr. Niklason their desire for a Baptist church, Mr. Niklason had made the casual comment that he would give a thousand dollars of his life savings to see a Baptist church in Anchorage. Chaplain Halsell had not forgotten the remark, so with the first thousand dollars in his pocket, he drove to the Niklason home and told Mrs. Niklason of the need for another thousand dollars. He then went to the place where Axel was working and asked him to accompany him to the bank. When the two men stood before the bank teller, the chaplain stated that Mr. Niklason wanted to draw out one thousand dollars from his savings account. When the teller presented the papers, Mr. Niklason signed them and Chaplain Halsell picked up the fifty twenty-dollar bills and proceeded on to the Federal Building to conclude the purchase of the property. The woman was sent for, found sober and still wanting to sell. While waiting for her to arrive, Chaplain Halsell was handed some mail. He found enclosed in one letter a check for five dollars; he then had a total of $2,011.28 in his pocket. The transaction of transferring the property took place at the office of the United States Commissioner on November 28, 1943; the Commissioner charged ten dollars for his service. The church was left with a balance of $1.28.

Seventeen of the twenty-two members of the church were tithers and weekly offerings averaged about $80, but much money was needed to renovate the fire-gutted residence. Southern Baptist papers in several states carried the story of the church's organization and a request for help. On January 2, 1944, the first services were held in the newly transformed church plant. Thirty people were present that day; four responded to the invitation for church membership.

Among Eddie Kuntz' papers was a bulletin from First Baptist Church dated January 9, 1944, which had the history of the church, including the organizational meeting, first baptism, locating and buying property, and converting the house into a suitable auditorium and six Sunday school rooms. All of the repairs were made with volunteer labor with the men working nights. The history ended with a plea for prayer that a civilian pastor might be supplied of the Lord.

After Chaplain Foster rotated, Chaplain Halsell wrote friends in Arkansas, "We need and must have a civilian pastor. . . . Won't somebody answer our call?" On January 10, 1944, Chaplain Halsell received a letter from Chaplain (Major) Ralph Wheeler, who had served as a Presbyterian missionary in Alaska for eight years before entering the chaplaincy, which said in part: "For several reasons I'm recommending that you be transferred to A.P.O. 729 . . . be-

cause I disapprove of your spending so much effort on establishing
another competitive church in Anchorage." Halsell believed the
action by Chaplain Wheeler to be merely another attempt to defeat
the Baptist work in Anchorage. His services for the church were
strictly on off-duty hours and in addition to his military responsibilities and evangelistic services at the Eklutna government school
for native children.

The exile of Chaplain Halsell to the Aleutian Chain was not
in vain, however. Within a few weeks a group of seven soldiers
who felt called to the ministry met together and began an "Aleutian
Seminary" with Chaplain Halsell conducting regular seminary
classes in a Civilian Construction Corps camp building. Civilians
employed at the camp established an endowment fund to aid the
young men to receive seminary training after the war.

In Anchorage, responsibility for carrying on services rested on
individual members after Halsell's rotation. Gifts and contributions
came from many states, and by May 1, 1944, the debts on the
church property had been paid off. On May 7, 1944, the property
was formally dedicated.

Bill Petty, a student at that time in Southern Baptist Seminary
in Louisville, had spent the summer after his graduation from
Ouchita Baptist College in Wrangell, Alaska, working in a salmon
cannery. He saw the need for Baptist work in Alaska and planned
to return after finishing seminary. Chaplain Halsell corresponded
with Mr. Petty, and the Anchorage church extended him a call to
be their first civilian pastor. He and his wife and baby son arrived
in Anchorage in June 1944 and he preached his first sermon to the
congregation June 11 on the subject "What Is Love?"

Meanwhile, the pastor of the First Baptist Church of Karnack,
Texas, Felton H. Griffin, had been greatly impressed that God was
calling him to go to Alaska to help establish Baptist work. He
promised that if God would provide the funds, he would go. A
druggist in town had heard of conditions in Alaska and offered to
pay Mr. Griffin's expenses. Two days after Griffin promised God
he would go, the druggist, A. T. Jobe, wrote out a check for the
necessary travel expenses. Griffin wrote to Chaplain Halsell:

Karnack, Texas
6-1-44

Dear Major:
MOVE OVER. I'M COMING IN.
Anything I should bring with me?

Felton H. Griffin

Felton Griffin secured the necessary permits and travel reservations for his trip in spite of criticism from friends. On the day he was to leave, two of the children were sick, but Mrs. Griffin insisted that he should go ahead. Four months passed before she and their three children could join him. He arrived in Anchorage and joined First Baptist Church on July 23, 1944, taking a job as a house painter to support himself. When Mr. Petty resigned the pastorate of the church in 1945 to devote himself to the establishment of a Bible school and orphanage, Mr. Griffin preached for the church for several weeks and accepted the call to become pastor in May 1945. Mr. Griffin submitted a "Fourteen Point Program" to the church and launched an aggressive Southern Baptist program.

A letter dated June 1, 1950, showed that the foundation for Baptist work in Alaska was laid on solid ground:

Anchorage, Alaska
June 1, 1950

Eddie J. Kuntz
Hot Springs, Ark.
Dear Eddie:
    You boys will never know what you started here. Just to give you an idea: We have started two missions from this church and they are both now organized churches, one on Government Hill and the other in the Spenard District.
    We also have a mission at Palmer and one at Girdwood.
    We now have a church in Fairbanks, Juneau, and Ketchikan.
    We have native missions at Fairbanks, and on Annette Island.
    We are publishing a monthly paper, The Alaska Baptist Messenger.
    We have an orphanage almost completed located six miles south of Anchorage.
    The Anchorage church now has 400 members.
    We have bought the house and lot next to the corner from the old property and have a nice building on the vacant lot but it is only a third large enough.
    We have had 303 for a record attendance in Sunday school, and our building is packed for every service. We had 96 in weekly prayer meeting last Wednesday evening.

Our offerings average over $2,000 a month locally.

God was surely leading in the organization of this church and He has smiled on us every day. We have additions every Sunday. For three years we have averaged around 250 additions per year. We baptize over a hundred a year. We have had 20 young men surrender to preach and several of these are already in schools in the States.

God has given us many victories here and we look forward to the time when we will have a really great church with a building that will seat at least 800 for the preaching services. Pray that God will provide for such a plant and when we get it that His power will be with us for a larger soul winning program.

We thank you for your continued interest in the work. May God's blessings be with you every day.

Yours in His wonderful service,
Felton H. Griffin
Pastor, First Baptist Church
Anchorage, Alaska

The Hot Springs Historical Society record contains the comment: "The parents, loved ones, and friends of these service men must have felt proud—everyone who learns of their activities can share this pride, and as the struggle continues to rear the next generation, to teach them the Lord's way, we know when they are old, they will not depart from His ways."

During early years the work of the convention was closely related to activities and members of Anchorage First Baptist Church. When Petty resigned the pastorate of the church, he set about establishing a Bible training school for natives and reported its progress in the *Alaska Baptist Messenger* he was editing.

The September 1947 *Messenger* stated: "Studies in the New Testament are now taking place at the Baptist College of Alaska in Anchorage. This is another milestone for the Baptist work here. The campus was purchased with the help of gifts from friends and relatives. A large seven room dormitory home is nearing completion. This structure includes emergency classrooms."

The next year a new city zoning law prevented them from operating as a school, but the classes continued to meet in the house the editor built. Petty reported in the May 1948 *Messenger:* "The school has been ministering to about twenty-five young people a week for the past eight months." He went on to state the need for practical training courses.

There were no Bible stores in Anchorage in the early days, so one concern of the convention was to establish a Bible book store. The store was set up on the porch of the Griffins' house. Every month the *Messenger* ran an advertisement, for Bibles at first, then for Bible story books and other religious materials.

Felton Griffin was pastoring First Baptist Church at the time he served as the first executive secretary of the convention. The other unpaid executive secretaries were members of the church. Pastor Griffin said about these men: "B. C. Evans helped us much in missions. He came up from New Mexico and spent a number of years here. He was a member of First Baptist Church. He taught school, was a principal, worked for the government in various capacities."

The August 1947 *Messenger* carried the article, "As a result of the contacts made by B. C. Evans while he was in New Mexico, Alaska will have a new Baptist work in Ketchikan. Carpenter has been employed by the New Mexico Baptist Convention as a field worker in that state."

Griffin continued:

> Another of our executive secretaries for a brief period was Bill Lewis. He was an active layman in First Baptist Church. He was interested in the activities of the convention and lived next door to the church and was accessible to those who needed to reach somebody. The convention did not have an office in those days, so we needed someone who could be found easily.
>
> Russell Simmons worked for the federal government. He was very active in the church and was always available to help in any way he could. Russell was an intelligent young man who made himself a servant of the Lord to the extent that people had great confidence in him. He always attended the sessions of the convention, was always reachable, and when we needed somebody to serve as executive secretary, the convention elected him. He did a good job without any pay. Our organization in those days was very crude; about all we did was act as a clearing house for those who sent funds for missions in Alaska.

Mrs. LaVerne Griffin related the story of her coming to join her husband and serving with him in the work in Anchorage as follows:

> The deacons of the church there in Karnack thought that anyone who would go to Alaska deserved to go to hell to get warm, and they told Felton so when he decided to come up here. Although the

church was not behind him, a man who was lost gave him the money to make the trip. The three children and I moved into smaller quarters while we waited for him to make arrangements to find us a place to live. We read with interest his letters about the fabulous country and were anxious to join him. He worked at all kinds of jobs, even as a dishwasher, to make enough money to send for us.

We spent about four days on the train to Seattle, then five days on the boat *Alaska.* Coming across the Gulf of Alaska, we had a blackout. Coast Guard boats had accompanied us part of the way to make sure we were safe, and they decided to disembark us at Whittier instead of Seward where Felton was waiting to meet us. Two women attached themselves to me, one with four children and the other with two. One of them began crying at the depot because her husband was working for the Alaska Railroad and she didn't know how to contact him. There were no hotels, so I told them to stay with me and at least we would have a roof over our heads.

When Felton came, he found twelve of us waiting for him. The mother with four children went on to Fairbanks the next day, but the other one stayed with us until she could find a place to live.

We lived on the base for about nine months, but because of the need to get the church finished, he resigned his job on base and we moved into the little building behind the church which had once been a horse stable, then a garage. It was quite cold and all that held the floor up was seven layers of linoleum.

Those were days of little privacy for our family because servicemen seemed to congregate in our home. We expected them to show up early in the morning and to stay late at night. We ate very few meals without them. They were our joy. We served hundreds of barrels of coffee and hot chocolate to those boys. Many of them surrendered to preach and gave their lives to Christ while they were in Alaska. We also had many native girls stay with us, including expectant mothers. We kept them because there was nowhere else they could go. When they wanted to give up their babies, we tried to find good, Christian homes for them.

Dr. Bruce, president of East Texas Baptist College, came to Alaska to preach a revival in our church. He asked if there were not some natives who would like to come to his college on a scholarship to get an education. We found two native girls in the Kodiak children's home who wanted to go, so we raised the money to send them down to the college. The girls proved worthy of their scholarships and made passing grades; they came back home and married after that year. Their lives were a credit to the trust invested in them.

Felton Griffin related some highlights of the church throughout the years:

We started the building in 1945. It would seat about 225 on the upper floor and had a full basement under it. We expanded it then so we could care for 450 people. We had just finished everything when it burned down. I was out visiting Tom Krause, doing some ice fishing, when a friend flew out in his plane and said, "Your church burned last night." By the time I got back to town the men had already made arrangements for us to meet in the Carpenters' Hall on Sunday.

We rebuilt a much larger building because we wanted room more than beauty in those days. The earthquake didn't damage our church. I was home getting ready for the Easter cantata when it happened. I had shined my only pair of shoes and had put them on. Now, I generally wear boots. The people from Texas won't let me quit; they keep giving me boots and Stetson hats because they want me to keep advertising Texas up here. Some folks accuse me of causing the earthquake because I had taken off my boots and put on shoes for the Easter program, and they beg me not to ever do it again. Every time I get those shoes out and look at them, even my family begins to tremble a little bit, and I admit that I haven't had the courage to put them back on since.

One of the most marvelous gifts I ever received in my life was $15. While preaching for a Moravian Bible Conference in Bethel one year, I traveled upriver and visited a children's home the Moravians operated there right in the midst of the wilderness. All the children there were Eskimos. I spent the night in the home with the children, spoke to the children, and we got to know each other pretty well. I didn't even count the little offering the Eskimo people gave me for the Bible conference; I just handed it back to them and said, "Take it up to the children's home and use it for them." Some months later our church building burned, and in just a few days I got a letter from the superintendent of the home. He wrote, "We heard on the radio about your church and the boys and girls here in the home decided to see how much money they could get together to send you to help rebuild your church." It was mostly in nickels and dimes—fifteen dollars in all.

In the early days Sixth Avenue was residential. Fourth Avenue was the only business area, and that wasn't much. Our church had four lots on Sixth. J. C. Penney's had built their building, which was shaken down by the earthquake, right across the street from us, They wanted additional parking space. We agreed to let them use our parking space, so they paved the lot. They began to try to buy our property, but at first we weren't interested. Then when office buildings began to go up, it became increasingly hard for us to operate our Vacation Bible Schools and the like because there was no place for the children, so we thought it would be better to go a little further out. Eventually we found an ideally situated piece of property about five blocks from town and right across from the Park Strip. We sold our property to J. C. Penney and bought the property where we are located now. Our present building is a dream of mine come true.

Many young men from our church have been called to preach. The reason is that God placed us where many young men are, lonely, away from home, ready to listen to what God has to say. We have some now serving with the foreign and home mission boards, and some serving as pastors of good churches. Among the young men who surrendered to preach was an F.B.I. agent named Dean Duke, a tall, handsome, college graduate. He was a dedicated Christian and at the present time is serving in Baranquilla, Columbia, as a foreign missionary. Others include Mike McKay, who had studied for two years for the Catholic priesthood before being saved in our church; Freddie Chapman, who pastored churches in Texas, and is now a pastor in Nashville, Tennessee; Charles LeClair, a young Indian man from Oklahoma, who was the first American Indian to become a Chaplain in the U. S. Army. Maurice Murdock was the Provost Marshall for the air base and greatly feared and respected by the men out there, and by his own testimony a rough man, but he began coming to services and was saved. He has been an outstanding soulwinner and lay preacher ever since.

One Sunday soon after Murdock was saved, I was to be gone in a revival. It was to start on Sunday evening, so I asked him to take the service at First Baptist. He said he didn't know how to preach, but I prevailed on him and he agreed to conduct the service. I heard about the service from others. He got up and forgot everything he meant to preach about. He began to give his testimony, then he gave an invitation and seven military men came forward to accept Christ. From that day to this he has always been available to fill pulpits and has worked very fruitfully for the Lord.

Part of First Baptist Church's program from the beginning was to conduct two revivals a year. Some of Southern Baptists' greatest leaders and evangelists have preached there. Among them are Dr. R. G. Lee, Angel Martinez, James Robison, Johnny Bisagno—whose services resulted in the largest number of additions—96, Fred Swank, nearly every evangelist from the department of evangelism, and many more. The revivals and program of perennial evangelism have resulted in hundreds of baptisms. Griffin related:

I've been accused of some terrible things, and one of them is that I baptize just everybody that comes along, and they give an example which actually happened in our church one Sunday evening. I got up and announced that all who were to be baptized should go with the baptismal committee through a certain door. I went up and prepared for the baptismal service. I baptized four or five candidates, then went back in, and soon came time for announcements and recognition of visitors.

I asked, "Who's here for the first time?" A boy about twelve years old sitting right in front of me on the second row with his hair all plastered down raised his hand.

I said, "Son, is this your first time here?"

He answered, "Yes, sir, it is."

I said, "Didn't I just get through baptizing you?"

He answered, "Yes, sir, you did."

I said, "How in the world did you get in the baptistry if this is the first time you've ever been to this church?"

The boy said something to Mr. Brooks, who was sitting beside him, and Brooks stood up and said, "He said he was just going back to try to find the rest room."

So in all probability, I have the most efficient baptismal committee of any Baptist church in the entire world.

On June 30, 1958, when the United States Senate passed the statehood bill ending Alaska's territorial status, wild celebrations erupted over all of Alaska. That evening a crowd, which newsmen described as the largest ever to be assembled in Alaska, met for a celebration in an Anchorage park. Two ministers, a Roman Catholic priest and Felton Griffin, had parts on the program. Perhaps this incident is indicative of the status the evangelistic endeavors of Southern Baptists had achieved in their first fifteen years in Alaska.

On the occasion of celebrating their fifteenth anniversary in 1959, First Baptist Church had many distinguished visitors, including Territorial officials. The following expressions of congratulations are representative of the many received by Felton Griffin and the church at that time:

> I take this opportunity to congratulate you and your congregation. You are to be commended for the outstanding part you have played for civic, economic, and spiritual betterment in Anchorage and Alaska. Under the inspired leadership which you have shown, your congregation has been a potent force for good. May the ensuing years bring a like harvest of success to you.
> —William A. Egan, Governor of Alaska

> Felton Griffin is a pastor whose preachments extend to practice far beyond the realm of his congregation and that of his fellow-believers in the Baptist faith. His has been a great influence for civic betterment ever since he came to Alaska, when I had the privilege of first knowing him, nearly 20 years ago. His has been a vital force for morality, for progress, for the public good. Just as leadership is essential in democracy, so, likewise, is it in all the various ramifications of our community life. Felton Griffin's personality and character have been projected beneficially and beneficently into the work of

his church, which, as a consequence, has grown rapidly, both in membership and in influence.

—Ernest Gruening, United States Senator

My warmest greetings to you upon the occasion of the fifteenth anniversary. I greatly admire the inspired and devoted manner in which you have carried on the Lord's work under the leadership of your good pastor, whom I hold in the highest personal esteem. May your talents increase and your labors grow ever more fruitful.

—E. L. "Bob" Bartlett, United States Senator

The 1968 watchnight service provided the setting for the twenty-fifth anniversary of the church. This was a time of recognition for many who had served the church through the years, such as Roger Laube, who had directed the musical program of the church since 1947, except for a two-year period, and Irene Laube and Jimmie Trietsch, pianist and organist.

＊　＊　＊

When Curtis O. Dunkin, a student at the Acadia Baptist Academy in Louisiana, read of the work begun in Anchorage by Chaplain Aubrey Halsell, he immediately wrote to learn more about opportunities in Alaska for Baptist work. Mr. Dunkin had left a business career to enter the ministry, and in middle age was preparing himself to preach. Before he received Dunkin's inquiry, Halsell had been transferred to the Aleutians. He wrote telling Dunkin of making tentative arrangements with Bill Petty, a young man from Arkansas who was just finishing his third year at Southern seminary, to come as pastor of the Anchorage church in June 1944, but went on to write:

> However, if God lays on the heart of a man a definite call to this needy section, *I would say come on*—there are in Alaska at least a dozen towns that could and would support a Baptist church NOW if someone with faith would tackle the job. . . . People, Place, Provision, Power, Pay—are there; all that is needed is the Person, the *Parson*, if you please, to perfect the organizations and go to work Winning, Witnessing, Worshipping, Baptizing, Building, and Bringing in the Sheaves.
>
> There could be no more prosperous mission field around the globe than Alaska—no language to learn, no customs to overcome— just Christ to preach and the devil to fight. Any one of the larger towns in three months' time could support a pastor and pay him at least $200 a month salary. The first month we were in our building

at Anchorage, January of this year, we had 12 additions, all adults, and the offerings were over $800, more than $500 from local members, and the strength of the church is 34. Money in Alaska is always plentiful; in fact, pennies are not used at all. On a per capita basis Alaska is richer than any state in the Union.

I could go on and on telling you about these glorious opportunities, but I trust God will not let you loose until you arrive in Alaska *if He has called you here.* May God richly bless you always.

Christ's servant,
Aubrey C. Halsell
Phil. 4:13

As soon as he received Halsell's letter, Mr. Dunkin wrote back that God had definitely called him to come. On March 24, 1944, a second letter from Halsell was sent to answer a few of the many questions Dunkin had asked. Before answering the questions, Halsell wrote, "To hear you say that you are coming thrills my heart and *His too,* I know." He went on to explain that driving to Juneau would be too difficult to attempt, and that because of the war, living quarters were difficult to find. "I urgently suggest that you come alone and let your family follow via boat from Seattle at least three months after your arrival at Seward. In this way you could save hundreds of dollars because you would be able to fully understand all the situations involved in coming to this great territory." He told of the plans Bill Petty and another young preacher were making to come, and ended his letter: "It would be glorious if you three servants of God could come up together. God grant it shall be. The Anchorage church is doing better and better. Souls are being saved. $1,340.00 in the treasury. Longing for the day when the civilian pastor arrives. God bless you and yours. Yours for Christ in Alaska."

Mr. Dunkin applied for permits to travel to Alaska, thinking that he would remain in Seward to begin Baptist work. After arriving in Anchorage and hearing of the need to begin work in Fairbanks, he decided to go there. He secured employment as a city fireman, then began looking for some Baptists in order to establish a Baptist church. It took him two weeks to find the first Baptist in the city, but on September 17, 1944, the day the Anchorage church celebrated its first anniversary, the Dunkins conducted the first Baptist worship services in Fairbanks. The work was begun as a mission of the First Baptist Church of LaFayette, Louisiana.

The dining room of the Masonic Temple served as the first

meeting place for the group, but soon they needed more space and rented the upstairs lodge room and another smaller room for Sunday school classes. In April 1945 the Masons rented the lower auditorium to a Church of Christ group. Feeling too crowded for comfort, the Baptists initiated plans to secure property, and by summer had purchased lots at 805 Sixth Avenue and begun construction of a thirty-two foot by fifty foot basement. When they celebrated their first anniversary on September 16, 1945, First Baptist Mission, Fairbanks, reported an average attendance in the Sunday morning service of twenty-nine and in the evening of twenty. Sixteen members had joined by letter; thirteen had come on profession of faith and one by statement.

By Thanksgiving of 1945 they were able to begin meeting in their almost-completed basement which had four Sunday school rooms, a baptistry, and a small auditorium. The property was valued at $12,000, with an existing debt of $4,000. One highlight of the first year was the conversion of Ivan Jordan, an Eskimo from Bethel, Alaska, who surrendered to preach. The *Fairbanks Daily News Miner* reported in June 1946 that Ivan Jordan, a member of First Baptist Church, attended the Baptist General Convention of Texas that convened at Mineral Wells and was given a place on the program. "Ivan is an Eskimo and he is preparing for the ministry at the present time at the Acadia Academy at Church Point, La. We anticipate great things for him when he returns to work among his own people. It was good, too, that he could represent this church at the convention."

In January 1946 Mrs. Dunkin was treated for cancer at Mayo Clinic, and when the Dunkins returned to Fairbanks in February, they made plans to leave Alaska, but first they wanted to see the mission constituted into a church. On April 17, 1946, the First Baptist Church of Fairbanks was constituted with a charter membership of thirty-two.

Meanwhile, in the 128th General Hospital in England, an X-ray technician asked a young army nurse a destiny-deciding question, "Will you go to Alaska with me?"

For several weeks Mabel Risse, the nurse, had been expecting a question, but that was the wrong one. She answered "yes" anyway, and Orland Cary's next words were the ones she had wanted to hear: "Let's get married." At Whitewell, Flintshire, Wales, they were married on January 3, 1945, and spent their honeymoon in

Scotland while Alaska hovered vaguely in the future. They traveled all over England together and made dear friends among the English people. Cary was able to preach in some rural or village church almost every Sunday. He wrote, "This, to me, is one of the interesting things about being drafted into the army. I probably preached about as many sermons in England as I would have if I had been a civilian pastor in the States. I suppose that it took this army experience for me to realistically learn that the Lord could override any obstacle once the man was completely depending upon the Lord."

For Orland Cary hadn't planned to join the army at all. He had graduated from Baylor University in 1934 and pastored quarter- and half-time churches in Texas for several years, supporting himself by teaching high school. In 1943, while pastoring the First Baptist Church, Peaster, Texas, he was asked by the War Manpower Commission to quit his teaching job at the Caddo High School and become an inspector in a plant in Ft. Worth. The school board was displeased with his decision, and since the same board served as the draft board for the community, they had him drafted into the army before he could leave Caddo.

Later he wrote, "I found myself a private in the army before I could find out what was happening. That was quite a jolt, and I was told that I was steam-rolled into the army, and at first it was the hardest trial that had come my way. But, realizing that the Lord knew all about it and perhaps that even though it did not look right to me, there was a purpose in it, I later saw that it turned out to be the greatest blessing that ever came my way. First, it taught me to rely completely on the Lord; and second, I found my wife."

After induction Cary applied for the chaplaincy, but the Southern Baptist quota was full, and it was not until he returned from overseas and was eligible for separation that the army was ready to commission him.

While stationed at Camp Beale, California, Cary met Mabel Risse at a chapel service. He introduced himself as an X-ray technician, but the next day she found him on her ward as a ward boy; "just temporarily," he assured her. After a few weeks they decided to marry some day, but because they were both up for overseas assignments, agreed to wait. Mabel was sent to England a few months before Cary, but when he was stationed nearby, they were able to see each other for a few days about every two weeks. Cary had been alerted for shipment to the Pacific when the war with Japan ended. He was discharged in September 1945, then had to wait in the States for Mabel until she was discharged in January 1946.

Orland Cary had realized while stationed in California that the Lord was calling him to Alaska, so he planned to go as soon as possible after the war was over. Since he and Mabel were discharged in the middle of the winter, they decided to wait until spring to try to travel the highway to Alaska. In the meantime Cary became mission pastor of the First Baptist Church, Brownfield, Texas. He had resolved to set himself up either in the bakery or photography business in Alaska to support himself while doing mission work, but while pastoring in Brownfield, he met Felton Griffin's parents and learned more about the needs in Alaska. When First Baptist, Fairbanks, became pastorless, Felton Griffin sent the church Cary's name, together with others, and the church called him as pastor. He found out later that the pulpit committee had written to every name on the list, and because he was the only one who responded, they called him.

As soon as the school term ended, Orland and Mable loaded up their furniture, visited her family in Wisconsin, and proceeded up the Alcan Highway, a 5,600 mile trip. They arrived in Fairbanks July 8, 1946, to find the sun shining brightly at eleven P.M. Though they were exhausted, they had to unload their furniture in order to have a bed to sleep on that night. They moved into a small apartment in the basement of the church.

They soon learned that only eighteen of the church's thirty-six members were resident and five of these were children. When the church had become pastorless, the Interstate Baptist Mission, a group of Baptist churches in Washington, Oregon, and northern California, agreed to send $225 a month to be used for a pastor's salary if he would give full time to the church. The Interstate churches, however, soon joined the California Baptist convention and began sending their money to that convention, and the expected salary did not materialize. Undaunted, Mr. Cary challenged the ten wage-earners among his members to tithe, and from the beginning they paid him a full salary, $375 a month at first, besides furnishing the apartment.

John Robert, the first of the Carys' nine children, was born

August 31, 1946. He didn't miss a church service all the next year although the temperature often went to sixty degrees below zero that winter. Mrs. Cary organized a W.M.U. and a Cradle Roll, and in a few weeks' time fifteen women attended the W.M.S. meetings and fifteen babies were enrolled in the Cradle Roll.

One of the first actions of the church under Cary's leadership was to ask for membership in the Brownfield Baptist Association in Texas. Writing to A. A. Brian, pastor of First Baptist Church, Brownfield, Cary asked: "Can we come into the association there and participate in the program of that organization as a regular member? That would solve our problem and do two things for us; first, it would give us an opportunity as a church to have a part in the Cooperative Program. As I understand it there is no set-up for foreign missions in this group of churches, or if there is, the people in this church have not heard about it. The second thing it would do for us is that it would make us feel like we belonged to someone, denominationally speaking, and not be just a group of stray mavericks."

Writing again to Mr. Brian after being in Alaska a month, Cary said:

> We have a lot of fun along at times. You, of course, know about this principle of *comitia* as practiced by the churches in this section. Well, this is in the "Presbyterian sphere of influence," and the man who represents that church here feels like we are impostors. Recently we went up to the hospital to see a lady who was Baptist, but not a member of our church. The Presbyterian man was there and said some foolish things, making light of our church's denominational stand. I felt like fighting, but somehow found grace enough to keep my mouth shut. A day or two later this lady told me she was coming into our church. A couple visited our church yesterday morning, two of his Sunday school workers, and I preached on tithing. These people were objecting mostly to the way their church was financed—food sales, rummage sales, bazaars. It looks as if we are going to take some of his members by preaching the very thing that he, seemingly, is afraid to preach.

On Sunday, October 13, 1946, Mabel led five of her junior girls to make a public profession of faith in Christ. Two of them did not join the church because the mother of one was a drunkard and the father of the other ran a liquor store. Soon after that Sunday, Orland realized that he "would soon have to get rid of that Texas hat and get something to cover my ears"; before December the temperature had dropped to fifty-five degrees below zero, and at this time Cary wrote: "We had lunch today with one of our members out at Ladd Field and we had to let the car sit out for about five hours. We had a little difficulty getting the car to roll again because the bearings were frozen to the wheels and the shock absorbers were frozen to where it was just like riding on the axle. . . . We have pure Prestone in the radiator."

Social conditions in Fairbanks presented constant problems. Mr. Cary wrote soon after coming to Fairbanks:

> There is a situation here in regard to the native women that we hope to do something about as soon as a way is opened up. Fairbanks is unusual in a number of ways and one of them is the number of old bachelors that it has. Many of these old men came up here because of some anti-social phase of their life. One of the professors out at the university recently said, "This is not a frontier; it is an escapist's paradise." There is a saying here, "Half the people in Alaska came here to get away from something." Now, when that condition is coupled with the fact that the natives are without our sense of moral values, a bad social situation naturally arises. Some of these girls have repented and come forward trusting Christ as their Savior, but their lack of any background as we understand morality, when subjected to these old men that just lie in wait for them, has made it almost impossible for us to keep the three that we have reached out of the dives. One of our most substantial church members is the Matron of the Detention Home and we live just two doors away from it. In order to be able to do anything with this situation, it is our opinion that we will have to have something like a rescue mission where these girls can stay until they have located proper employment and can have training and supervision.

Within one four-month-period during Cary's first year at Fairbanks three young men surrendered for the ministry. Two of the young men began conducting a mission Sunday school in the Federal jail, with fifteen to twenty attending the class. Until cold weather closed down Twenty-Six Mile Camp, Cary preached there regularly every Thursday night and had two conversions and one surrender to preach. He surveyed in the neighborhood of the university, which was then six miles out of town, and began corresponding with churches in Texas about the need to buy lots and start work out there. Later he led the church to purchase three lots near the school.

Growth the first year of Cary's ministry included ninety-six additions, with thirty-three coming by baptism and thirteen others awaiting baptism. The church sent more than $1,000 to the Co-operative Program and used $11,150 for local expenses, including $3,500 on the building. Sunday school classes were organized for every age group and the average attendance was sixty.

The month he arrived in Fairbanks, Cary wrote to the Home Mission Board asking if the church were eligible for a loan. Dr. Lawrence's secretary wrote back stating, "The Executive Committee of the Southern Baptist Convention has ruled that the Home Mission Board is not to do any work in Alaska. We would therefore be inhibited from making a loan to your church." He then wrote to the architectural department of the Sunday School Board explaining their need and received a floor plan that enabled them to add a thirty-two foot by seventy-two foot wing to the existing basement, with the men of the church doing the work. In December 1946, the church received through the Home Mission Board over $600 that had been sent by the churches in Waco, Texas, and designated for Fairbanks. This gift helped purchase materials for the new basement.

During the next two years the church issued bonds, first $20,000, then $10,000 more, which made possible the construction of their first building. The Sunday school rooms were all in use but not finished when Cary again wrote to Dr. Lawrence in 1949, saying that his family had been living in the basement for eighteen months, and that although the living room was used for a nursery for thirty babies during the preaching services, the church was badly in need of all the space being used by the family. Once again he asked if it would be possible for the Home Mission Board to invest $10,000 in the work. The following month he repeated his request to Dr. Courts Redford. The request was presented to the Administrative Committee.

The answer came back: ". . . The local congregation has practically exhausted its ability to finance this project, and in view of their splendid achievements and sacrificial contributions, we recommend an appropriation of $10,000 from Capital Needs Fund for the completion of this building, with the understanding that this Board is to take a gift lien contract for the amount thus invested and that the gift lien contract will be subordinated to outstanding bonds on the building which will not exceed $30,000."

The money was used to finish the three-story structure which provided an auditorium seating three hundred fifty people, an

apartment for the pastor's family on the third floor, facilities for a
kitchen and banquet room in the basement, and adequate Sunday
school space. Mr. Cary wrote to the *Alaska Baptist Messenger:*

> Our plans are to get the inside of the building finished by April
> 18th which is the fourth anniversary of the organization of the
> church. There is very little work to be done on the outside. The
> men have already started to work on the apartment, and we are
> eagerly looking forward to moving up above the surface of the
> ground where we can look out. After these years in the basement,
> we will enjoy living in our new quarters. We have just received
> notice that the rest of our heating plant has finally been loaded on
> the boat in Seattle and is on its way to us. Part of that was ordered
> months ago but got lost somehow. We have all the basement on
> central heat now and even with the temperature at forty degrees
> below zero it has been working like a charm.

Orland Cary served First Baptist Church, Fairbanks, until
November 1958. During his ministry the church received 1,589
members by baptism and transfer of membership. For two years
before his death on November 19, 1961, he pastored the Airport
Road Baptist Church, Fairbanks. In addition to his work as a
pioneer pastor, he was a leader and president of the Alaska
Baptist Convention and helped organize the Tanana Valley Baptist
Association.

The first seven years the church averaged baptizing one person
for every four resident members. The Native Baptist Mission was
a mission of the church during the time of the building of First
Baptist's superstructure. The North Pole Baptist Church, Big Delta
Baptist Church, St. John's Baptist Church, and the Tok mission
have been sponsored by Fairbanks First Baptist Church.

In 1959 Donald Davis, who was saved, baptized, and surrendered to preach in the church, and who had graduated from
Baylor and Southwestern Seminary, was called to pastor Fairbanks
First Baptist. In December 1961 a dedication service for a new
church plant was held. The service ended ten months of meeting
in rented halls since the former building burned in February.
Pastor Davis said, "We are glad to be home again and back in
business at 805 Sixth Avenue. We believe that the greatest evidence
of the glorious future of the church is the wondrous fact that God
has been with us and has led us."

When Oliver Marson resigned the church in July 1968, the
church again called Don Davis, who is the present pastor.

2

"Though Thy Beginning Was Small . . ."

Job 8:7

From *Minutes of the Business Meeting of the Organizational Meeting of the Alaska Baptist Convention*, held at the First Baptist Church, Anchorage, Alaska, March 27-28, 1946.

Bro. B. C. Evans acted as Chairman.

Rev. Felton Griffin elected Temporary Chairman.

Rev. C. O. Dunkin elected Temporary Secretary.

Rev. C. O. Dunkin and Bro. B. C. Evans appointed By-Law Committee.

Rev. Bill Petty and Bro. Baber appointed on Resolution Committee.

Dr. Spurling and Mrs. Keynote appointed on Nomination Committee.

Motion: Dr. Spurling made a motion we call ourselves the Alaska Baptist Convention. Motion seconded; no discussion: motion carried.

The Alaska Baptist Convention meeting in March 1946 at Anchorage, Alaska: Whereas we have now organized the Alaska Baptist Convention and whereas the Alaska Baptist Convention embraces the whole of Alaska in its work and whereas other Baptist groups proposing to do work in Alaska and seeing the need for co-ordination and cooperation in Baptist work throughout the Territory; THEREFORE: Be it resolved that all Baptist groups desiring to do work in Alaska shall be invited to do such work through the office and officers of this convention except for the work already established, and a copy of this resolution sent to all the major Baptist groups in the States.

Report of the Executive Board and their recommendations read by Rev. Bill Petty as follows:

1. Rev. Felton Griffin—Executive Secretary.
2. That we publish a Baptist paper for the convention.
3. The name of this paper shall be *The Alaska Messenger*.
4. Subscription price to be $1.00 per year (12 issues).
5. Rev. Bill Petty to be the editor; Bro. Bill Baker, Assistant Editor one year; John Keynote, Manager for two years.

The Resolution Committee suggests that the Convention empower the Executive Board to form a charter to be submitted to the Territorial Government so that our Convention can be incorporated and have proper legal protection. . . . Motion was seconded and carried. The Executive Board proposed this recommendation to be in force until the August meeting of this convention concerning the disbursement of undesignated gifts be as follows: five percent to be placed in a reserve fund, twenty five percent for miscellaneous use, the remaining seventy percent to be used for Mission funds. . . . Motion seconded, no discussion, adopted.

Message by Bro. C. E. Baber, Songs and Handshaking.

From *Minutes of the First Annual Meeting of the Alaska Baptist Convention,* Fairbanks, Alaska, August 22-23, 1946.

RESOLUTION:

WHEREAS, the liquor industry is a great burden to the spiritual, moral, and social life of Alaska, and

WHEREAS, the laws of the Territory do very little to combat the evil powers of the liquor traffic as it sows unhappiness and sorrow among the people of Alaska,

THEREFORE, be it resolved, that when the Territorial Legislature is again in session our clerk shall send to the Senate, the House, and the Governor of Alaska a recommendation that some laws be passed to curb the power of the liquor industry in its corrupting influence, and in bleeding her people of funds that should be turned into constructive business channels.

Be it further resolved, that a copy of this resolution be sent to the above named people.

Be it also resolved, that a copy of this resolution along with commendations for their stand against the evils of liquor advertisements in magazines be sent to the *Alaska Sportsman.* . . .

From *Minutes of the Second Annual Meeting of the Alaska Baptist Convention,* Juneau, Alaska, August 30-31, 1947.

A motion made, seconded, and passed that the Convention withhold any further financial assistance to missions and missionaries, with the exception of designated funds, until their position in the Convention, their doctrinal beliefs, and their meeting of the conditions of the constitution be determined.

Motion made, seconded and carried that our funds be allocated as follows: 60% for Alaska missions; 40% for Cooperative Program. Amendment passed to send immediately $50.00 a month to Cooperative Program.

Motion made, seconded and passed that the Executive Secretary be instructed to make request to the Texas General Convention for assistance in the Alaska Baptist work to this extent: the General Convention of Texas to send a general field worker into Alaska with the Alaska Convention helping in his salary as much as possible.

Motion made, seconded and passed that Odell Lene be approved by this Convention to continue his work on our behalf in Texas at a salary of $250.00 per month if there is no objection from J. Howard Williams, General Secretary of the Texas General Baptist Convention.

ALASKA BAPTIST CONVENTION BEGINNINGS

From the time Felton Griffin arrived in Anchorage in July 1944, he felt that all Baptists in Alaska should unite and form an Alaska Baptist Convention for fellowship and evangelization. He worked as a painter when he first arrived, then in 1945 accepted the pastorate of First Baptist Church, Anchorage, after Bill Petty resigned to work with needy native children. Griffin believed his first responsibility was to stabilize his own church as a Southern Baptist organization. He wrote that he had "some Northern Baptists who were bucking the program," so he instituted his now famous "Fourteen Point Program" to insure loyalty to denominational literature and mission programs, and to "fight modernism." Griffin felt that unless the same loyalty could bind together the churches, they would soon split into small, weak factions just at the time the people of the territory needed to see the unity and cooperation of a dynamic, democratic, denominational organization.

The Foreign Mission Board had at first encouraged Chaplain Halsell about the possibility of helping, but were not able to follow through with any funds. The Home Mission Board hesitated to help Alaskan churches until the Executive Committee of the Southern Baptist Convention gave approval. Dr. J. B. Lawrence promised help if the Northern Baptists didn't occupy the field. When he brought the matter before the committee in June 1945, they instructed him to contact the Northern Baptist Home Mission Society as to what their plans were. They replied that they were making plans to expand their work to Anchorage and would try to work out details with the Anchorage church.

The society's idea of working out details was put in the form of a proposal to the First Baptist Church: "We will finish your church building and build a parsonage if the church will deed its property to our society and accept our choice of a pastor." Griffin and his church stopped laughing only long enough to reject this ridiculous proposition; Griffin then notified the Home Mission

Board, SBC, that Southern Baptist churches in Alaska could never enter the Northern Baptist Convention.

Felton Griffin, who had been elected president of the Territorial American Federation of Labor, enlisted the assistance of Governor Ernest Gruening and Congressional Delegate E. L. Bartlett, as well as other leading governmental figures in the territory, to urge the Home Mission Board to begin work in Alaska. Early in 1946 Griffin wrote Dr. Spurlin at Juneau and C. O. Dunkin at Fairbanks, inviting their churches to come to Anchorage in March 1946 for the purpose of organizing a convention. Messengers from the three churches met in Anchorage on March 27 and 28 to form the Alaska Baptist Convention.

In May 1946 Felton Griffin sent a petition to the Executive Committee of the Southern Baptist Convention, meeting during the Southern Baptist Convention in Miami, requesting admittance of the Alaska Baptist churches. The committee telegraphed him back that they had no power to admit churches into the convention which was composed of messengers representing individual churches. The Alaska churches thus assumed that if they had sent messengers, they would have been seated at the convention.

C. O. Dunkin resigned the Fairbanks church shortly after the Alaska organizational meeting. The church called Orland Cary, who arrived on the field in June. The next month he wrote back to the pastor of his home church in Brownfield, Texas, stating, "As I understand it, there is no set up for foreign missions in this group of churches, or if there is, the people in this church have not heard about it." He went on to ask, "Can we come into the Brownfield Association and participate in the program of that organization as a regular member?" Thus, two philosophies of the best way to carry on Southern Baptist work in Alaska were set in opposition to each other.

In August Orland Cary wrote again to his former pastor, A. A. Brian, of the Brownfield church:

> I have been in somewhat of a quandary the past two weeks. About the time I received your letter, I also received a letter from a Mr. Wadsworth of the Cities Department of the American Baptist Home Mission Society saying that he had been invited by Bro. Griffin of Anchorage to attend the convention that was meeting here on the 21st and 22nd. I could not figure out what they were trying to do, so I wrote Griffin a letter. It was so close to the time that these

Northern Convention men were to be here that I just decided to wait until they cleared out before putting it before the church. I was afraid that someone might talk out of turn and foil the thing for us. There were four men here from the Northern Convention, one from the home office in New York and three from the church at Kodiak. Bro. Wadsworth from New York really tried to get some things done, but he did not get anywhere as far as I know. He let it be known that he wanted us in the Northern Convention. When he realized that he was not getting anywhere, he tried to get us to draw up a resolution saying that we would cooperate with the Northern Convention in the work here and take the Kodiak church in as a regular member but allow it to carry on just as it is. The Kodiak church is known as the Community Baptist Church, and seems to be as much Methodist and Presbyterian as Baptist. He could not get that done, and then he tried to get us to promise that we would not affiliate with any other convention for at least another year. He had quite a lot to say about us just being an independent group. He put out quite a little bait. He dangled out in front of this church the possibility of a pastor's salary. I could have told him that the church had averaged over a hundred dollars a Sunday for the past two months, but I just let him talk. . . . This thing of not being affiliated with an established group is hurting the work here. It puts us in the category of offbrand Baptists and that makes people stand off and look at us for a while before they join the church. In our next business meeting we will get the things done that will enable you to present this church's request before that association.

Lincoln Wadsworth had visited each of the new Baptist churches before the first annual convention which met in Fairbanks August 21-22, 1946. He hoped to get them into the American Baptist Convention, but was not successful at either place. He revealed to Felton Griffin that because of the comity agreement through the Alaska Committee of the Federal Council of Churches, Northern Baptists were limited to Kodiak and other islands off the mainland. According to the agreement, they could not enter the mainland.

The bulletin of Fairbanks First Baptist Church for September 22, 1946, carries the announcement: "On Thursday of last week, September 12, this church was received, as a regular member, into the fellowship of churches comprising the Brownfield Baptist Association, the Baptist General Convention of Texas, and the Southern Baptist Convention. We have been participating in the work of these churches for some time through the Cooperative Program and other agencies." The advantages of such a move were described as "giving us the moral support of that great group of churches" and that it "would bring the work in Alaska closer to them in a more realistic way."

The Fairbanks church clerk wrote asking Felton Griffin for a statement each quarter as to the disposition of funds sent to the Alaska Baptist Convention. He answered that the itemized statement was placed in the paper every month, but sent the report with the answer to some questions that had been asked:

Now I would like to explain about the gifts from the Interstate Baptist Mission. These do not come to the Alaska Baptist Convention. I am the regularly elected "Director of Missions for Alaska" of the Interstate Baptist Mission. These checks come to me personally as the Director of the Interstate Baptist Mission. They tell me to place these funds as I see fit. If I chose, I could place them all in one church or one mission. These funds are not the property of the Alaska Baptist Convention until I give them to the Alaska Baptist Convention. I have placed them with the convention and have done my best to make a proper and fair distribution of these funds. The Executive Board of the Interstate Mission receives from me a report on the distribution of the funds sent to me from their treasurer. . . .

I would like to point out further that not one penny of this money goes to any person for salaries other than to Odell Lene. The convention voted in the last session to pay him $200 a month and he is giving full time to the work. Now this is a profitable investment for the convention. As a result of his work in Waco, four churches have sent in money to the Home Mission Board. These offerings total more than $600 and they represent just a few days' effort on his part. These offerings have not reached my office yet, but they will just as soon as they clear through proper channels. . . .

May I say also that I HAVE NEVER HAD ANY DOUBT THAT WE SHOULD SOME DAY ASSOCIATE OURSELVES WITH SOUTHERN BAPTISTS, NOR HAVE I EVER DOUBTED THAT SOME DAY SOUTHERN BAPTISTS WOULD RECEIVE US. I have written more letters and done more work than anyone else in Alaska trying to tie the Alaska Baptist Convention in with Southern Baptists. I had hoped all along that we would wait until the time was right and then go into the Southern Convention together. This is an inevitable relationship I am sure. I have always been a Southern Baptist and always will be.

Regarding the letter that Griffin wrote, Cary wrote the following to A. A. Brian:

We have the Alaska Baptist Convention on our backs—the *Executive Secretary* wrote me a letter saying he had hoped that we would wait and all go into the Southern Baptist Convention together. . . .

Well, anyway, I felt it was the thing for us to do (affiliating with the Brownfield Association), and I felt good the other day when I got a letter from a Rev. Farmer who is director of the Brotherhood and Sunday School work in the California state convention, saying that my name had been given him through a church in Washington and saying that a group of churches in Washington and Oregon had recently asked to be admitted into the California Baptist State Convention of the Southern Baptist Convention.

This is how that came about. A group of churches in Washington and Oregon broke off from Northern Convention and formed the Interstate Baptist Mission. This group had been sending a little money up here from time to time, and recently when acknowledging same to the secretary of this group of churches, I told him that we had come into the Southern Baptist Convention through the Brownfield Association of Texas and this fellow is the only one that I know of that could have possibly gotten my name and address. The reason I mentioned that to him was I knew that the churches in the Interstate Baptist Mission wanted to become affiliated with the work of the Southern Convention. It looks as though some of these churches grasped the precedent that the Brownfield Association set when it received us, and they asked to be received into the California state convention on the same basis.

This is the irony of the Alaska Baptist Convention. This group of well-established churches in Washington and Oregon that were able to send help to the churches in Alaska did not feel that they were too big to be received into a state convention. But Griffin at Anchorage wanted to wait until the time was right and be received as a convention, even though neither of the three churches is quite out of the mission stage.

In the spring of 1947 J. B. Lawrence of the Home Mission Board wrote to Felton Griffin suggesting that Alaska send as many representatives as possible to the Southern Baptist Convention in St. Louis and ask for admittance into the convention. He stated, "The convention will admit your churches, I am sure. This will open the way to the Executive Committee. . . ."

Griffin sent copies of the letter to Dr. Spurlin and Orland Cary, with the notation on the bottom: "The time is now ripe; we can walk in the front door and down the center aisle. God is leading and we should go in at this Convention. This is the letter that I have been trying to get ever since I have been in Alaska. I received a small check today from the Executive Committee of the Southern Baptist Convention marked Cooperative Program, so they are in agreement evidently."

Messengers from Alaska were present in St. Louis in 1947. As a result, the Executive Board asked the Home Mission Board to request the Southern Baptist Convention for the right to enter Alaska with a mission program. Fred McCaulley, Field Worker in the Western States for the HMB, visited the churches in Alaska in the fall of 1947 and submitted an account of his impressions. After the visit, McCaulley became an enthusiastic supporter of Alaska Baptists.

Meanwhile, Dr. Lawrence asked Felton to get all the information he could about every church and their needs, and assured him that the Board would give Alaska wide publicity that year. In an appeal for information, Griffin wrote to Cary:

> Porter Routh, Duke McCall, and J. Howard Williams are making arrangements to present a petition to the next Southern Baptist Convention for the work here. Now they say that it will be necessary for the Alaska Baptist Convention to take official action at our convention meeting in August, prepare a petition for presentation to the Southern Convention next year and send this to the Executive Board before the meeting of the Convention as did the Kansas Convention. After this is favorably acted on, the Territory will be wide open for Southern Baptists. UNTIL THE ALASKA BAPTIST CONVENTION IS RECOGNIZED AS AN ACTIVE PART OF THE SOUTHERN BAPTIST CONVENTION THE TERRITORY ITSELF WILL NOT BE CONSIDERED SOUTHERN BAPTIST TERRITORY. This makes it necessary for us to stick together in order to get the needed work started here in the Territory.
>
> Now I know that you have some objections to me personally and to some of the work that the Alaska Convention is doing. That is your privilege and I will tell you that I am willing to surrender every position and place in the Alaska convention that I have if it will help get things going here. I will be happy to do so if it will mean a closer cooperation among the churches here. I will go that far and I am asking that you shall help us do this much needed job.

Responding to this letter, Cary reminded Griffin that when California with eighteen churches, heavy supporters of the Cooperative Program, tried to get into the SBC in 1942 in San Antonio, a stormy fight ensued on the floor; then Kansas with thirty-six churches petitioned to get in and their request had been referred back to a committee for the last three years, and concluded, "I wonder if it is logical for us, three churches who have been asking mostly for help, to expect that same convention to recognize us as a state convention?" Cary went on to state his feelings that if Alaska Baptists were concerned about missions, they should be led to actively support the Cooperative Program; if they were concerned for holding the territory, where was a single instance where Northern Baptists were aggressive in establishing churches and doing evangelistic work? He still held out that if Alaska were an association in some state convention such as California's, it would have a better chance of recognition by the Southern Baptist Convention. He wrote, "Of course, there would be this difference. I would not be able to write 'Recording Secretary of the Alaska Baptist Convention' after my name and Spurlin would not be able to write 'President of the Alaska Baptist Convention' after his, and someone else would have to condescend to the title of 'moderator' or 'clerk' and we could not all be Big Shots and become famous in the history of Southern Baptists of Alaska, but I believe it would make it easy for the Home Mission Board to get some good constructive work done sooner, and there would be nothing unlawful or unethical about it."

When Felton answered the above letter, he explained that he had received conflicting advice from all the leaders of the Southern Baptist Convention, but he had been told repeatedly that until "we are recognized as an active part of the convention as an Alaska group, they can not do anything to expand their work. It has to be through some organization here. Frankly, that was the reason for the organization of our own work here. We didn't care what it was called. We just wanted some sort of an organization so we could work together. . . . I have failed in my effort to keep the work united here. This I regret more than anything else. I have certainly messed things up along that line. It is certainly not to my credit that I failed to get our churches together here. . . . In my blundering way I want to help you. We have prayed much for the work in Fairbanks as well as sent our money there."

About a week later Griffin wrote another letter to Cary inviting him to come down to preach the fall revival. He said at the end of the letter, "Now I understand that you and I do not see eye to eye about all things, but I know where you are from and I believe that I know the kind of preaching you do. The gospel message is one thing that we can agree on, and I am sure that your coming to us will be a real blessing if God so leads you." Cary responded that "your asking me to come has made me feel humble indeed."

The New Mexico Baptist Convention sent the B. I. Carpenters to Ketchikan to begin Baptist work in 1947. When Cary heard of it, he wrote to Griffin, "I am very happy to know this; if other state groups would do likewise, that might be the solution to our present problem of reaching all these communities with the Baptist message." He went on to tell that the pastor of the Brownfield church would be with him in revival and would be making a survey of the needs of Alaska to present to the Texas state board.

When he got back to Fairbanks after the Alaska Baptist Convention met in Juneau in 1947, Cary wrote to Brian in Brownfield:

> It seemed strange for four men to carry on the work of a convention, but that is what we did. When the discussion regarding possible aid in doing mission work up here from the Texas convention came up, I told them that it was my opinion that Texas Baptists would definitely do something for the work up here if the churches that are already here were properly identified with the Texas work. When they wanted to know just what that would be, I told them that it was my opinion that the Baptists down there would want an affiliation with some association similar to what we have with the Brownfield association. Spurlin expressed a willingness to present the matter to his church, but Griffin was noncommital until I asked him point blank what he thought about it. He said he would be willing to do that if Dr. Williams would advise him to do it.

Cary went on to express his feelings that Lene should not be sent back as a fund raiser and that the budgetary designation for Alaska missions should be sent through the Texas office. He added, "I have come to the conclusion that any man sent up here from Texas or anywhere else ought to be able to raise at least part of his salary on the field he serves in order to insure a healthy atmosphere for growth and that they might be expected to do something towards missions regardless of their local needs."

Cary was concerned about the fact that the Juneau church had not contributed to missions, and when he had an opportunity to preach to them on Wednesday night, he preached on "The Mission of the Church"; Dr. Spurlin told him the church had been living within themselves and should be giving out more.

Cary wrote that the meeting he preached for Anchorage First Baptist was one he would never forget. He said the Holy Spirit was completely absent. He had lunch with B. C. Evans, "an ordained preacher and principal of a grade school in Anchorage," and told Evans that he thought he was wasting his time trying to preach under such conditions. Evans wanted a meeting to "lay all the cards on the table." Cary would not agree at first, but then decided that it might clear the air. He wrote, "Lene and his father, Griffin, Bill Petty . . . B. C. Evans and myself met on Sunday afternoon." They hashed over all the arguments: Cary's refusing to send mission money through the Alaska Baptist Convention, Griffin's refusing to talk to his church about joining a Texas association; Cary's wanting a general worker and Griffin's sending money directly to Dunkin at the Fairbanks Native Mission, etc. "Finally they put it to me on what it would take for us to cooperate in a general program for all the churches up here, and after 'beating the devil around the bush,' I told them what it would take: Griffin would have to resign as executive secretary, and we would want some assurance that whoever was elected to take his place would function through the board members by mail and not on his own hook."

Griffin resigned and "they asked me to suggest a man to take Griffin's place. I think Evans will be the man. He had been president of Montezuma Baptist College in New Mexico and has had a lot of experience and seems to be very stable." Cary led the Fairbanks church to vote to "cooperate with these churches up here under the new setup." On the basis of their weekly offerings, they would send $45 to the Alaska work and $31 through Mr. Springer's office in Texas. The only difference was that the money they had been sending to Texas designated for Alaska would now be sent directly to the Alaska office.

A short time later the Brownfield Association cooperated with the Alaska Baptist Convention in supporting a general worker for Alaska. The man, L. L. Richardson, went first to Juneau to try to help that church get on its feet. Dr. Spurlin had resigned in the interim. Cary reported, "The Anchorage church has agreed to send their mission money in the regular way through the treasury of the State Convention of Texas. I, personally, feel as if we have made some good headway toward solidarity and cooperation. We now have a contact in the regular way with a duly constituted agency of the Southern Baptist Convention, the Brownfield Baptist Association of the Baptist General Convention of Texas of the Southern Baptist Convention."

At the SBC in Memphis in 1948, Dr. W. C. Boone of Kentucky made a motion during a miscellaneous business session that the Home Mission Board "be requested to investigate the desirability and possibility of a mission program in Alaska, and that if favor-

able, the board be authorized to proceed with such a program."
There was no dissent nor discussion on the motion. As a result,
Dr. Courts Redford, in the fall of 1948, came to Alaska on a survey
trip and preached at the Alaska Baptist Convention. In December
he made his report to the Board. They immediately appointed the
B. I. Carpenters, who had at first been supported by New Mexico,
as the first Southern Baptist missionaries to Alaska. The Board also
set $5,000 for a salary and $1,400 for travel expenses for a general
worker.

In 1949, Dr. C. E. Matthews, Superintendent of Evangelism for
the Home Mission Board, led the five Alaska churches in their first
simultaneous revival crusade. Matthews preached at Anchorage
First Baptist; Dr. David Gardner, editor of the Texas *Baptist
Standard* preached for the Juneau church; Dr. Ramsey Pollard,
pastor of Broadway Baptist Church, Knoxville, preached for the
Fairbanks church; Dr. W. D. Wyatt, pastor of First Baptist, Muskogee, preached for Anchorage Government Hill Church; and Dr.
James Middleton, pastor of the First Baptist Church, Atlanta,
preached for the Ketchikan church. The revivals resulted in ninety-
five additions to the churches by baptism. The crusades have continued annually. Felton Griffin has stated, "These crusades have
done more to advance our work in Alaska than any other one
thing."

In the summer of 1949, the Home Mission Board, in cooperation
with the Baptist Student Union, inaugurated a student summer
mission program. Coming to Alaska that summer were Walter
Scott, Baylor University; William Cowley, Georgetown College;
Katie Sullivan and Richard A. Miller, Southwestern Baptist Theological Seminary. That fall the Board made its first gift for erecting
an Alaska Baptist church building. First Baptist, Fairbanks, received $10,000, with the Board taking a gift lien on the building.

When the Alaska Baptist Convention met in Fairbanks in 1949,
they adopted the petitionary letter asking to be recognized as a
"cooperating constituency" of the Southern Baptist Convention. Dr.
Porter Routh presented the petition to the SBC meeting in Chicago
in 1950, and moved that the request be referred to a committee to
be composed of one member from each state convention. Dr. James
Middleton was named chairman of the committee. The committee
met in February of 1951 at Nashville. Dr. John Barnes of Mississippi was elected acting chairman in the absence of Dr. Middleton.

Several questions arose: "How did the spirit of the Southern Baptist Convention differ from that of the Northern Baptist Convention? What consideration did Alaska want—was it prestige as a state convention? Should Alaska be put on probation for five years? Should they require ten thousand church members before acceptance? Should the Board set up a special organization for developing territories such as Alaska?" Willis J. Ray sent a telegram from Arizona favoring the petition if Alaska "becomes a district association of some state convention."

Before the meeting was over, however, the committee voted unanimously to recognize the "fact of fellowship and our desire for mutual helpfulness," and for those reasons, to recognize Alaska as a state convention.

I was present at the Southern Baptist Convention in San Francisco in 1951 when the committee presented its report. Messengers from Alaska churches were seated, and the petition was accepted with the stipulation that Alaska be given representation on the boards, commissions, and committees of the SBC when total membership reached 25,000. Thus, the petition of five churches in Alaska set the precedent for future admission of new state conventions.

The Chugach association, the first Baptist association in Alaska, was organized September 10, 1950. Comprised of three churches, the new association's first important action was accepting the Turnagain Children's Home as a gift from the Alaska convention and assuming the responsibility for its operation. The organization of the association was a result of action taken at the fifth session of the Alaska convention meeting in August at Calvary church, Anchorage, which approved the recommendation of the Executive Board to organize associations in the Territory.

In June 1951 representatives from the Anchorage Baptist churches met at First Baptist Church with a group of Negro Baptists to help them organize a Baptist church. With seventeen charter members, they named their organization the Greater Friendship Baptist Church and called Charles Kennedy as pastor. The new church became the seventh Baptist church in Anchorage. In the first five weeks after its organization, the Greater Friendship membership had grown to one hundred members. They requested admittance into the Alaska Baptist Convention in August 1951, becoming the first Negro church to be a part of the convention.

When fire destroyed the First Baptist Church two years later, Kennedy and his people offered to clear away the debris if they could salvage usable material for their own building program. The *Messenger* commented, "This is real evidence of Christian zeal and love for Christ in the great Northland." The second Negro congregation, Shiloh Baptist Church, was constituted in 1952 with some members of Greater Friendship going into the new work.

The Northern Baptist congregation at Kodiak sent messengers to Alaska state conventions until 1951. After the 1950 convention in Anchorage, Dick Miller wrote:

> I could not help wondering why thirteen Baptists, unattached to the Alaska Baptist Convention except by the fraternal bonds of love and devotion to the same Lord and faith, would charter a plane and fly three hundred miles to attend a Baptist convention. Mrs. Marian Howe gave the answer. . . . During the sessions at Fairbanks in 1949 she was inspired and blessed by the wonderful spirit of fellowship in the group and left knowing she had been blessed. When she returned to Kodiak and told of the blessings received, others saw what it had meant. She said, "I suppose the people could tell just how much it had meant to us." That night the church voted to charter a plane for a group to fly to the next convention. . . .

After the 1951 state convention in Kodiak, Mrs. Felton Griffin wrote:

> Say! We sure missed you in Kodiak—and we had the most fun ever. Surely B. I. and Forrest can bear witness to it, and they missed the highlight closing. We had a grand street meeting. Some flaunted in front of Felton while he was preaching, but many listened, and, oh, how they stopped when Mable (Cary) sang and played the violin. It was beautiful. Velton Walker closed the service and brought a wonderful message. People fairly tumbled down the aisle coming to dedicate themselves to the Lord.
>
> At the close of the last sermon there were close to a hundred decisions . . . it was the high point of the convention. We will be looking for all of you and your people next year.
>
> The Lord was even with us when we landed at home. We joked about the eight fire trucks following us until we landed and got out and found that one motor had caught fire and our hydraulic system didn't work and the wheel had to be pumped down and we had no brakes. There were no hysterics. The Lord was good.

J. B. Dyal, pastor of the Kodiak church, had invited the Alaska convention to meet with their church. Others who gave reports at early conventions included Howard May of the Cordova Northern Baptist Church, and Mrs. Loretta Burgardt, who worked with the Moravian missions on the Kuskokwim River. She was from an independent Baptist church in Philadelphia and later united with the Anchorage Calvary Baptist Church. After B. I. Carpenter went to Ketchikan, he maintained friendly relations with the Northern Baptist church in Prince Rupert, British Columbia. He preached a revival for the church, and Ketchikan youth attended the Few Acres Baptist Camp near Terrace, B.C., for two summers. In 1952 Eual Lawson preached the first week of simultaneous revival in Ketchikan, and the second week in Prince Rupert. In September 1950 pastors of Regular Baptist churches in Vancouver and Prince Rupert visited Carpenter to seek to establish a fellowship with the Ketchikan church. Carpenter told them of the Southern Baptist work in Washington and Oregon and suggested that they contact Executive Secretary R. E. Milam of that convention if they were interested in the Southern Baptist program. The church in Vancouver, pastored by Ross MacPherson, later became the first Southern Baptist church in British Columbia, and he edited a paper, *Baptist Horizons,* which told of Southern Baptists in the province.

"Welcome to Alaska! God is here. What took you so long?" This sentiment was repeated many times after the Home Mission Board approved entrance into Alaska, and leaders of the denomination began arriving for revivals and conventions. The visitors always took a bit of Alaska back with them and tried to share what they had found. Writing for *Home Missions* in 1951, Dr. C. Y. Dossey said:

> Three weeks before the campaign started, the territory was seized with a severe polio epidemic. The public schools at Fairbanks were closed immediately preceding the revival there. In spite of the hindrances, God gave some marvelous victories.
>
> In the First Baptist Church at Anchorage, a man who tried to commit suicide on the first Sunday night of the campaign was gloriously saved the following Tuesday night and gave his testimony at the fellowship breakfast on Wednesday morning. In the First Baptist Church at Juneau, a lawyer was ordained and plans now to start a Baptist Church at Seward. At the Palmer Mission there was a man saved who now plans to see that a church building is erected there. The writer saw a seventy-three-year-old Eskimo and his wife saved and baptized at Fairbanks. . . . There were eleven conversions among the Eskimos.[1]

In the December issue that year, Mrs. J. B. Lawrence recounted:

Anchorage, with a population of approximately 35,000, has 250 liquor stores within the city limits and many more outside the city. Prostitution, gambling, and other vices are well represented throughout the Territory. It is said that among the natives—Eskimos and Indians—there are only two classes: alcoholics and truly converted Christians. Suicide and murder cause most of Alaska's deaths. One of the most touching situations in the city areas is the large number of children left homeless because of drunken and lawless parents. . . . They (natives) are needy people, for the white man has succeeded in degrading them with liquor and lusts.[2]

Dr. Courts Redford wrote in 1953:

It was a lazy plane flying more than an hour late that carried us from Seattle, Washington, to Anchorage, Alaska, on the morning of May 16. The plane flew the last few miles from Seward to Anchorage between the snowcapped mountains which wore their capes of fir about their shoulders. Alaska is a beautiful land.

One's first impression upon landing in Alaska is that of action and growth. Everything is on the move in Alaska. This is expecially true during the summer season because there are only five or six months in which outdoor construction can be carried on. It seems that everyone in Alaska is building something. . . . Anchorage is a city of contrasts. Small wooden structures built in the boom days share the downtown business area with modern concrete buildings which rise seven or eight stories above the streets. When I first visited the city in 1949, the population was only about 10,000. Today the Chamber of Commerce boasts a city of 55,000, exclusive of thousands of military personnel stationed in nearby camps.[3]

Mrs. B. I. Carpenter told about the Ketchikan convention in 1953 as follows:

God provided what was perhaps the most colorful setting for any Baptist meeting in the world when 175 messengers and visitors attended the eighth annual session of the Alaska Baptist Convention. The group met in the church farthest north on the continent of North America, the First Baptist Church of Fairbanks, Alaska,. September 21-24, 1953. It was not enough that the dark green and usually drab colors of the mountains and hillsides were dressed up in gorgeous autumn frocks of red and gold with fresh white snow caps, but glaciers sitting here and there added the beauty of their peculiar blue. Late travelers had a special show of God's own fireworks, the Northern Lights. Preachers and laymen felt God's presence before this mighty display, and his presence carried through each session of the convention.[4]

Dr. C. E. Wilbanks, director of Mississippi evangelism in 1955, who directed the Anchorage area revivals and preached at Calvary Baptist Church, was quoted in the January 1955 *Home Missions:*

> After the nine-inch snow had melted from the Anchorage area, three of us stood in the chilly night watching the early display of the Northern Lights. Bluish, green, yellow-tinted, and occasional crimson streaks, standing still, now sliding over each other, or disappearing entirely to reappear again in another form and spot in the north, those playful lights held our rapt attention. They seemed to leave a parable with us, too, as we stood there behind Calvary Baptist Church on Government Hill.
>
> The parable was that the whole Alaskan peninsula is as unpredictable as are the far-famed Northern Lights which are seen so vividly at times. No man knows whence they come or whither bound. So it is with the Alaskan territory.
>
> Alaska is a land of complexity, where schools and churches thrive, where riches of mines, soils, and streams allure, and where every vice or virtue known to man pawns itself for the control of the people. . . . Pray, oh, pray for Alaska, our last continental frontier where we are with "Too little too late!" [5]

Dr. Wade H. Bryant, pastor of the First Baptist Church, Roanoke, Virginia, who preached at the First Baptist Church, Juneau, wrote in the same issue:

> Two facts surprise most people. The first is that Alaska is on the same latitude as Denmark, Norway, and Sweden, and not at the North Pole. The second is that it can support a population of ten to twelve million people. The pressure of world population is growing greater and distances are growing smaller. . . . As the western states fill up, homesteaders, farmers, miners, lumbermen, fishermen, fur trappers, traders, merchants, manufacturers, teachers, doctors, lawyers, journalists, preachers, engineers, government workers will move up the coast to Alaska, and the sixth boom will far exceed the others in size, power, and permanence. The tide is already running that way. [6]

A meeting of Baptist pastors of the Fairbanks area was held at the North Pole church in the summer of 1954 to organize an association. The vote was unanimous that the association be called the Tanana Valley Baptist Association. Those present were Orland Cary, H. A. Zimmerman, John Dickerson, Charlie Alsten, Carl Smith, Fred Pelosi, and Carl Elder. The first annual meeting of the new association was in August 1956.

When the Home Mission Board began work in Alaska, one of

its first objectives was to appoint a general missionary to direct the Board's activities in the Territory. In 1950, Dr. Arthur Hinson was appointed contact man for the Board and pastor of Anchorage Calvary Baptist Church. He served seven months before returning to the states. John DeFoore came next to the church under the same arrangement. In January 1954, the Board resumed its attempts to provide a general worker and Walter Haley from Texas was appointed, but the Alaska convention could not raise their part of his salary. By that summer, the convention's financial condition had improved, and messengers at the Juneau convention asked the Board to appoint a worker. A call was extended at that time to Dr. W. C. Fields, but he did not accept the position.

Until 1955 all pastors who received support were counted direct missionaries under the Board. That year the Board planned to put $3,000 a month into salaries; in August 1955 the Alaska convention and Home Mission Board reached a new agreement. At that time Alaska came under the Cooperative Missions Department, and work began to be conducted on the same basis as in the States. The Board assumed direct responsibility for all non-institutional native mission work the following year. It would make loans available for church buildings and make grants for church sites, as well as make allocations to the convention for mission pastoral aid. A superintendent of missions was to be employed to direct this new program.

The new arrangement with the Board was adopted at the Valdez convention in 1955. After L. A. Watson from Colorado spoke at that convention, the Executive Committee brought a recommendation that Mr. Watson be offered the position of superintendent of missions. He accepted and came to Anchorage in January 1956 to assume the position in addition to the duties of executive secretary-treasurer and editor of the *Alaska Baptist Messenger*. The first Baptist offices for the Alaska convention were set up in the basement of Watson's home at 1038 Sixteenth Street. The addition of extra staff members caused overcrowding, and in May 1958, a house at 419 Seventh Avenue, directly behind First Baptist Church, was purchased to house the convention offices.

❀   ❀   ❀

One of the first recommendations ever made at an Alaska Baptist convention session was to publish a Baptist state paper.

The birthdate of the *Alaska Baptist Messenger* was November 24, 1944, when Anchorage pastor W. A. Petty printed and sent out information concerning Southern Baptist work on a single mimeographed sheet. The first issue contained a plea for more Baptist preachers to come to Alaska to begin churches. At that time the paper was sent free to Baptists in Alaska and friends and boosters in the States. It attained a circulation of more than 300 by the end of the first year.

After a few months of publication, articles in the *Messenger* led to correspondence with men interested in coming to Alaska. Soon, C. O. Dunkin came from Louisiana to start a Baptist mission in Fairbanks and Dr. J. T. Spurlin came to Juneau from Detroit. Two more preachers also had arrived in Anchorage, Felton Griffin and B. C. Evans. The *Messenger* carried communications about the possibility of organizing an Alaska Baptist Convention.

When the convention was organized in March 1946, the *Messenger* was given official status and placed upon a paid subscription basis ($1.00 per year), with Petty continuing as editor until Mr. B. I. Carpenter of Ketchikan was elected editor in September 1948, at the Third Annual Meeting of the convention. At that time the paper was changed to headquarters in Ketchikan and was printed by a local newspaper press. The editor's job had been non-salaried from the beginning, but he had part-time help with typing and mailouts. Mrs. B. I. Carpenter was elected assistant editor to aid her husband.

For several years the paper was unique in that it was sent out entirely by airmail because surface transportation was too slow and irregular to insure delivery.

Editor B. I. Carpenter called convention-wide Baptist attention to Alaska and greatly increased the circulation of the *Messenger* when he arrived at the Southern Baptist Convention in Oklahoma City in May 1949 with a 35-pound Alaskan king salmon. The big fish became the talk of the town, and Carpenter let it be known that more fishers of men were needed in Alaska. He stated at a dinner at the Skirvin Hotel that he'd heard "the way to a man's heart is through his stomach. I brought you the best fish of northern waters for you to eat, hoping that at the close of the meal you may find Alaska on your heart."

"How did the fish get here?" someone asked.

"This is one time a fish flew. Contrary to popular belief, this fish was not frozen. In the salmon capital of the world, Ketchikan, Alaska, a new process has been discovered for shipping fish. They are chilled to 33 degrees, placed in a special wrapper and sealed. This then is put in a carton aboard an airplane and flown to its destination. The fish only loses one degree of temperature every three hours even in the hottest weather. They arrive just as fresh as if they had only been taken from the ocean," Carpenter explained.

"Why not freeze them; then there'd be no danger of spoilage?" someone wanted to know.

"If you have never eaten salmon right out of the water, then you cannot understand the difference between fresh and frozen fish. Freezing the fish breaks its fiber down and makes it a little watery."

The king salmon was prepared by the chef of the Skirvin and served to fifty guests from many states. Mr. Carpenter reported that his picture, and the salmon's, appeared in the daily papers with a story about Baptist work in Alaska. "I am not sure but that the fish was more popular than I, but at least the giant king got us a lot of publicity."

After Carpenter stood on the convention platform during the Home Mission program while Dr. Redford told about the work in Alaska, he was met by lines of people waiting to greet him and ask questions prompted by interest in the land of ice and snow. He reported clearing up erroneous conceptions about Alaska and promised to send the *Messenger* to many new subscribers who were interested in hearing more.

The following letter from a serviceman is typical of those received through the years by the editors of the *Messenger*:

Mascoutah, Ill.
July 1, 1955

Dear Brother Carpenter:

Though we have been gone from Alaska for over a year now, our hearts are still there and we could not think of doing without the *Messenger*. My heart especially will always be with Brother Griffin's church in Anchorage, for that is where I found Christ as my Lord and Savior. . . . On June 2, 1955, the Lord gave us a baby boy (we have three girls), and he is named Aubrey Dale—named after Chaplain Aubrey Halsell, who started our Southern Baptist work in Alaska.

Please send our regards to our many friends in Anchorage and

Fairbanks and please renew our subscription to the *Messenger,* only
this year send it air mail.

Christ's servant,
Harold D. Haines

B. I. Carpenter continued to serve as editor of the *Messenger*
until January 1956 when L. A. Watson, the newly elected executive
secretary, arrived to set up convention offices in Anchorage and
become the new editor.

The importance of the *Messenger* in its role of historian, recording the events and experiences of Baptist work, was emphasized
every year in the Annual Minutes of our convention. In 1957, L. A.
Watson wrote:

> Baptists have been a people of history, but negligent people in
> recording history. Most of our past is known from the pens of
> enemies to our cause. If Baptists had recorded their historical events,
> knowledge of our perpetuity would not be so faint that so many of
> our Baptists would get lost in ecumenicalism as they attempt to
> stroll back through the haunted corridors of ecclesiastical history,
> with the mile posts marked by Baptist blood. The history of the
> martyrs would take on new life, if Baptists could read the account
> from unbiased pens.
>
> If Baptists had recorded history, the outbreak of the Reformation
> would have a different hue. The average Baptist could point a proud
> finger to a Baptist preacher, whose name is unknown, that caused
> Martin Luther to take such a firm stand against Catholicism; to a
> Baptist's preacher's widow who caused John Calvin to break with
> the Catholic church. He would be proud to claim kin to millions of
> Baptists whose blood sickened the earth until she regurgitated and
> turned the world into reformation, trying to recuperate from pagan
> Romanism into a new era of God-fearing peace and love.

The importance of the *Messenger* to inspire and influence our
people for good was the gist of Watson's 1962 report. He stated
that much printed matter was like a river of pollution besmirching
the mind, and quoted as follows from Dr. R. G. Lee:

> The vicious influences run on the successive harvests of evil. The
> crushed rattlesnake bites no more, a lion with a bullet through his
> brain devours no more, a spent bullet wounds no more, but a bad
> book continues to destroy, it continues to agitate a current of the
> world's thoughts and life, planting the seeds of disillusion and misery,
> chilling religion, and lowering the moral tone.
>
> You can kill a bandit or imprison a criminal and stop their evil

conduct, but you can't kill the evil started and maintained by an evil book. The influence of a criminal is but a few short years, while that of an evil book that corrupts the imagination and influences the compassions may be for ages. What a scourge is an unclean book! It helps build insane asylums, penitentiaries, dens of shame. While plagues count their bodily victims by the thousands, a bad book has deposited tens of thousands in the morgue of the morally dead—power to bring putrefactions in the land.

Reading an evil book is like jumping through a hedge of thorns to get one blackberry; like swimming through fifty yards of sewerage to one teaspoon of truth; like jumping in a volcano to see if fire burns. Burned be the book that tries to make crime attractive, hypocrisy noble, and impurity decent! Cursed be the infidel book that summons the Scriptures to appear at the bar of human reason, that persuades men to give up the gospel and spiritual religion as a myth, that blatantly declares God is a nonentity, that persuades people to give up the church of Christ as a useless burden on humanity's back, that asks youth to give up good morals as an infringement on personal rights and expression!

Felton Griffin served as acting editor of the *Messenger* after Watson's resignation. In the 1963 Annual Minutes he wrote, "People become what they read; churches cooperate when they know. Our one reading source of information on Baptists in Alaska is the *Alaska Baptist Messenger*. It is our medium of information for all our people. Every Baptist in Alaska should read every copy." When W. H. Hansen became executive secretary and editor later that year, he reemphasized the need for all to read the *Messenger* and was able to report in 1964 that all churches in the convention had it in their budget, with the circulation standing at approximately 1,700. Mr. Hansen's report in the 1964 Annual Minutes contained the following quote from the *Arkansas Baptist Newsmagazine:*

An Arkansas pastor tells of his church's decision to drop the Baptist state paper from its budget as an economy move. The pastor said that it was the biggest mistake a church could make, in the vital area of keeping the people informed and enlisted in the support of the church and its world mission program. He said that there was a drop in attendance and contributions from the day the paper was dropped, and that the church offerings averaged $200.00 a week less for the next six months!

"Baptists who know, care." And how can they care if they don't know? And what better way to help them to know than to send the state paper to them every week, both to those who come to church at least occasionally and to the other half "who never darken the door of the church"?

Jane Perkins was interim editor after Hansen's resignation in May 1966. When E. W. Hunke arrived to be executive secretary and editor, he led in having the *Messenger* incorporated into the unified convention budget. The complimentary mailout was increased to include public libraries, senators and legislators, the governor, and seven institutions of higher education in the state. Later the mailout was again increased to include Pioneer 2000 Club members and display reading at the Anchorage International Airport. Hunke instituted a new format which included a regular picture feature on page three. From 1966 to 1970 the *Messenger* circulation increased from 1,700 to 2,800 copies each month. During the summer complimentary copies are sent to Glorieta, Ridgecrest, Alaskaland, and the Southern Baptist Convention.

3

". . . In the Days of Thy Youth . . ."

Ecclesiastes 12:1

From *Minutes of the Third Annual Meeting of the Alaska Baptist Convention*, Anchorage, Alaska, September 8-9, 1948.

42. A motion made by Odell Lene that the land offered for a Children's Home be accepted by the Alaska Baptist Convention and that the Convention express their appreciation and thanks for this gift. Motion carried. . . .

Children's Home Committee of the Executive Board:

We, the Children's Home Committee of the Alaska Baptist Convention, make the following report:

We have deeded to the Orphans Home Committee of the Alaska Baptist Convention twenty-two lots in the Mountain View area to be sold and the proceeds used to establish a home for needy children.

The Committee recommends that the Convention accept the gift and authorize a Board of Trustees to administer the same in keeping with the wishes of the donor, Miss Mildred Thomas, and in keeping with Southern Baptist usage and practice.

Resolutions:

6. BE IT RESOLVED: That the telegram from Dr. Bill Marshall be acknowledged with a letter and that the clerk of the convention be instructed to express our appreciation of the work of the students who spent several weeks in the Territory this summer serving the church at Fairbanks and the two churches in Anchorage, and expressing the desire that Wayland College will be able to serve the territory next summer.

Realizing the results of a Vacation Bible School program, we recommend that through the Home Mission Board an effort be made to enlist additional college and seminary students for the summer, to be engaged in Vacation Bible School and other evangelistic efforts.

When Mr. William Petty resigned the First Baptist Church of Anchorage in April 1943, he began devoting part of his time to the establishment of an orphanage for needy children. The first gift toward the home came to him from the T.E.L. class of the Main

Street Baptist Church of Hattiesburg, Mississippi. Mr. Petty turned this offering of $13.75 over to the convention executive secretary with the hope that "appropriate action would be taken at the next convention."

At the first annual session of the convention in Fairbanks, August 1946, Mr. Petty brought a recommendation to the executive committee that a fund be collected to establish a children's home. The motion was amended to request the chairman to appoint a committee to study the possibility of starting such an institution.

Mildred Thomas, who worked in a parachute shop, was a warm-hearted young woman with a sincere desire to promote a worthy work for Christ. Her opportunity came when an investment of a $300 piece of land was dedicated to God; the increase was like the ten talents.

On June 21, 1948, B. Clarence Evans sent out this wire:

A WOMAN IS GIVING 22 LOTS IN MOUNTAIN VIEW FOR AN ORPHANAGE. LOTS TO BE SOLD AND MONEY SAVED TILL WE ARE READY TO BUILD ORPHANAGE. NO RESTRICTIONS. YOU (Orland Cary) ARE ON COMMITTEE. SHE WANTS THE COMMITTEE TO HANDLE PROPERTY. MUST COMPLETE DEAL THIS WEEK. WIRE ME YOUR CONCURRENCE.

A Christian children's home near Anchorage was a need that was obvious from the beginning of Baptist work. Mrs. Felton Griffin wrote the following article in 1949 under the title "Do We Need a Children's Home?"

Two weeks ago, a little baby twenty-two months old was picked up in an abandoned home by the welfare of Anchorage. He could neither walk nor talk. He had become so hungry he had chewed his tongue until it was abnormal. The clothes they put on him frightened him until he tore at them. When he was able to stand in his crib, he was not able to get down unless he fell, and his brittle bones seemed to just snap. He was suffering terribly from malnutrition. His wet diapers had made his skin become very red and sore. This was a white baby. Our women went to his aid, but someone had taken him temporarily until the father, who was in the States, could be contacted. The welfare worker advised us there were many more. "Don't worry," she told us. "There are lots of them." This child had already been in a city nursery when we heard about him. They have no room for him, and the nursery head had asked that he be removed because of his need for special attention.

B. Clarence Evans, executive secretary of the convention, took the lead in promoting and supporting the home. He wrote to Lt. Ashton in November 1948:

> I appreciate your interest in the Children's Home project in Alaska. Here are the present facts.
>
> Miss Mildred Thomas, member of Government Hill church, gave the convention twenty-two city lots located in Mountain View community. Proceeds from the sale of these lots to be used for a children's home. A local realtor is handling the sale. He has sold eighteen lots for $100 down and $50 per month. The gross price is $565.
>
> Our big problem has been to find a suitable location with sufficient ground for future expansion. Several of us scoured the country and could not find anything. One day I discovered a 160 acre homestead six miles south of town, ¼ mile from the main highway leading to Seward and the Kenai Peninsula.
>
> I paid $1,500 cash for the improvements—a log cabin, a road, water, and some clearing. I have added a few hundred dollars in other improvements. It will be possible for me to prove up next September. When I have made final proof, I intend to offer to build the home for the convention. There is an abundance of timber on the land. Until then I am offering to secure the convention for the use of what money I use, by my home in Anchorage. I have the home arranged in three apartments plus one large attic room which I reserve for myself when I need to stay in town. I am getting $250 a month income. I have the house listed at $12,000.
>
> I have talked with the Land Office head, Mr. Puckett. He showed me Interior rulings to the effect that building the Children's Home would not interfere with my homestead rights.
>
> My own family expense has made the carrying of the $1,500 a heavy burden. I asked the committee for a loan to enable me to hold this land and at the same time take advantage of purchasing some material and equipment. Miss Thomas, now Mrs. Lene, has approved the transaction. You are a member of the Home committee. I would like to have your reaction.

After Mr. Evans finished building the basement, he and his wife took in the first few children. The first ones were small and helpless. One little girl asked a visitor one day, "Does your Daddy beat you? My Daddy does, and he threw me against the wall." The nightmare never left her mind; she never outgrew beating her head against the wall or on a pillow at night. In 1949 Mr. Evans wrote to Orland Cary:

> I was laid off last week because of a reduction in force. I would like to give full time to the mission and the orphanage. I am helping

build the home now. I don't intend to look for a job, but give all my time to this work. Do you suppose you could interest some group down home to assist me with a modest salary so I could devote all my time to the work?

We are putting the roof on the Home today. The building is frame. I think we'll be in it by Thanksgiving. I am looking forward to doing a good work.

Carl Rylander of Anchorage helped build the upper part of the home. One major problem at first was the well. Mr. Evans dug the first one by hand, only to have it cave in; another one had to be dug, and this one was used for fifteen years. Fourteen children were allowed as the maximum at first. Baptist women from the churches helped out with the laundry; baths had to be rationed.

In August 1950 when the convention met at Calvary Baptist Church of Anchorage, some of the messengers believed the convention was not ready for institutional work. After much discussion, the convention reversed previous actions and refused to accept the responsibility for the orphanage.

For some time Mr. Evans supported this endeavor almost alone, but in September 1950 the newly organized Chugach Baptist Association voted to take the responsibility for the work. In November 1951 the First Baptist Church, Anchorage, assumed its care and indebtedness, which included $5,000 on a farm loan. The property transferred included one hundred acres of land, a house, farm machinery, and two cows. Mr. Evans later decided to sell the remaining forty-seven acres of his homestead, and the church purchased this property for $20,000, paying $3,000 down and $150 per month. This debt was paid off in 1959. From 1950 until 1956 the property was held in the name of the First Baptist Church and activities were directed by a Board of Directors elected by the church, then later by Chugach association.

At Valdez in 1955, immediately after the convention had accepted a new constitution, Felton Griffin moved that a committee be appointed to investigate the possibility of the convention sponsoring the Turnagain Children's Home. This action was approved by the messengers. The New Enterprise Committee brought a favorable report to the convention which met at Faith Baptist Church in August 1956, and the convention voted unanimously to accept the orphanage.

Accurate records were not kept in the beginning, but the known records show that 129 children have been registered and lived at the Turnagain Children's Home, as it was named. Many others have received temporary emergency care. Every boy and girl old enough to make a voluntary decision has accepted Christ as Savior. Regular Bible reading, prayer, and activity in church have always been a part of the home's program.

Mr. and Mrs. Evans served the home for five years until her health broke under the load. One particularly hard time for her was Christmas 1951 when almost all the children had mumps and Mrs. Evans caught them too. At that time Mr. Evans wrote, "Due to the dry weather, the water supply has been very limited, but we rejoice that our two cows have held up marvelously in milk production during the cold months and have furnished all the milk and butter needed for the 14 children."

Those who have served the Turnagain Children's Home in addition to the Evanses include: Mr. and Mrs. Frank Miller, Mr. and Mrs. Arthur Purnel, Mr. and Mrs. Stanley Sanders, Mr. and Mrs. Harold Jones, Mrs. Felton Griffin, Mr. and Mrs. Ted Twinley, and since June 1957, Ed and Ruby Knutsen. Through these last years Mr. Knutsen's mother, "Bestamor," has been a loving grandmother to all the children. Until a bad heart condition limited her activities, Bestamor was the faithful baker and mender also.

Many good adoptive homes have been found for the children. Good reports have come from every one. Recently a letter came saying, "If it hadn't been for you, Mama, Ruby, and Ed, I don't know what I'd be today. I'm trying to teach my little girl all that you taught me."

Funding the home has always been the greatest problem. No state funds have been accepted. Military help has made one of the major contributions through the years. Churches, W.M.U. organizations, and civic and charitable groups have given much.

Once after preaching at Kiana, L.A. Watson took the responsibility for taking a fifteen-month-old baby boy to Anchorage to be cared for at the Turnagain Children's Home. The baby's mother accompanied them to Kotzebue, took care of him that night, and prepared him for the journey the next day.

When they got up the next morning, John Thomas, missionary at Kotzebue, decided to fly the baby and Watson to Fairbanks. Since Watson had to care for the baby, they became inseparable companions on the trip. Arriving in Nenana early in the day, they decided to fly on to Anchorage. Harvey, the baby, wasn't fed at Nenana so he became unhappy and cried for two hours until they finally had to land at Talkeetna. Darkness had overtaken them.

As soon as the plane landed, a man offered to take them to his home to feed the baby. Harvey was happy after that, giving everyone big smiles, until at the roadhouse he saw a fellow with whiskers all over his face. Not being accustomed to seeing bearded people because Eskimos do not grow beards, he was frightened at the sight and really let it out for a while. Watson hugged him close, but began to think they were not going to get him settled down that night.

Because the roadhouse was not equipped with baby beds, they attempted to sleep on three twin beds. Watson lay with Harvey until he had gone to sleep. After moving to his own bed, he heard Harving whining and got up to see about him. He found that Harvey had rolled off onto the floor. He wasn't used to sleeping on a bed in the first place. Watson put him back on the bed and slept with him the rest of the night to keep him from rolling off again.

Since Harvey was short on diapers, the decision of whether it would be better to wash the dirty ones or carry them had to be made. They decided to wash. John Thomas, the missionary, and L. A. Watson, the executive secretary of the Alaska Baptist Convention, had a big laugh over the sight of the two of them trying to get those diapers clean. Watson voiced his gratitude that there was not to be a week of this.

It had started to rain during the night, and the next morning after they took off the clouds closed in, forcing them to return to the landing strip to wait for the ceiling to lift. Fortunately for their extra passenger, who was becoming quite a concern, the rain let up later in the day, and they continued on to Anchorage where Harvey was delivered to his new home.

Georgia Greatreaks came to the home in 1959. By the time she started to school, Georgia had already accepted Christ. One Sunday evening in May 1970, I attended a G. A. coronation service at University Baptist Church in Anchorage and saw Georgia advance to the Princess step. All the children from the home were there to watch her achieve this honor.

✿   ✿   ✿

Student summer missionaries have made invaluable contributions to Baptist work in Alaska. In August 1946 I attended California's first Baptist Student Union retreat. Our guest speakers were Bob Denny and Bill Marshall. Dr. Marshall thrilled us by telling how students were going everywhere, even as far away as Hawaii and Alaska. Later I met two of the first Alaska student workers, Miss Favor and Sid Davis, both from Buckeye, Arizona. Sid and his family belonged to the same church we belonged to in Phoenix, and we served together in enlargement campaigns. Orland Cary wrote to B. C. Evans in August 1948, "Miss Favor is an excellent soloist and pianist. Sid Davis is leading the singing here and he is good, and also sings well as a soloist."

Baptist Student Union work began at the University of Alaska in 1956. The new organization had nine in attendance at its first meeting. Pastor-advisor John Jeffcoat stated that the group was indebted to James Whisenhant for his tireless efforts and profound interest in Baptist work on the campus. James was a junior transfer student from Texas A. and M. The Texas B.S.U. made possible the group's first B.S.U. secretary, Elwyn Gunn, a student from Texas University.

Many of the summer missionaries have come back to Alaska to stay. Perhaps the best known of these are Dick Miller, Opal Hammond Miller, Valeria Sherard, and Louise Yarbrough. Louise served as W.M.U. executive secretary for Alaska Baptists for twelve years, and the others have worked for many years with the Eskimo people. Even those who don't stay or never come back again, always remember Alaska and never tire of telling about its mission needs and opportunities. When I attended the Baptist Center Christmas service in Jerusalem in 1968, Dr. Lindsey introduced me as coming from Alaska. After the service I met the other missionaries who serve our Baptist churches in that part of Israel, the Norman Lytles, and Norman wanted to hear all about all the churches up here; he had been a summer missionary here one summer.

Some former summer missionaries, like Carol Ann Holcomb, come back to Alaska as school teachers. Carol Ann came as a summer missionary for four years, then after graduation from Mercer, she began teaching on an island in the Aleutians. This year she is teaching on Elmendorf Air Force Base. Other summer missionaries leave missions behind that grow into churches. Dr. J. T. Burdine related the story of one such young man in the June 1963 *Home Missions*.

the year ¿
went
there

BSU summer missionary from Georgia Institute of Technology, Jerry Jarrell arrived in Fairbanks in the summer of 1962 to help the University Baptist Church of College start mission work around Clear Site, located about 90 miles from Fairbanks. The area is a part of the Air Force Ballistic Missile Early Warning System; two other communities of missile employees are here. One is Rex, consisting of two large trailer courts. The other is Anderson.

Jerry and I drove out to survey the field. In the long daylight of June we drove until 10 or 11 P.M. Knowing no one, I pulled the station wagon off on a side road in the woods at night where we blew up air mattresses, crawled into sleeping bags and went to sleep.

A tailgate breakfast in the early morning started us off for more surveying. We had only begun when a black bear came out by the side of the road to gaze, but as we slowed the car, he gave us a once over and headed back to the woods. . . .

Portland, Oregon, has the nearest Baptist Book Store, but we rounded up surplus Army and Navy hymnals, a surplus tent for living or services, Sunday school literature from the church, canned goods for food—and a motorscooter. . . .

The motorscooter was of uncertain vintage, mail ordered into Alaska some years before. One of our members had bought it especially for the mission and had fixed it up with what was at hand. It coughed, but it ran. Chips in the paint showed several layers for the vehicle's several owners. One was green, another orange, several were in between. Its present color was golden, but that was not its disposition.

With the entire load of gear in the station wagon, we took off for Clear. I frankly did not know where Jerry was to sleep as there were no hotels or motels in the area. I mentioned the tent. Jerry mentioned the bear.[7]

They found a spare room to rent for Jerry and a place to hold services in a large wanigan (a building attached to a mobile home). By the time Jerry ended his summer, he had begun worship services in both communities and held Vacation Bible Schools for two weeks in each place. At the Rex Mission, 75 people were present for the Parents' Night program. Eighteen persons came into the fellowship of University church from the missions. The motorscooter became a familiar sight and sound in both communities and the 15-mile-road between the two became accustomed to its wheels. Finally, it refused to go any longer, and before repair parts arrived, Jerry was on his way back to Georgia Tech. Now a pastor is on the field.

✤   ✤   ✤

After serving as a student summer missionary for two years,

Still there *serving the Lord in 1984*

in August 1950 Dick Miller, a graduate of Mississippi College, was
appointed by the Home Mission Board to serve in Ketchikan as an
assistant to B. I. Carpenter. Dick, an accomplished musician, had
charge of the music program at the Ketchikan church. He also
worked with the home Bible fellowship at Annette Island and
was associate editor of the *Alaska Baptist Messenger*. After about
eighteen months there, Dick next served as interim pastor of the
Fairbanks Native Baptist Mission, and in the summer of 1953 he
was appointed by the Board to begin Baptist work in Kotzebue.

He rented a small cabin in Kotzebue, and by knocking out a
partition, made enough room to hold services. The first was on
August 8, 1953, and by the third Sunday there were nine in Sunday
school and fifteen in an evening preaching service. In September
the Home Mission Board bought a two-story building facing the
beach and provided $2,000 for repairs. Tom Willock assisted in the
remodeling of the building. The Christmas service on December
20, 1953, was the first service in the new auditorium. Dick wrote
about preparations for the service in a story "One Won" in the
March 1954 *Messenger*.

He first met Fred Flood in August. Between then and December, Fred was in trouble with the law, but he was back helping
Dick change the former pool room into a church auditorium for
Christmas. After dismantling and storing pool tables and cleaning
out the room, Dick began to wonder where to find a Christmas
tree. There were some spruce across the bay, but they were
twenty-five miles away.

Fred offered to take his dog team, so they made the thirty
mile trip in minus nineteen degree weather and came back with a
tree and enough branches to decorate the church. About ninety
persons crowded in for the program.

On Christmas Day, Fred accepted Christ. For some time he
was the only boy in the village attempting to live as a Christian.
He soon began teaching a junior class and became president of the
new Training Union.

Those who remember studying the 1954 mission book written
by Harold Dye may also remember feeling somewhat sorry for
Dick, the young man in Kotzebue who was unmarried and seemingly stuck away off from all hope of finding a wife. But we didn't
know the whole story. Opal Hammond Miller can fill us in:

Before I graduated from college, California had begun to participate in the student summer mission program. That year they planned to send two to Hawaii. I was chosen to go, but at the last minute they decided that instead of sending both of us to Hawaii, I would go to Alaska.

I spent my first night in Anchorage with Louise Yarbrough on a couch in John DeFoore's basement. The next day I traveled on to Valdez where I was to work. At the end of the summer, I stopped by the state convention which was meeting in Juneau, and that's where I met Dick. The convention was one in which all the messengers slept at the church, the women on one side of the basement and the men on the other side. I remember Dr. Carpenter asking Dick and Valeria out to eat with him at a restaurant, and as a kind of afterthought, he asked me too. We got quite well acquainted, but after the convention, I went back to Golden Gate seminary and Dick left for Kotzebue where he was working.

We corresponded from August until the end of the year, then in January we were married back in Texas. I feel that our meeting each other was in the plan of God, because in his work at Kotzebue, Dick rarely had the opportunity to meet any girls.

We stayed in the States about a month, then went home to Kotzebue in late February. It was a pretty good time. The days had begun to get longer and warmer, so we could look forward to breakup coming before long.

I married a family of sorts. Willie Hensley,* an Eskimo boy of about twelve years of age, was living with Dick. We had talked it over and agreed to continue to care for him. He lived with us another year and a half, then when he graduated from eighth grade, he went to school in Tennessee.

The summer after we were married, Dick built a mission building at Selawik; the summer before he had built one at Kobuk. The next summer he built the new building at Kotzebue, then next at Kiana, so we were in a building program every summer.

I think one of the highlights of our ministry in the Arctic was the many guests we had. We constantly had people from the Home Mission Board or somewhere. These people were interested in the work and really wanted to know more so they could help us.

One happy occasion was when the Kotzebue church constituted. The members located in Kotzebue, Selawik, and Kobuk missions were granted letters from the Native Baptist Church, Fairbanks. We had thirty-one charter members.

From Kotzebue we moved down on the lower Yukon to Mountain

---

* Willie Hensley is a state representative and Democratic chairman today and often figures prominently in the news of Alaska, especially in native claims issues. In May 1970 he filed for the Kotzebue area's single Senate seat. He served two years as chairman of the Health, Education, and Welfare Committee.

Village. We had services in our little cabin the year we lived there. We decided that since the little Mission Covenant Church there was preaching the gospel, we would go further on down where there were nothing but Catholic churches.

We decided to stay in Emmonak. I felt it was a place that was more needy than anywhere else I've been. There was no gospel witness at all. There were no teachers, so we offered to teach the children. An educational specialist from Bethel came to see us and had us wire for our transcripts and records. In a few days we got word that they couldn't use us. The priest had agitated the people by telling them, "First they'll be ringing the school bell and then the church bell. It will never work." Finally, another educational specialist was sent in to finish out the year.

One of the most touching incidents that we had on the lower Yukon came one night when we heard a knocking on our door about 1:00 A.M. Some girls had come downriver from another village. A friend's baby was desperately ill, and they wanted Dick to come and fly the baby out to a doctor. He had the only plane in the area. Dick worried about this sort of thing for fear some tragedy would occur, but this time he got the baby to a doctor in time.

We built a building in Emmonak also. A summer worker helped us. I remember one frustration was that the generator didn't arrive until long after the building was completed. I would like to go back now and tour all the villages where we worked and visit with the native people again.

I'm so glad that Willie and Martha Johnson are in Emmonak now. He was the mayor of the village last year, and he is also their doctor, lawyer, everything to them, because he is Eskimo. They came to us for everything too, but we had to be careful, especially in doctoring anyone, because we knew if anything should ever go wrong, we were in trouble.

We went Outside from Emmonak and that time we didn't know whether we would come back or not. By then we already had the three older boys. The first two were born in the hospital at Nome during our missionary time in Kotzebue. When time came for the third one, I left the older boy in Mountain Village with Dick, and I took the younger one with me to Texas where Mother could help take care of us all. George and John were born in Sitka after we came back from our year in Mississippi.

After their eight years in Sitka, Dick and Opal moved to Anchorage in the fall of 1969 to help begin a new work there. Dick taught history at the Orion Junior High School on Elmendorf Air Force Base that year.

❖   ❖   ❖

Valeria Sherard accepted Christ at the age of twelve and from the first wanted her life to be an influence for Christ. She, however, began to plan her own life without consulting God about his will. The adults in her Mississippi community thought that a high school diploma was as much education as any girl needed. Valeria wanted to get more education. She had always enjoyed reading and treasured books. She decided that she could be a librarian and have the environment she loved, at the same time using her influence for Christ. She made plans to get her B.A. and then go on to the only school in the country at that time which gave a master's degree in library science. Her ultimate goal was no less than to be the head librarian in the Library of Congress.

God opened the way for her to enter college the fall after she graduated from high school. During her freshman year at Blue Mountain College, she knew God was calling her to mission work. "I was aghast," she said. She felt she had no ability to be a missionary and refused to say yes to the Lord. Gradually she lost all interest in books and libraries. To have to read a book became a real torture to her. She thought that when summer came everything would be different; the rush and tension of campus life must be responsible for her confusion and loss of interest in studying and the repugnance she felt when doing research in the library.

Because of her mother's ill health, she stayed home from college the second year. About January her mother improved, so Valeria found work in a civic clerk's office. The work was so interesting that she decided not to return to school. The following fall a preacher, who was a stranger to her, stopped by the office one day and began talking to her and was soon trying to encourage her to go back to college. Through his persuasion she began thinking about returning. Her grandmother surprised her by offering to lend her the money if she would resume her studies. By that time school had already opened. Valeria called the president of Blue Mountain College and he told her to come on and they would find her a place to live. She entered school that year with no definite plans for her future.

After graduation she taught social science in a secondary school. She enjoyed it so much that she decided to get a master's degree in social science. Her way was blocked the first year because she had applied too late for a room in the dormitory. Her father's death prevented her going back the next year. The summer following his death, in the quietness of the rural area, she had time to think and to listen to God. Valeria says, "He revealed to me that if I continued to teach school, he had no reason to let me remain any longer on the earth. I argued with God at first that the school would not accept my resignation, but God promised to take care of that for me. Finally, I promised God that if he would reveal to me definitely that he wanted me to do mission work, I would be willing to yield to him and go anywhere in the world." He granted her request through the inner workings of his Holy Spirit, and when she surrendered to missions, she was filled with peace for the first time in her life.

After graduation from New Orleans Baptist Theological Seminary, Valeria stayed to help close the dormitory. One day that week she walked into a room where Fred McCaulley was having interviews. He said, "Valeria, you're the one I wanted to see. Would you like to go to Alaska?"

She said, "No." When he asked why not, the only reason she could think of was that it was too cold. He asked if she would go talk to Dr. Courts Redford; she agreed to do so, but to herself she asked, "What difference does it make? I'll not go to Alaska; that's for sure."

The first thing Dr. Redford said was, "This will only be for ten weeks because the Home Mission Board does not employ single women in Alaska." She told him that she wasn't looking for a job, especially in Alaska. Several times that afternoon Dr. McCaulley called her room to ask if she had her bags packed. Later both men came to the dorm and brought her an application form to fill out. They told her that she could go by train to Seattle and fly from there to Anchorage.

She thought, "Fly? I'll never do that!" She was afraid of planes and had always said that she would never put even one foot inside a plane. They got her to promise to pray about going; after struggling all night in prayer, she filled out the application in the early morning hours.

When she got into Seattle, the only flight available was on an unscheduled airline that had experienced motor trouble all day. Valeria reports, "As the hours went by before the plane took off, I would have given anything if a bus depot had been nearby; I would have taken a bus straight back home." She spent the time talking with God, and when the plane was ready and she walked up the steps to board, the last of her fear disappeared and she was very calm.

The Home Mission Board contact man in Anchorage did not know when she would arrive, so no one met her when the plane landed about 2 A.M. Valeria decided not to call him until a more suitable hour. During the hours spent waiting, she saw sin in all its ugliness and realized how great the need was for many in Anchorage to learn of Christ. By mid-summer Valeria knew that the Lord wanted her to stay in Alaska. The question was, how? The Home Mission Board's not employing single women closed that avenue, and the Alaska Baptist Convention was made up of few churches; these were small and had their own financial problems. She left her need of support in God's hands and to her surprise, one of the Anchorage pastors approached her about staying in the area and serving as an associational missionary, working with native people.

When she expressed her interest, plans were made to begin a mission for these people. One Eskimo woman grabbed her and squeezed her tightly when she learned that the first service for Eskimo and Indian people would be held. She laughed and laughed and laughed; even after closing the door to her room, Valeria could hear her laughter. It was many months later that the reason for the woman's response became clear. One night in a testimony service, the woman told how for years she had been praying that God would send someone who cared enough for her people to lead them in a mission of their own, and when Miss Sherard came, it was the answer to her prayer.

When Valeria gave the report of her first two months' work to the Chugach association in October 1952, she had taught four Sunday school classes, visited in one hundred sixty-five homes, helped take census in seven communities, taught two study courses, brought three devotionals, made six talks, made nine hospital visits, led four committee meetings, worked nine days in the Turnagain Children's Home, had four personal conferences, written nineteen personal letters about the new work, spent three days at camp, led three people to Christ in personal visitation, and attended forty-five church services, plus numerous other responsibilities she had taken on in order to help the native people. The association was pleased with their new worker, and her zeal did not flag during the three years she worked in Anchorage. She began to visit the jails regularly and to see Eskimo women who worked in the bars and taverns in town. A member of Calvary Baptist Church gave her a 1949 Ford after she had worked two years as a "walking" missionary. The car had been overhauled, had new seat covers, and was furnished with gas and oil for her needs. More and more she began to pray for a door to open for her to work among the Eskimos in the villages, and finally in the summer of 1955 the Home Mission Board asked her to go to the village of Selawik for a few months.

Selawik is located in a rich fur area among numerous small lakes and large rivers. The countryside is tundra with a few small trees along the rivers. It lies just above the Arctic Circle and is one of Alaska's most needy villages, both economically and spiritually. In Valeria's heart was a great deal of fear of going into a strange village where the Eskimo language was spoken. Fear became real to her when a woman at Kotzebue told her that she was praying for her to go to Selawik because she knew what the people there were like.

She walked into the little log cabin where she was to stay in Selawik and immediately thought she must have made a mistake. The place had been closed up for months. Drying skins covered the walls. "God, surely you don't want me here, not here in a place like this," she whispered. That night as she went to bed, she realized that the door was not securely fastened and that anyone could push into the room. She thought again of the old woman who had said, "I know those people." In her mind she could picture them coming after her with knives and guns. Real terror filled her heart, but God spoke to her saying, "Fear not, for lo, I am with thee." She closed her eyes and immediately slept soundly.

Because of missing materials, the door between her cabin and the church auditorium did not have a knob. One night when she was very tired, Valeria decided not to nail up plywood over the door; instead, she merely leaned the piece of plywood against it. In the night she heard someone stumbling through the church, coming toward her room. Quickly catching up her robe, she started toward the door, and as she reached out her fingers toward the hole in the door, fingers from the church came through and clasped her hand. The fellow had been drinking. He said, "I want to sing." Valeria tried to persuade him that it was not the right time to sing, but he would not leave until he had sung "What a Friend We Have in Jesus," mixed with some other songs, then he began to repeat over and over, "I not a bad boy. I not mean to hurt you. I just want to sing." When he left at last, she lost no time nailing the plywood over the door.

One woman became a social outcast in the village after she accepted Christ. Her child was not allowed to play with the others. Valeria went to see her, hoping to encourage and strengthen her against the persecution, but the woman said, "I find in my Bible that Jesus said for us to love those that hate us; people hate me, but I love them like Jesus say." Valeria went away comforted herself. Pressure against the woman continued to increase. She was in fish camp when the pastor came for baptismal services, so a note was sent telling her that if she did not want to come back to the village just then, they would understand and she could be baptized another time. On Sunday morning as she was playing the organ, Valeria looked out the window and saw the child coming and knew the mother would be following close behind. When the woman arrived, she said, "I could hardly wait for morning to come. I wanted to hurry to the village. I wanted to be baptized. I wanted to follow Jesus."

One woman helped for two weeks in Vacation Bible School. She was not physically strong, so it took all her strength to work with the children. She did not try to set a net or fish during the school. At the end of the school she set out her nets which were old and full of holes. Just in front of them were some new nylon nets. She came by the mission saying she was afraid she would catch no fish that year. The next morning she came back by the mission, this time rejoicing because her nets had been full of fish. The new nylon nets had caught very few. She gave God the praise for taking care of her.

Usually, home life of the villagers is very simple. Large families often live happily in a small one or two-room house. To someone who might try to trace a family tree, family life may be quite confusing, however. Sometimes the fact that many mothers and perhaps many fathers live in one household cause exact relationships to be unknown. To the question, "How many children do you have?" one mother replied, "I had four but I gave the last one away." Although they are devoted to their children, they always seem willing to share them by giving them away to people who need them. The custom of exchanging children has resulted in many mixed families in some Eskimo villages.

A public health nurse said, "I have never seen such a religious group of people in my life. They are always reading the Bible and singing hymns." It is true that many Eskimos are very religious, but few know Christ. Their religion consists of going to church—perhaps not the same church each time—superstition, and a negative kind of life. An often heard remark is, "I used to be a Christian." Early missionaries to the villages confronted such pagan practices as cannibalism, polygamy, incest, and wars between Eskimos and Indians. The natives always worked seven days a week and the significance of Sunday as a day of worship seemed incomprehensible to them. Their struggle to exist was so great that they felt each day, indeed, every waking moment, must be used for the securing of food and the necessities of survival. Even today, giving the Lord's day its rightful place is one of the most difficult truths for the natives to grasp.

Missionary work also suffers because of the lack of church loyalty. Many natives who come to town for personal business will not seek out church services. Because their employment is usually seasonal, they do much moving around and are soon lost to the church. Perhaps the greatest obstacle to living a Christian life is the curse of alcohol which completely demoralizes the natives who have contact with it. If liquor cannot be bought, they add yeast to strong coffee and let it sit over night and get drunk drinking it.

The health problem in a village like Selawik causes great concern to those who love the people. Venereal disease and many viruses plague the people. An average of fifteen persons from the area will be in hospitals with tuberculosis, and others will receive treatment at home. Of six deaths during the first winter Valeria spent there, four were young people.

When Baptists first came to Selawik, community life had centered around the one church there which had no formal membership. The people were told that Baptists would throw them in the river, meaning baptism. Those who came to services were ridiculed and called "little Baptists," but in spite of this, the average attendance had reached sixty by spring and two were waiting baptism when breakup came.

In July 1956 Dick Miller conducted the first Baptist service in Kiana. After a Vacation Bible School, many residents of Kiana expressed the desire to have a Baptist church there. In 1957 work was begun and a mission building built. From January 1959 until the present time Valeria Sherard has worked with the Baptists of

Kiana. When she first approached Kiana by plane, the first thing she saw was the mission building because it is located on one of the highest hills in the village. The path to the door of the mission was already well-trodden. The inside was not finished and borrowed lumber lying across boxes furnished the seats. The stove kept people nervous with its puffs and groans, and the folding organ seemed to make more moans than music, yet the mission was already filled to capacity for services.

From the beginning Valeria was impressed with the friendly people of Kiana. Many of them came by to help "settle" her. Some brought meat and other foodstuffs. Over and over she was told, "We are glad to have a Baptist mission here." Within six days of her arrival, she had announced G.A.'s, R.A.'s, and Sunbeams, and for the first meetings had twelve, ten, and twelve, respectively, in attendance.

Writing to *Royal Service* early in 1965, Valeria said:

> With sunshine twenty-four hours a day, the days are still not long enough for the busy schedule day after day. Last Sunday we had a "mountaintop experience." We had a baptismal service in the beautiful Kobuk River and four of our villagers followed the Lord in baptism. Not many came close enough to help with the songs, but many stood on the riverbank. Johnny Smith, a seventy-year-old man, came to the door after putting on dry clothes and said, "I want you to see the new Johnny."
>
> During the worship service that night we observed the Lord's Supper. This is something new to our people here. After Johnny had taken the bread, he said aloud, "Uh-te-gue," which means "too small."
>
> Elsie Hunicutt, whom you and Miss Hunt visited in our village, was also baptized. What a radiant Christian she is! [8]

Later she wrote again:

> We started our second week of Bible school today and we have enrolled eighty-eight. Last week our lowest attendance was seventy-six. The smelt (little fish) arrived the first day of Bible school. They are here not more than a couple of days. However, the Bible school workers were faithful enough that they came to Bible school. One of them told me that they went to get smelt after Bible school. And in just a short time they had more than the people who had been here all day. She said that she remembered Matthew 6:33, and they told the others that God had helped them because they had given some of their time to him. The other people laughed at them and called them "preachers." [9]

In the summer Valeria has to carry all her water in five gallon cans up the steep path from the Kobuk River which runs just below the mission building. In the winter she either chops through the river ice for water or melts snow to provide for her needs. Before winter sets in, she must have about a hundred fifty-gallon drums of fuel rolled up the hill if she is to have any heat. She confessed that she gets some of the village boys to help her if no Baptist visitors happen along at the right time. On one occasion, Leonard Everman from Muldoon Road Baptist Church had "happened along." He had left the last few drums for Executive Secretary Hunke and Missionary Chron to work on when they visited the village a little later. They also unbeached her boat which she found sitting high on the river bank when she returned from the state convention. Thinking back on that visit, Mr. Hunke recalls, "Everything about Kiana looked good to me that day—the beautiful tree-lined river with its sandy beaches, the friendly children who rushed to meet us when our plane landed on the short, once-graveled-but-then-full-of-chuckholes runway, and especially the freshly baked cake and can of corned beef that Valeria opened for us—because we had been eating just fish for several meals."

The following letter sent out in January 1965 is typical of Valeria's newsletters and the spirit of the work she does:

The first Sunday night in December a teenage girl made a profession of faith. She talked to two of her friends and they made professions. During December the three girls spent most of their spare time in my home. One of the girls said, "I like to stay here so I'll be away from wrong and not be tempted." However, the newness and first enthusiasm is disappearing—so pray for them that they may be faithful and grow in their Christian life.

Sunday before Christmas the beginners agreed to make some cookies as gifts. When we were ready to wrap the cookies, it took some "tall" talking to get them to agree to put a name on the package. They wanted their own names on the gifts. Most of them did give them to others. One threw a tantrum when he thought someone else was going to get the cookie.

On the 22nd the G.A.'s and R.A.'s went Christmas caroling. We had ordered apples, oranges, pears, tangerines, grapefruit, and bananas (we asked the store to judge about the weather and sending the bananas—they didn't send them) from Fairbanks. Uneasy minds became glad when the fruit arrived just a few hours before they were needed. We were to give the fruit to people over sixty years of age. I prepared twelve boxes. First we took three boxes to the far end of the village. After warming our toes and fingers, we took seven boxes to people in the central section of the village. I did not go into any home—there were too many for all to go inside. At one place I heard an elderly man say, "Praise the Lord!" At another place an elderly man came to the door as we sang. He was so grateful for the singing and the fruit. Two boxes were left over—I had counted one woman who is not yet sixty. The other box was the one for the Friends' missionaries. But since there was a light in their church and everyone was so cold, I suggested that the carolers eat the fruit. Each one had almost a half of an apple and orange, about one-eighth of a pear, tangerine, and grapefruit. They called it a "feast." For most it was their first time to taste a pear, tangerine or grapefruit. The grapefruit was a *surprise* and caused all kinds of faces, remarks and laughter. But with sugar or salt, I think most enjoyed it.

Our mission building is eighteen feet by thirty feet—from this subtract room for a platform, organ, stove, Christmas tree, and book cases—and in the rest of the room on the 23rd, one hundred eighty people were jammed! Although the room was cold at first (heat was turned off), it soon became stuffy and hot even with the door open. In spite of the stuffy, hot, crowded room, the program was good and through a playlet, "Gifts to the King," the message of salvation was given.

We did not have a mail plane after the 22nd of December until late afternoon of the 31st. It took so long for the postmaster to sort the mail that I did not have time to open my mail before R.A.'s. Immediately following R.A.'s began one phase of our night watch service. The presence of the Lord could be felt and the spirit was good. Most rededicated their lives anew. About 12:30 A.M. everyone had gone. I made myself comfortable and with mail piled around me, thoroughly enjoyed letters and Christmas cards until 2:30 A.M. At that time I decided papers, packages, etc., could wait for awhile.

I planned to go to Selawik the 26th. There has been none of our workers in the village since last summer. I was ready to leave that morning by 9 A.M. I spent the day waiting. The next morning I got ready. I then sent word to the airlines that I wanted to go January 2. Again I spent the day waiting. The 3rd I got ready. And I waited the 4th and 5th. So I "give up for the present."

We are depending upon your support in this year ahead as you often present our names and needs to God in prayer.

THE FIRST BAPTIST CHURCH OF ANCHORAGE, ALASKA

On September 19, 1943, at 3:00 P.M., in the Post Chapel of Elmendorf Air Force Base, the 1st Baptist Church of Anchorage was organized with the seventeen charter members pictured above. The 2nd Baptist Church of Hot Springs, Arkansas, where seven of the charter members held membership, extended an arm to the new work (Home Board Photo).

When 1st Baptist Church was seven days old, it conducted its first baptismal services. With the temperature at 35°, the church gathered on the banks of Otter Lake where Chaplain Aubrey Halsell baptized Corporal Herbert Dennis (Home Board Photo).

Halsell raised $2000 down payment and agreed to pay $100 per month for this fire-gutted home on 6th Avenue in Anchorage to house the newly constituted 1st Baptist Church. The seven-story Penney Parking Garage in Anchorage now stands on this location (Home Board Photo).

FIRST BAPTIST CHURCH OF FAIRBANKS, ALASKA

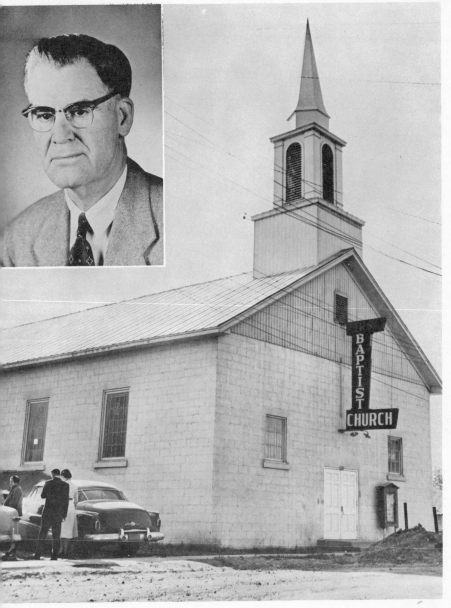

This Fairbanks First Baptist Church building was completed and dedicated in 1950. This building burned in 1961. *Inset:* Orland R. Cary.

FIRST BAPTIST CHURCH OF JUNEAU, ALASKA

Charter members on the first Sunday in February 1946 when the church was organized at the American Legion Hall on Second Street. *Front:* the Spurlin family, Donnanell, Jimmy, Mrs. and Pastor Spurlin. *Center:* Wilma Jenkins, Mrs. Harold Cargin, Mrs. A. Peterson, Thomas Horn, and James Parsons. *Top:* Harold Cargin, Mrs. J. Parsons, Miss Hilda D. Krause, and William Bastion.

The church met first in the American Legion Dugout (1945).

The people purchased this home with 234 steps to third floor (1948).

Frank Allen, Frankie Allen, Miss Francis Black, Jean Bastion.

EXECUTIVE SECRETARY-TREASURERS
OF THE ALASKA BAPTIST CONVENTION

Felton H. Griffin
1946-47

B. Clarence Evans
1948-49

Will F. Lewis
1950

Russell G. Simmons
1951-55

L. A. Watson
1956-63

William H. Hansen
1963-66

Edmund W. Hunke, Jr.
1966-71

A seven-car caravan from Anchorage traveled to Fairbanks (1946).

The convention caravan stopped for a bridge to be built on the trip (1946).

Historically the host church provides a fellowship meal for out-of-town guests attending the convention (Fairbanks, 1949).

STATE OFFICE BUILDINGS
OF THE ALASKA BAPTIST CONVENTION

he home of state secretary L. A. Watson served as
e first office building.

The home at 419 Seventh Avenue
was purchased for the offices
(1970 photo).

The Seventh Avenue property is seen here
across the dug-out basement for the first building of Anchorage First Baptist Church (1945).

The staff and state executive board of the
Alaska Baptist Convention considered constructing a new office building (1970).

IN MEMORY OF TWO PRESIDENTS WHO DIED IN OFFICE

Above: John R. Canning, pastor of Anchorage Calvary Baptist Church, elected ABC president in 20th Session; died in 1966. *Right:* J Aubrey Short, pastor of Anchorage Faith Baptist Church, elected ABC president in 18th Session; died in 1964.

TURNAGAIN CHILDREN'S HOME OF ANCHORAGE, ALASKA

Children line up in front of home to go to Training Union (1967 Home Board Photo).

Ruby and Ed Knudsen pause for a coffee break to introduce a newcomer (1968).

Turnagain Children's Home has been owned and operated by the Alaska Baptist Convention since 1949. This early photo portrays a thanksgiving for the food.

Dedication of Ketchikan building with Edkin, Carpenter, J. B. Lawrence (1951).

HMB leaders Courts Redford and A. B. Rutledge receive appreciation scroll (1962).

W. D. Wyatt, Odell Lene, C. E. Matthews at first simultaneous crusade (1949).

Summer missionaries Opal and Dick Miller pioneered Alaska Eskimo work (1956 photo).

"Atauvakartok" (happy) are the Akins to receive check from McConnell (1968).

Hunke, a Texas layman, and Griffin confer with Jack Stanton of HMB (1967).

The Third Annual Alaska Baptist Convention met with the First Baptist Church of Anchorage on September 8-9, 1948. Orland R. Cary preached the annual sermon. J. T. Spurlin was elected president and B. Clarence Evans became executive secretary-treasurer for the Convention.

The Fifth Annual Alaska Baptist Convention met with the Calvary Baptist Church of Anchorage on August 15-17, 1950. Odell Lene preached the annual sermon. Orland R. Cary was elected president and W. F. Lewis became executive secretary- treasurer for the Convention.

PHOTOS FROM THE THIRD AND EIGHTH
ANNUAL STATE CONVENTIONS

Pastors and leaders attending the Third Annual Alaska Baptist Convention: (l-r) J. J. Mahoney, B. I. Carpenter, L. L. Richardson, Courts Redford, W. A. Petty, Felton Griffin, Orland Cary, Odell Lene, C. O. Dunkin (September 1948).

Pastors and leaders attending the Eighth Annual Alaska Baptist Convention: (l-r) *first row*, Thomas Miller, George Harrivet, J. L. Holliday, Robert H. Jackson, Orland Cary, Russell Simmons; *middle*, Avery Richey, Dan Tyson, John Dickerson, Donald Davis, Harry Wilde, James Rose; *back*, Carl Elder, Jimmy Bolton, J. C. Denton, E. H. Herman, Felton Griffin, Dick Miller, B. I. Carpenter (September 1953 Home Board Photo).

SCENES OF EARLY MISSION WORK
IN THE ANCHORAGE AREA

The Faith Baptist Church of Spenard conducted a kindergarten (1961).

Members of Calvary Baptist Church on Government Hill turned out in large numbers to construct a new building (1953 Home Board Photo).

The Thomas Miller family led in developing the Native Mission (1953 Home Board Photo).

C. Y. Dossey of the HMB division of evangelism preaches at Fairbanks First Baptist Church during the second annual Simultaneous Revival Crusade (1950).

Pastors and evangelists preaching at the churches of Tanana Valley Baptist Association gather at College, University Baptist Church during 16th Crusade (1966).

'. W. Hunke, Jr., newly elected executive secretary, is welcomed to the 21st Annual laska Baptist Convention by (l-r) President Oliver Marson, 2nd VP Leo Josey, 1st P Edward Wolfe, and Missionary Willie Johnson (August 1966).

THE STORY OF 25 YEARS AS PASTOR OF ONE CHURCH

Jerry Griffin and his dog play in front of 1st Church pastorium (1945).

First church building received wing on each side before burning down (1946 photo).

This building, completed in 1953, withstood the 1964 Alaska earthquake.

Laverne and Felton Griffin after four years in God's work in Alaska (1948).

Roger Slwooko, an Eskimo from St. Lawrence Island, is baptized (1961).

The present $1.2 million dollar building is located at 10th and L Streets (1967).

ALASKA BAPTIST MISSION LEADERSHIP, 1960-1965

Native Training School teachers and officers, Anchorage, 1960: (l-r) Felton Griffin, Warden Mann, James Henderson, Allen Meeks, Mrs. Virginia McKay, Mike McKay, Roger Laube, and L. A. Watson.

Native Mission Conference, Fairbanks, February 1961: (l-r) *back row,* Harry Wilde, Charlie Sheldon, L. A. Watson, Martha Johnson, Callie Thomas, Tom Willock, Willie Johnson, Lillian Isaacs, O. W. Marson; *front,* Mike McKay, John Isaacs, Valeria Sherard, Emily Barr, and three unidentified ladies.

Alaska Baptists at Home Mission Week, Ridgecrest, 1965: (l-r) William Hansen, Bernice Gillespie, Norman Harrell, Gunita Harrell, Edward Owens, Louise Yarbrough, O. W. Marson (Home Board Photo).

Direct HMB missionaries (1957): *back row*, Mike McKay, John Jeffcoat, L. A. Watson, Dick Miller; *front*, Bob Craun, Virginia McKay, Valeria Sherard, Charlie Sheldon, Opal Miller.

Cooperative ABC-HMB missionaries (1968): *men*, Harley Shield, Don Rollins, Mike Brown, John Isaacs, Don Wright, Eugene Mockerman, Willie Johnson; *women*, Martha Shield, Marianne Rollins, Valeria Sherard, Virginia McKay.

4

". . . So Were the Churches Established . . ."

Acts 16:5

From *Minutes of the Third Annual Meeting of the Alaska Baptist Convention,* Anchorage, Alaska, September 8-9, 1948.

Motion was made by Felton Griffin that the Petitionary letter be accepted and approved by the Convention and the Government Hill Baptist Church messengers be seated.

"Whereas, the Government Hill Baptist Church is of like faith and order as the other churches cooperating in the work for the Alaska Baptist Convention, And Whereas, the Government Hill Baptist Church in adopting its constitution and by-laws designated that all mission gifts should go through Alaska Baptist Convention channels, And Whereas, we believe that we can best serve in this missionary field by joining hands with you, Therefore, we, the Government Hill Baptist Church, petition the Alaska Baptist Convention for admittance into its fellowship."

Petitionary letter accepted, and messengers were duly seated. . . .

From *Minutes of the Fourth Annual Meeting of the Alaska Baptist Convention,* Fairbanks, Alaska, August 24-25, 1949.

Letter from First Church, Ketchikan, requesting admission to the Alaska Baptist Convention, was read.

Recommendation: That messengers be seated as submitted by churches and that First Church, Ketchikan, be admitted as a member of the Alaska Baptist Convention.

Motion was made that recommendations be adopted as read; passed. . . .

From letter for admission to convention, First Church, Ketchikan: The First Baptist Church of Ketchikan was organized September 19, 1948, with 42 charter members. Because there were not enough visiting Baptists present to form a council, we asked Rev. H. F. Burns and Mrs. Burns, members of the First Baptist Church, Grand Prairie, Texas, to observe and counsel with us in the organization of our church. . . .

From *Minutes of the Fifth Annual Meeting of the Alaska Baptist Convention,* Anchorage, Alaska, August 15-17, 1950.

TO THE ALASKA BAPTIST CONVENTION:

Having been led by the Holy Spirit of God to unite in the fellowship of a local church, members of Spenard Baptist Mission assembled on May 28, 1950, for the purpose of organizing FAITH BAPTIST CHURCH.

During the two months of the church's existence, rapid growth and gain have been made through the grace of God. Six members have been added and work has begun on the church's own building.

Because we desire to combine our strength, prayers, gifts, and influence with those of other churches and because we wish to cooperate with fellow Baptists for the ongoing of the Kingdom, we do hereby apply for membership in the ALASKA BAPTIST CONVENTION.

Pledging our prayers and full cooperation in the work as planned and executed by the Convention, we ask for consideration of this petition by the Executive Committee and by the delegates meeting with the Calvary Baptist Church, Anchorage, Alaska, August 15-17, 1950.

FAITH BAPTIST CHURCH

By Order of the Church, August 6, 1950.

/s/ E. A. Davis, Clerk
/s/ H. E. Allison, Pastor

In 1947 First Baptist, Anchorage, leased land on the top of Government Hill for $6.00 a year and began the Government Hill Baptist Mission on November 2, 1947. Thirty-nine persons met in a quonset hut on the property where the present educational building stands. When Odell Lene returned from Texas where he had served as a representative of the Alaska convention, he had requested First Baptist to help in the erection of a building on the leased Government Hill land. They had made a loan of $4,500 to cover the cost of the first building. Four months later the note was paid off.

The new mission moved forward rapidly. When they organized into a church on February 18, 1948, they called Odell Lene as pastor. During 1948 the church adopted a constitution, held its first revival, and sent messengers to the Alaska Baptist Convention. In 1949 an annex-basement was built to serve as a parsonage and classroom building. The name was changed to Calvary Baptist Church. Pastor Lene wrote about the work at that time:

It is difficult to put into words the struggles and progress of the church. But here are a few of our accomplishments and plans for the future.

During the month of June we completed the concrete work in our new basement by pouring the floor. We are in the process of partitioning the rooms for Sunday school classes and for a three-room apartment as a temporary parsonage. The apartment is the initial step in the full support of a pastor.

The slow progress is discouraging, but we are progressing. We look forward to the time when the pastor will be able to give his full time to the work. At present he is working forty-eight hours a week as a carpenter-timekeeper, and finishing living quarters for his family. The balance of the time he spends caring for some of his pastoral duties.

In every step of our program planning we have tried to take the long look. We are waiting to enlarge the basement to the full length of our property before building the superstructure, and because we are paying as we go, we will not be able to do additional enlarging this year. We are confident that our plans are not overdrawn because only this week the senate okayed a recommended appropriation of several millions of dollars for the housing of some seven hundred families on Government Hill and the suburb adjoining.

We are thankful to God for the added strength, wisdom, and funds that have been given us for the church plant with which to serve the people. We are thankful, too, for your prayers and encouragement.

Later in the summer of 1949 the church purchased a bus to serve its people and also began an outreach ministry. In September, Lene wrote, "Last night I preached at Girdwood, about thirty-five miles south on the Alaska Railroad. There has never been any religious service in this little community. There were forty who met in an unfinished schoolhouse. Four accepted Christ as Savior and about fifteen rededicated their lives to him." When the convention met at Calvary Baptist Church in 1950, the church had a membership of fifty-two and the church property, valued at $20,000, was debt free.

For seven months during 1951, Dr. Arthur L. Hinson, former superintendent of Baptist City Missions, Augusta, Georgia, served Calvary church as pastor. Mrs. Hinson wrote in the summer of 1951, "We have a Sunbeam Band which has grown from six to twenty-two children and three workers. This morning twenty of them were present. Our leader, Mrs. R. C. Perkins, a young mother of two children, was converted just last August. The Lord is using her in a wonderful way." Dr. Hinson enrolled eleven R. A.'s who met every week. Mrs. Hinson wrote again, "In January 1951, we started our G.A. with one little girl. By the end of May we enrolled sixteen. On the night after Mother's Day we gave a Mother-Daughter banquet. Our recreational room was crowded. Mrs. Hamilton, the other counselor, and I were happy indeed. You see, none of them had ever heard of a G. A. until we started this one at Calvary. . . . Our W. M. U. sponsors all the young people's organizations."

In the fall of 1951 Mr. and Mrs. J. N. DeFoore came to the Calvary church from Mississippi. Mr. DeFoore received the B.D. and Th.M. degrees from Southern seminary. He served five years in the army and was discharged a major, having served in the South Pacific and Philippines. Mrs. DeFoore had a degree in piano and violin. During October and November the church had six additions. They placed new equipment in their nursery and beginner departments and new pews in the choir. All were constructed by the men of the church. They also put a new roof on the basement and a new coat of paint on the outside. Under DeFoore's leadership the church leased from the Alaska Railroad the triangular piece of property they now occupy. They were able to obtain the property because of an act of Congress passed in June 1952. Purchase of the property triggered immediate spontaneous gifts into a building fund. The church installed a Carrier Current Transmitter to broadcast services and teaching activities. The transmitter was built by Carl Meeks and his son Mike. The station gave coverage for Government Hill and part of the city of Anchorage, with broadcast periods from 7:30 to 10:00 P.M. on weeknights and 10:00 A.M. to 10:00 P.M. on Sundays.

Pastor DeFoore and his congregation moved into a new, still unfinished auditorium for a special Christmas service held on Christmas Day, 1953, at 5:00 P.M. The largest crowd ever to attend a single service was present to share the victory with the voluntary laborers who had been working through the winter, often in sub-zero weather. The Lottie Moon Christmas offering was taken and two young ladies surrendered to special service during the Christmas service. In spite of heavy building costs, the new budget of the church called for an increase from ten to twelve and one-half percent to the Cooperative Program. Gifts to the Anchorage Native Mission were raised from $25 to $50 a month, and to the Chugach

Baptist Association gifts were increased from $100 a month to $125 a month.

On Easter Sunday, April 10, 1954, the church held a dedication service for the finished auditorium which seated 543. The total indebtedness on the building was $58,000. The architect who designed the building evaluated its worth at $180,000. The church had installed a new Baldwin organ, grand piano, and new pews. Immediately following the dedication services for the new building, the congregation adjourned to the outside to break ground for a new educational annex. They planned to move out old buildings and begin excavation as soon as breakup allowed digging. The membership of the church was 372, with average Sunday school attendance being 253. Again, the members contributed labor. The buildings were financed through several bond issues, the last of which was retired in 1970.

The first parsonage was purchased in 1955 and occupied primarily by Jack Turner, who became pastor in 1956 and served until 1961. Under Mr. Turner's leadership the church completed the educational building. The Sunday school expanded to take the shape of the new facility and the church program grew during his years with the church.

John R. Canning began his pastorate of Calvary September 1, 1961, and served until his death in 1966. The church advanced in internal organization under this seasoned pastor.

The March 1966 issue of the *Alaska Baptist Messenger* carried the following story:

> The seventeenth president of the Alaska Baptist Convention, Rev. John R. Canning, was called home to be with the Lord on February 3. Brother Canning, 54, was preaching in a revival at Tacoma, Washington, at the time of his death.
>
> Since September 1961, Brother Canning had been pastor of Calvary church, Anchorage. Coming to the church from pastorates in the Northwest—the latest at Longview, Washington, Mr. Canning's stable influence was felt for more than four years in Alaska.
>
> The pastor was elected president of the Alaska convention only last August. Almost since his arrival in Alaska, he served effectively on the executive board of the convention, where he was chairman of the education committee.
>
> Brother Canning pastored for twenty-five years. During World War II he was a chaplain in the Air Force. Between pastorates in Oregon and Washington, he was for three years Sunday school

secretary for the Oregon-Washington convention. He had also served as president of that convention.

Funeral services were held February 7 at Hale, Missouri, with burial in Avalon, Missouri. Calvary church had a memorial service on February 6.

Brother Canning is survived by his wife Charlotte; three sons in college; and two married daughters; besides a multitude of Christian friends.

The same issue of the *Messenger* revealed that Glen Canning, John's son, had been named by Senator Ernest Gruening as first alternate for appointment to the Naval Academy.

In 1962 the old parsonage in Turnagain was sold and another house bought, located three blocks from the church. After Canning's untimely death, Dr. William H. Hansen, then serving as executive secretary of the Alaska Baptist Convention, became interim pastor of the church in February 1966, then pastor in June. Mrs. Hansen became state W.M.U. president in 1967 and teaches citizenship and literacy classes which are held at Calvary Baptist Church.

Dr. Hansen wrote to the church early in 1968, "The steady, even expansion of our beloved church causes each of us to thank God for his blessing. It also makes us want to give ourselves unselfishly as have those before us, to advance the kingdom of Christ. Others sacrificed to give us the tools; we must use them for God's glory."

❈   ❈   ❈

When B. I. Carpenter and his wife and daughter came to Ketchikan as missionaries sent by the New Mexico convention in 1947, there was no Baptist work there. A lay-preacher had tried to hold some Baptist services, but no other attempts had been made to establish work in the town of 5,500 population. Carpenter rented a small building in the heart of town, put a few chairs and a piano in it, and held the first service on October 15, 1947. Mr. Homer Crowther was the only one present besides the three Carpenters. Others began to come, and when they organized as a mission of the First Baptist Church, Albuquerque, the mission had seventeen charter members.

Felton Griffin preached their first revival in the spring of 1948. They held their first baptismal service in May 1948 and baptized three, two young women and a young man who was a converted

Catholic. The service was in the Seventh-Day Adventist Church, which had the only baptistry in town.

Before the spring revival in 1949, B. I. Carpenter led in taking a census of Ketchikan. One worker, who contacted nineteen families in one afternoon, found only one family that attended church. Another worker contacted fourteen families and found that although some had belonged to churches in the Lower 48, not one had joined a church since moving to Alaska, and none of the children were in Sunday school. One Baptist man over seventy years old was found living alone about nine miles from town with no means of transportation. He had not been in a Baptist church for thirty-five years.

Dr. James W. Middleton, pastor of First Baptist Church of Atlanta, led in the revival in March 1949; at this time a building fund was begun to buy lots and construct a church building. During the revival Dr. Middleton received a phone call from Dr. J. B. Lawrence, executive secretary of the Home Mission Board, asking him to officiate at Dr. Lawrence's wedding. Dr. Middleton promised to do so if Dr. Lawrence would agree to certain stipulations that would be explained upon Dr. Middleton's return. The workings of the deal are vague, but they resulted in a $25,000 loan to the Ketchikan church from the Board. At the time of the revival the church was renting the Assay Office for their intermediates, a club across the street for adult and young people's departments, the barber shop down the street for the juniors, and was looking for a place for the nursery to meet.

In May 1949 Carpenter performed the wedding for Vicky and Warren Hoyle, the first Baptist wedding ever held in Ketchikan. Mrs. Hoyle taught Sunday school for the church.

In August 1949 Southeastern Alaska was shaken by earth tremors. The Ketchikan church was in the middle of its song service when the shaking began. Mrs. Carpenter, at the piano, thought, "My, I'm getting dizzy." Then as the tremors grew more severe, she said to herself, "I'm going to faint and fall off this piano stool." When she stopped playing to try to steady herself, she found that it was the building and not she who was shaking. Everyone walked out and waited for a few minutes for the shaking to subside, then calmly walked back in and continued the service. None of those present had ever been in an earthquake before. Pastor Bolton at Juneau reported that no one in his service thought the shaking was an earthquake because their seventy-five-year-old building always shook that way when cars passed outside. Their services continued uninterrupted.

In October 1949 the church organized their W.M.U. At that time the church was sponsoring services on Annette Island and Carpenter reported that attendance was good. He was flying over on an amphibian plane to hold the weeknight services in a home on the island. In February of 1950 the W.M.U. sponsored the first school of missions to be held at Ketchikan. Mrs. Frank Edwards, whose husband was employed by the weather bureau on Annette, brought the message and captured the hearts of the audience with her consecration to the Lord's work. Mrs. Helen Carpenter repeated part of the testimony of Frank Edwards in the June 1953 *Home Missions:*

> "How did you happen to be in Alaska?" the inevitable question comes, if you are a "Cheechako" in this great northland.
>
> Frank Edwards told us: "After I had my degree, the call came to students trained in meteorology to serve with the weather bureau in the Territory of Alaska. The good salary and the adventure of going to the land of the Eskimos seemed to satisfy both of us. We landed in Yakatat in July 1949 at 11:30 P.M., with the sun shining like mad. . . .
>
> "The unbelievable midnight sun, the indescribable Northern Lights, fishing in the icy waters of the northern Pacific for fifty-pound king salmon, and picking wild cranberries that covered the lower mountain slopes were all wonderful experiences." . . . After a few months in Yakatat, they were transferred to Annette Island where they found an unlimited and ceaseless opportunity to witness for Christ. . . . One afternoon as Frank sat in the doctor's office in Ketchikan, after having broadcast the weather report that morning, he heard two women across the waiting room discussing the weather.
>
> "I'd like to get hold of that weather man. He said it wouldn't snow until tomorrow; and look at that!"
>
> Frank didn't look because he knew that the southeast wind was blowing snow in at almost blizzard pace at that moment. He just quietly eased down in his chair and put his magazine up to hide his face, praying that no one would speak to him lest his voice give the "weather man" away.[10]

In March 1950 the church purchased two lots on Nadau and First Streets, directly in front of the largest elementary school in the city. Construction began some time later; in leveling the lots it became necessary to use a diesel shovel to dig out a caterpillar

Ke.tchiKAN 1950

which mired up in the muskeg. Progress continued slowly despite many long periods of inclement weather, and when the building was completed, it was rated third on the list of new buildings that had been added to the city that year. It was the second of only two brick buildings in the city. The first and second awards went to a low rent housing project and to an apartment building.

On July 9, 1950, Miss Irene Chambers, W.M.U. field worker who was visiting Alaska that summer, led the G.A.'s of the First Baptist Church in their first coronation service. The two queens crowned by Miss Chambers were Helen Ruth Carpenter and Madge Silsbee. When the church celebrated its third anniversary, Dr. J. B. Lawrence and his wife represented the Home Mission Board on the program. Charles Ashcraft came to Ketchikan for the fall revival in 1951 as the representative of the young people and intermediate youth camps of New Mexico who had raised the money for his trip. On Christmas of that year the church received a check for $1,140 sent from the First Baptist Church of Eunice, New Mexico; this gift allowed construction to be resumed to complete the basement.

During the summers of 1952 and 1953, the young people of Ketchikan Baptist Church joined the Canadian Baptists in their youth camp in British Columbia, with Miss Irene Berryman acting as director of the camp in 1953. An unusual feature of this camp was the day the girls all joined to harvest a field of oats adjoining the camp ground. The field belonged to the woman who cooked for the camp, and the girls decided to forego a scheduled hike that day in order to help out the cook. They finished the job in one afternoon and furnished a practical illustration of the Good Neighbor Policy.

Among the stories Miss Berryman told about her experiences was the following published in the March 1953 *Home Missions:*

> For some time Jerry Barron had felt the leadership of God drawing her to surrender for full-time Christian service. On Thursday night, July 31, 1952, during the Alaska Baptist Convention in Ketchikan, she made public her decision to commit her life to God's service. . . .
>
> The street was almost deserted, for it was in the very early hours of morning in Los Angeles on April 26, 1952. A young woman had been to an all-night picture show and because she was nervous, discouraged, and had a heavy burden on her heart, she was walking up and down the streets in the cool quietness of the morning.

She came to a small building on the front of which was the word MISSION. Curiosity drew her inside, but God had provided a kindly-faced woman to tell the story of Jesus' love. That morning Jerry Barron became a child of God and for the first time she had peace in her heart.

Two days later Jerry was on her way to—she knew not where. But she knew that she must get away from her old friends and associates if she ever found real happiness in her new faith. Later she said, "Ketchikan, Alaska, is where the Spirit led me." She arrived there on May 9, 1952. . . . She is a radiant testimony to the power of God in the human life which is dedicated to him. She was baptized into the First Baptist Church of Ketchikan May 26, 1952. She attended all the activities of the church regularly. She worked nights at a cab stand where she witnessed to the people who came to wait for a taxi. She attended the evening Vacation Bible School class for intermediates. She read and studied her Bible many hours each day, meditating on its wonderful messages to her heart. She brought many to church with her, five of whom gave their hearts to the Lord, three uniting with the church by baptism. . . .[11]

Six weeks after Jerry made her life commitment decision, she left Ketchikan to attend Oklahoma Baptist University. Over and over she had said, "When people know about Christ, why don't they tell others about him? I wish I had been taught about him when I was a child; I would have become a Christian much earlier in life. I cannot remember an adult ever inviting me to church until I came to Ketchikan."

With the coming of the new pulp mill to Ketchikan, every boat in early 1954 brought new families. A young man from South America who worked at the pulp mill, for whom the church had prayed several months, was converted during the fall revival; twelve persons were baptized following the revival. Dan Tyson had succeeded B. I. Carpenter as pastor of the Ketchikan church. On October 22, 1954, Mrs. Marie Tyson spoke to the church in a called conference, telling them that the doctor in Seattle, under whose care Mr. Tyson had been since August, had advised against his return to Alaska because of the strenuous work a pastor has to do here. J. A. Pennington, evangelist for the revival, was authorized by the church to baptize the candidates, and commended the church for their faithfulness and revival fervor during the months of the pastor's illness. The church reluctantly accepted Tyson's resignation.

During December the members of First Baptist Church located

an apartment and filled the shelves with food supplies, then on January 4, 1954, they gathered at the Canadian Steamship dock at 8:30 A.M. to welcome their new pastor, Harry Borah, and his wife and son. Marion B. Dunham was the next pastor, coming to Ketchikan in March 1959.

Soon after Marion Dunham moved to Ketchikan, he received a letter from Byron O. Reed who had been converted in a revival Dunham had preached back in Louisiana. In the letter was a check for $200 and a message saying, "Use this to reach the most people for God the quickest." He took the check and note to prayer meeting and asked the church how to spend the money. The answer came back—"Radio." He told them that $200 wouldn't go very far, but agreed to use it to start a fund for radio work.

Immediately, another $100 came from a teacher in Hannibal Grange College who had been a friend of the Dunhams for many years. Soon more money had come in until the fund reached $515. Mr. Dunham worked out a deal with a local radio station for gospel broadcasting for an indefinite period of time. For five years he broadcast a ten minute message every night except Sunday, and since then the time extended to fifteen minutes.

One time came when funds were not available to meet the bill; the program has never been a budgeted item of the Ketchikan church. Mr. Dunham related what happened:

> The Saturday before the bill came due, a logger from a logging camp 120 miles away came into my study. His name was Don Meurs. He said, "The Lord and I have had some fine times together the years I've been a Christian. We can hardly get your program out where we live because of the high mountains, but we know it's just what is needed in Southeast Alaska. My wife and I want to have a little part in your program. She always writes out the checks, so since she isn't with me, if you'll just make out a check, I'll sign it for you."
>
> I wrote First Baptist Church, Ketchikan, and he said, "Write $2,000." When I just stared up at him bewilderedly, he said, "That's right. We want to pay for a full year's broadcasting, and if there's anything left over, you can buy equipment or whatever you need. We want this program to keep going."
>
> Other smaller amounts came along which enabled us to buy the professional equipment we needed to make these recordings for broadcast; that's been going on all through the years.
>
> Another couple who lived in Ketchikan for six months, and then moved to Michigan so he could start his own business, were the John

Clarks. Their name should be mentioned among those who have given much to the Bible Break. John and Lois have sent us from three to five hundred dollars at the end of every year to be used exclusively for the radio program. With the Meurs' and Clarks' gifts, the work has been able to carry on. Byron Reed and Don Meurs have both gone to be with the Lord now, but if the Lord wants the work to continue, I'm sure he'll raise up somebody else to contribute. We call it the Bible Break because it gives people just a few minutes out with God's Word during a busy day.

Shortly after we started the Bible Break, we noticed a new face in church. The lady had come because our church clerk had invited her. When she spoke to the lady about coming to church, the response was, "I've been listening to your preacher on the radio every night, and I've been wondering what I should do." It was only a few Sundays before I baptized her, and she was a radiant Christian, faithful to the church, until she moved away just a while back. She was one of the first fruits of the radio ministry.

One day as we started to camp and had the children already on their way, I had stopped by the grocery store to buy the few remaining provisions to take, when across the street I noticed a big policeman watching me. He had his little granddaughter up on his shoulders. His name was Arnie Cam. I went over to greet him and he told me, "Reverend, I listened to you last night."

I told him I appreciated it. Then he said, "I listen to you every night."

I told him I often wondered if the message were really getting through so that people could understand it. He replied, "I think I've gone as long as I can without talking to you to learn more. I've got to have help."

I had a tide to make, so I made a date with Arnie for nine o'clock Saturday night. Right at nine he burst through the church door; I met him, and we went up to my study. Arnie broke down and cried, "Can God forgive me? Can he save me?"

I assured him that Jesus died to save even the chiefest of sinners, and Arnie got down on his knees and accepted Christ that night. When he got back up off his knees, he said, "I can't understand why I didn't do this years ago. God has been trying to get at me for so long."

Doc Holman came up here from the Northwest when the pulp mill was built. He was an educated man, a man dedicated to his work. He had grown up in Georgia in a Baptist home, and had been in Sunday school and church until he married, but after that he got involved in too many things and had let his religious life suffer. The time came when his life began being stormy. He began drinking, and eventually his home broke up. We had never seen him in church until one day when we had the funeral for the head logger of the pulp mill who had been killed in a plane crash. Doc came that day, along with more people than we could get into the church. I didn't know the man who had died, but I preached the gospel to the living.

One Sunday a few weeks later, we saw Doc Holman sitting in a pew next to a window; for about six months we could always find him sitting there by that window. Soon, he started coming on Sunday night and then on Wednesday night. He licked his drink problem and became a man dedicated to God.

One day he wanted to talk to me, so we made a date for him to pick me up at Knudson Cove to take a boat ride and talk. Before we even left the harbor, he said, "You'll never know what you've meant to me the last four years through that Bible Break. After coming for that funeral, I never missed a night listening to it. That sustained me until I got back into church. That program brought me back. There are still two or three things to fall into place, then I want you to let me tell the church what God has done for me. He's worked so miraculously in my life." Doc was ordained a deacon in the Ketchikan church and has been Sunday school superintendent.

In 1949 the Spenard District of Anchorage was a fast growing area with some four hundred and fifty families already living there. Only one small Presbyterian mission and one small non-denominational church had located in the area. When B. Clarence Evans, executive secretary for the Alaska Baptist Convention, returned from New Mexico, he asked the convention to pay $50 a month rent on a meeting place, and began mission work. Mr. Evans had a full time position with the Alaska Railroad, but gave much time to lead out in the new Baptist mission without salary. When the mission organized into a church in 1950, the *Alaska Baptist Messenger* carried the following story under the heading "Birth Announcement":

> Alaskan Baptists are receiving congratulations upon the birth of a new church in Spenard, Alaska, on May 28, 1950. H. E. Allison, the officiating physician, states that the new arrival weighed twenty-one members, and has been named Faith Baptist Church.
>
> For one and one-half years the Alaska Baptist Convention anxiously awaited the arrival of a newcomer to its family. During those days a group of people from the First Baptist Church in Anchorage were meeting under the direction of B. C. Evans and H. E. Allison for services in the Community Club building of Spenard, Alaska. On May 28, 1950, the blessed event occurred when the Spenard Baptist Mission became a full-fledged church. There were twenty-one charter members present that day to sign as witnesses of the nativity. Assisting Pastor H. E. Allison on Charter Day were Felton Griffin, First Baptist, Anchorage, and Odell Lene, Calvary Baptist, Anchorage.

It soon became necessary for the new baby to have a name.
Because the church was born in a large community which presented
many needs and challenges for growth, it was necessary that it consume large quantities of faith during early infancy. Therefore, the
name Faith Baptist Church was voted on by the members. To the
diet of faith, continuous supplements of hard work have been added
by the membership.

After two brief months the baby has already shed its swaddling
clothes. Through gift and purchase, two well located lots have been
acquired for the new church. On these, construction has already
begun for the basement of an educational building. The activities of
the church will center here as its building program advances. Future
plans include units which will complete the church and educational
plant.

Membership has increased by seven and new Sunday school
classes and Training Unions have been organized. Provisions have
been made for youth activities. Prayer meetings rotate among the
homes of the members.

The first baptismal service was conducted on July 16 with two
candidates receiving the ordinance. Vacation Bible School enrolled
35 in June.

Mr. Allison is now leading his church in taking a religious census
of the entire Spenard area. His plans for the future include an intense
program of visitation since the census results are already showing
that one-half of the people in that area are prospects for the Faith
Baptist Church. He is also looking forward to the completion of the
church's own building.

Alaskan Baptists have every right to be proud and thankful for
their new offspring. You are cordially invited to visit the new church
when you come to Anchorage.

Marvin Lytle, with his wife and three children, arrived in
Spenard on April 1, 1952, to pastor the Faith Baptist Church. The
church had finished the basement and were having all their services
there, but had plans to be worshiping in a second-story building
by fall. They were not able to carry out their projected plans,
however, and when Mr. and Mrs. J. B. Dotson come to the church
in 1954, they found the members still meeting in the basement
with an average attendance of thirty in Sunday school. During the
eight years Dotson pastored the church, the basement was enlarged
with a two-story educational structure erected above. A pastorium
across the street from the church was completed. Each year the
church was among the leaders of the Alaska convention in baptisms and developed a full-graded, well organized program of
church activities. A mission was begun at Kenai under Dotson's

leadership, and a weekday kindergarten in the church blessed both the church and community. When Dotson was elected president of the state convention in the fall of 1961, he had already served in almost every elective office in the convention. He was connected with the seminary extension classes from the beginning and taught several courses at the center. He resigned the church in May 1962.

Aubrey Short was the next pastor of Faith Baptist Church. His wife Mary Lucy has written of their call and coming to Alaska. He was pastor at San Benito, Texas, when he saw Dr. C. E. Autrey at the state evangelistic conference at Ft. Worth in January 1959. Dr. Short had been invited to participate in Alaska revivals, but previously had been unable to go, so approaching Dr. Autrey, he remarked, "Dr. Autrey, I'm ready to go on an Alaska crusade if you'll ask me one more time."

To his surprise, Dr. Autrey countered with, "Can you go this February? The crusade is just three weeks off."

Aubrey was somewhat stunned, but managed to murmur weakly, "Yes, I guess I can."

The San Benito church agreed to pay the fare and caught the vision of having a share in soulwinning in what seemed to them to be the ends of the earth. The Shorts deliberated for days over what he should take to keep his skin from cracking with the cold; they felt sure he would stay half frozen all the time. He expected Fairbanks to be a solid cake of ice and thought he would have to eat Eskimo chuck and bunk in an igloo. Instead, he stayed in a modern hotel, where looking out of the window on the day of his arrival, he saw on the street a lady from home, and realized that he wasn't at the end of the earth at all. When he came home again and showed slides of Alaska: dog races, Eskimos, mining rigs, bears, moose, the university—and told hunting tales that he had heard and how he had spat out the window and the spit turned into an ice cube before it hit the sidewalk, he had all the men itching to go see for themselves. Aubrey always called his stories "blowing it up where everyone can see it." Then he told how he and Carl Elder had visited in an Eskimo hut with a dirt floor and a smell like cod liver oil and limburger cheese, and that the bears and Eskimos could have Alaska as far as he was concerned. However, God had other ideas.

Mary Lucy could tell that God was dealing with Aubrey, so was not too surprised one day soon after he returned from Fairbanks when he announced, "I'm afraid I'm going to have to go to Alaska. I can't get away from the feeling that I'll get a call." She knew then that she had to pray and be willing to accept the call when it came.

Her struggle was very great. She thought of their son George, a senior in high school and a star player on the football team, at home for probably his last year. They didn't get to see their daughter and three grandchildren often, but could get to them quickly if they were needed. Also, their parents were getting old. Then there were the accumulations of twenty-five years of marriage that would have to be sold. The hardest thing was leaving George, and even though he was left in a good home, for years afterward Mary Lucy would find the tears rolling down her cheeks as she remembered the loneliness of missing him and wanting to do things for him that a mother loves to do. However, she knew God would bless if she would submit to his will.

Soon, two letters came from Carl Elder of the Hamilton Acres Baptist Church in Fairbanks. The first thanked Aubrey for blessing the church during the revival; the second stated that Carl would be coming back to Ft. Worth that summer to finish seminary, and asked if Aubrey would consider coming as pastor of the Hamilton Acres Baptist Church. This was it. The decision had to be made.

Meanwhile, a church in Escondido, California, had written to Dr. Short. It was a struggling church with a very small building for their worship services. The juniors were meeting in a cattle barn nearby. The barn had a dirt floor covered with dried manure. The Shorts resigned their church, sold their belongings, filled a little house trailer with personal necessities, and started out to preach revivals while searching for God's will. None of their relatives could understand why they had left San Benito and were on such a wild trip, but Mary Lucy tried to explain that "when God stirs up your nest, you have to get out and see where he wants you to light." That was what they were trying to find—the place to light.

They stayed in Escondido for two weeks, never unpacked, but loaded the U-haul for which they had changed their trailer in New Mexico and waited on God. Across the highway was a mountain with a clump of trees at its base. Here Aubrey put out a secret fleece to know what God wanted of him. The church at Hamilton Acres was getting desperate to hear from him, so one night Seth Moore had called the sheriff in Escondido to ask him to locate Aubrey Short through the Baptist churches. The sheriff found him, the secret condition was met, and they were on their way to Alaska.

They shipped their U-haul from Seattle, bought winter clothes, and started up the Alcan as excited as a couple of kids. They were elated with the scenery, for soon the trees were bent over with snow and the mountains, lakes, and rivers were magnificent. They met wolves, deer, and buffalo on the road, and learned that recently a grizzly had killed a horse in a lot behind one of the service stations. They planned to stay in the Moore's home when they reached Fairbanks. They met the Moores on the highway between Big Delta and Fairbanks, stopped and talked with them, and got instructions as to what to do when they arrived.

The next day Mr. Short suddenly became seriously ill. Mary Lucy had never driven on ice, but she learned in a hurry. When she arrived in Fairbanks, a doctor who was in the air force and also a member of the church, arranged for him to be taken immediately to the hospital, where his condition was critical. However, he soon was able to be released, although he was not strong enough to begin preaching for a month. Mary Lucy found an apartment over the Dripping Faucet, a plumbing business. After 16 months in Alaska, Aubrey Short wrote:

> Alaska is truly a land of enchantment. Sunsets are made here and reflected elsewhere. The clear, cold, windless nights, the play of Northern Lights, gorgeous sunsets, moon-smitten snow, the midnight sun, the luxuriant foliage, and hundreds of silver lakes in green velvet valleys of tundra—make it a fairyland.
>
> There are wide stretches of land in Alaska where the foot of man has never been. Only three percent has been surveyed.

One day an announcement appeared in the *Alaska Baptist Messenger* that the pastor of Faith Baptist Church in Anchorage had resigned. Mary Lucy and Aubrey read it at different times, but both felt in their hearts that they would be called to serve there next. It was not long before they were contacted by Faith church and moved to Anchorage in September of 1962.

The last time Aubrey Short went Outside for a revival, he returned to Alaska and told Mary Lucy, "I don't want to ever pastor again in the Lower 48; the people are so indifferent and set in their ways. God would have to stick his head out of a cloud and holler loud to get me to move back down there." Of course, now Aubrey has had his last call from God, not to go back down, but to come up to be received into His own presence.

The July 1964 *Alaska Baptist Messenger* carried the story "Well Done . . ."; "J. Aubrey Short, 55, beloved president of the Alaska Baptist Convention and pastor of Faith Baptist Church, was killed in a light plane crash at 5:20 P.M. on Saturday, May 30. He was alone in the plane. An afternoon of visits with his wife preceded the plane ride. He had not been flying for nine years until he took some refresher lessons earlier this year. Practice landings on a small strip south of Anchorage were his aim; the crash occurred as he came in for one of those landings. A memorial service was conducted June 2, 1964; members of Faith church and friends from all over the state filled the church in tribute to his contributions to the work of the gospel in Alaska."

Ben Windham came as the next pastor, but returned to Portland, Oregon, in January of 1965. The Faith church was pastorless for several months until Richard Perkins from Galveston, Texas, arrived on May 9 to preach his first sermon as their new leader. Perkins' church in Galveston had an average attendance exceeding seven hundred; he had served as a vice president of the Arkansas state Baptist convention. The following year Perkins announced his resignation as pastor, effective August 21. He told his congregation that he was going on active duty in the army as a chaplain, and was to report to Ft. Wainwright, Alaska. Mr. Perkins told the church, "I am very pleased to be remaining in Alaska. I requested to be allowed to stay in the state, but was very much surprised that my request was granted."

Edward Wolfe accepted Faith Baptist Church's call and moved on the field on September 18, 1966. He came from the Hamilton Acres church where he had led in constructing a new educational unit and refinancing the church property. Wolfe was Alaska Baptist state convention president during 1968-69. During his ministry with Faith, the church has sponsored the Kenai mission at Mile 8 and Mile 15, while maintaining a steady growth.

5

". . . Out of the City
by a River Side . . ."

Acts 16:13

From *Minutes of the Fourth Annual Meeting of the Alaska Baptist Convention,* First Baptist Church, Fairbanks, Alaska, August 24-25, 1949.

> Orland Cary recommended that the convention secure land for summer encampment for all Baptists in the Territory. He also suggested a spot midway between Anchorage and Fairbanks near the Taslina Glacier area, and recommended a committee be appointed to form recommendations for such a camp. . . .
>
> Special order of business: Mrs. B. I. Carpenter made a resolution that the W.M.U. be recognized as an auxiliary of the convention. Motion was made that the resolution be adopted; passed.

During the week of July 18-22, 1949, Pastor Felton Griffin took nineteen boys and four men up to Mile 87 on the Glenn Highway where they spent the week boating and enjoying camping outdoors in Alaska. He conducted Bible study periods twice a day and the boys joined in singing and telling Bible stories around the campfire every evening. This was a significant beginning for a camping program by Baptists.

In 1950 young people from Juneau, Ketchikan, and Annette took part in the first Baptist youth camp in Southeastern Alaska. Twenty young people and sponsors traveled three hundred miles from Ketchikan to Juneau aboard the *Athero,* a fifty-foot yacht owned by O. R. Skagg. Miss Irene Chambers, representative of the Home Mission Board, spoke to the young people at the camp, located on Indian Cove, eighteen miles north of Juneau. Dick Miller and Bill Causey, student summer missionaries, assisted with the teaching. Pastors James Bolton and B. I. Carpenter directed the program.

On August 26, 1952, a group of Baptists left Anchorage in a steady downpour of rain for the first Chugach Baptist associational

camp, but by the time they reached King's Lake, near Palmer, the
sun was shining and continued to beam down warmly during the
three-day encampment. Enrollment reached sixty-three, not count-
ing the many visitors. Morning hours were devoted to classes and
worship, with chalk talks by Mrs. Avery Richey highlighting the
schedule. Velton Walker was camp pastor; Marvin Lytle, camp
evangelist; Avery Richey, camp director, and Mrs. Carlos Driggers
camp cook. Lowell Krise was in charge of the book store and con-
fections; Roger Laube was chief of police and song leader; Art
Purnell directed recreation, and Mrs. Ethel Lindley was camp
nurse. Jerry Griffin and his assistants kept the campfires burning in
the cabins as well as in the kitchen and recreation hall.

One junior boy created quite a stir when he landed two
eighteen inch rainbow trout from the pier. Felton Griffin and Jerry
couldn't stand to be outdone, so they sailed out on their raft and
returned with a poor, innocent loon. Other moments of excitement
came when a red fox, moose, beaver, and various muskrats visited
the camp. One afternoon Marvin Lytle took Mrs. Lindley for a
ride in the Griffins' rubber raft, and Jerry had to speed to their
rescue when he observed that the raft was beginning to deflate.
Could Mrs. Lindley have been carrying a hat pin?

Those attending agreed that the camp was worth every minute
of preparation and participation. One young man stated that he
had never attended a summer camp that had given as much spiritual satisfaction and enjoyment as this one. The camp closed with
extra funds to be used the following year.

In August 1952 Etheline Hamilton from Fairbanks wrote, "Did
you think all the important trails on this last frontier had been
blazed already? I did too until a group of junior and intermediate
girls and boys from First Baptist Church in Fairbanks and the two
missions, Native Baptist and 14 Mile Chapel, accompanied by a
few adults, rolled up their sleeping bags with a few other necessities, and started for the Baptist camp site by Harding Lake, fifty
miles southeast of Fairbanks."

She went on to describe the sounds of gaiety around the
church early on Monday morning, August 4. When everything was
ready to go, a big truck loaded with the boat, tents, army cots, and
other bulky items led the way. Next in line came the green church
bus driven by Pastor Cary. At each of its windows, two or three
smiling faces peered out. The Carl Smiths' pick-up truck rolled

along next with more camp equipment and an ample food supply. Dick Miller was privileged to drive the Cary's station wagon, then at the rear of the caravan came Charles LaFon, Frances Long, and Poe Hamilton.

Forty-eight miles from Fairbanks on the Richardson highway stood a sign which said "Bible Camp," and pointed off the road to the left. After turning left and traveling about two miles down a very rough road, all the vehicles came to a stop. Everyone asked excitedly, "Is this it? Why did we stop? What do we do now?"

Of course, this was not the camp site and what they had to do was load everything on their backs and pack down a trail to reach the camp. Everyone did his part, and by afternoon everything had been carried in and the boys began to pitch the tents, after chopping out the smaller stumps with axes. Back at the road, a strong cable was tied to the big truck and then attached to the larger stumps. On a backward move of the truck, the stumps were pulled out of the group and thrown aside. Proceeding yard by yard, Mr. Schmidt and the boys kept destroying stumps and edging the truck forward until late that night when they drove the truck all the way into camp. The narrow pack trail had become a road.

With plenty of good food inside and plenty of mosquito dope rubbed on outside, the campers zipped into sleeping bags and slept soundly after the excitement and hard work. At 6:30 A.M., Tuesday, George McDonald beat on a garbage can lid until everyone was awakened and out of the sleeping bags. That was the beginning of a full schedule. Dick Miller preached at the morning worship services and Orland Cary at the evening services. On Friday two junior boys made professions of faith.

The camp was made possible by the many hours of hard work donated by men of the Fairbanks churches and missions. Some of them had gone to the Harding Lake campsite on their Fourth of July holiday for a work picnic and had sore muscles for weeks afterwards. They had initiated a good thing; Harding Lake served as the site for Fairbanks area Baptist camps for the next eighteen years.

The Chugach Baptist Association, feeling the need for a camp program, made application in 1956 to the United States Department of the Interior Bureau of Land Management, under provisions whereby land could be obtained at a minimum cost.

The association filed on one hundred and sixty acres which had been previously filed on for a homestead by a Mr. William Rindge, who was attending college in Michigan. Because Mr. Rindge had made no effort to improve or establish residence on the homestead during the six-month period after filing his claim and waited beyond the prescribed time to request an extension, the government eventually ruled in favor of the association, but only after years of procrastination on the part of government agencies. Questions as to whether the land belonged to the federal or state government had to be settled. The question as to whether the land had been designated for school use also had to be decided. During this time the association used the camp site. Mr. Rindge, in a letter of appeal, wrote to the director of the Bureau of Land Management in July 1957:

> . . . we did not feel it would be a wise gesture to make any expensive improvements on the property until we were sure that it would be legally ours. We felt this would be clarified by the receival of our final clearance papers. We did not receive those papers until July 23. Evidently the Chugach Baptist Association did not feel that legal clearance was necessary, as when we made a trip to our homestead during that time, we found that in addition to a road, land had been cleared and a number of tents erected which were being actively used by the Chugach Baptist Association during the summer months as a recreation site for their congregation. From the residents at the beginning of the said road we learned that there were up to one hundred cars seen in there every Sunday. Naturally, all of this activity resulted in much defacing of land and was centered in the area which we had planned to use as a dwelling site. Also, we did not consider it prudent to construct a road parallel to that of the Baptist Association. Therefore, we decided to wait before making any improvements whatsoever until the legal right of the land was resolved.

E. E. Evans, chairman of the camp committee, in defense of the Baptist claim, wrote to the Bureau of Land Management in reference to Mr. Rindge's letter:

> . . . The land was not properly marked and there were no signs nor indications that anyone had been there or filed a location notice on the land. . . . At the time of Mr. Rindge's return to this area after his summer employment, the area in question was not being actively used. The Chugach Baptist Association had built a road, down the section line, into the area. They had also used the area for camping grounds only three times, for summer recreation for boys and girls of the territory; but this area was never used on Sunday, as our

recreation program permits the boys and girls to be in their own churches on Sunday.

During the period when it appeared doubtful that Baptists would ever receive final patent on the land, an opportunity came to purchase seventy-eight acres at the intersection of the Big Lake, Wasilla, Talkeetna highways. The association voted to purchase the property for $10,000 and use it as a camp site. The first camp was held on this property in 1962. But in March 1963 the association was notified that the application to the Bureau of Land Management had been approved for sixty acres that could be purchased for one-half the fair market price of $15,000. Two members of local Baptist churches made the down payment in the name of the association.

In 1964 the messengers to the Chugach association's annual meeting were in a mood to retain both the Big Lake and Baptist Lake properties, but in 1965 the camp committee recommended that the Wright homestead (Big Lake site) be developed as the permanent camp site. It also suggested that the Baptist Lake site be returned to the Bureau of Land Management and a refund asked. They thought the refund money should be applied toward the development of the permanent camp. They urged speedy development of the camp.

Accepting the report and its recommendations, the association allowed an amendment offered by Felton Griffin that First Baptist, Anchorage, be allowed to reimburse the parties which held the Baptist Lake site and continue the payments.

A major change in the budget was that the $100 a month previously earmarked for camp land purchase would now go for camp development.

The first state-wide assembly was held June 22-26, 1959, at Baptist Lake, a primitive wilderness area, hidden among the hills on the western edge of the Matanuska Valley. William Hall Preston, Sunday school worker from Nashville, was principal speaker. His theme was "Never Hit a Low Note." Mr. and Mrs. Robert Sherer, foreign missionaries to Japan, related their experiences and the history of Baptist work in Japan. Ben Hill, general missionary, directed the camp. The sixty-four persons enrolled camped in tents, cooking, studying, praying together, loaning sleeping bags and arranging air mattresses to make everyone as comfortable as possible.

Felton Griffin flew back and forth, landing his small plane on the lake which was about a mile long and one-half mile wide.

From July 27 through August 1, 1959, the east tip of a gravel-fringed island in the many-channeled Kobuk River buzzed with activity. Shouts of happy children playing echoed against the spruce-covered mountainside across the river. Canvas tents rising above the green willow brush, a parka-clad native woman working at a table covered with pots and pans, clusters of young people engaged in recreational activities—all resulted from months of intelligent planning. In the rugged wilderness forty-four boys and girls and staff members were conducting a successful R.A. and G.A. camp for the Kotzebue Sound area.

Kiana had been chosen as the location for the camp because of its centrality. Charlie Sheldon had brought his boys and girls by boat one hundred and fifty miles from Kobuk. Willie Johnson brought his group down the Selawik River into the lake, skirted its shoreline to enter the Kobuk Delta, crossed its maze of channels to enter the Kobuk River, and came down about one hundred miles. Those from Kotzebue had about the same distance to travel across the Kobuk Lake and up the river to Kiana.

Valeria Sherard, missionary to Kiana, had planned the camp, assigned personnel, and coordinated the program. Louise Yarbrough had enlisted the support of churches throughout the territory of Alaska to furnish the food. Many parcels of food came both early and late, but the bulk of it had come from Anchorage on a C-123 air force plane and arrived in Kotzebue the day the camp began. A large bush plane was quickly chartered to haul the food to Kiana. John Thomas's mission plane flew trips from Kotzebue to Kiana constantly up to 1:30 A.M. on Tuesday in order to transport all the children. After Willie Johnson left Selawik early Monday morning, the wind came up on the lake and caused such large whitecaps to leap into the boat that he put the children out to walk the beach while he ran the borrowed boat through the rough water alone, so his group got into Kiana late also. At the Kiana camp site, Valeria, Kotzebue missionary John Thomas, and Baptist Student Union worker Jim Leeman had worked up to the last minute erecting tents and cutting poles, then because their outboard had run out of gas, had rowed back to Kiana to replenish the supply and pick up their G.A.'s and R.A.'s, getting a later start than they had anticipated.

By the second day everything had gotten back on schedule. Louise was the missionary speaker and counselor; Valeria was camp director; Baptist Student Union workers Jim Leeman and John Strawhorn led recreation; Willie Johnson taught the Bible study; Charlie Sheldon was camp policeman; and Mrs. John Thomas cooked the meals. The young people also followed a program of study to enable them to advance in the R.A. and G.A. rank and forward steps.

The first Arctic Bible Conference was held at Kotzebue April 13-15, 1960. Forty-three persons from the villages of Selawik, Shungnak, Kobuk, and the missionaries from Kwiguk attended the conference. All of those coming had relatives or friends living in Kotzebue with whom they could stay during the conference. Since the area had no roads and the rivers were frozen over, preventing boats from navigating this time of year, all the people attending were flown in. John Thomas, missionary at Kotzebue, and Dick Miller, missionary at Kwiguk, used the two Home Mission Board planes to shuttle the people into Kotzebue and back to their villages following the Saturday services. Only three persons could be carried each trip. The Eskimos who came never dreamed of attending a meeting with so many Baptists as they met in Kotzebue. They went home determined to do more for the Lord. The program included much singing, for they enjoy singing and have many songs translated into their native dialect. One member of the church from Kobuk, a lady who could not read, had her songs written in hieroglyphics. She is the last person left on the Kobuk River who writes this language. The second Arctic Bible Conference was planned for 1961 in Kiana.

The first week of April 1962 the third Arctic Bible Conference was held at Selawik. People came by dog sled, by plane, and for the first time, one Snow-Go vehicle arrived with riders from Kiana. Because of bad weather, John Thomas, who did most of the hauling of people to the conferences, was delayed in getting some of them back to their homes at the end of the meetings. A high attendance of one hundred and seventy set a new record at the night services. Eskimo families in Selawik opened their homes to provide sleeping quarters for their friends, and the Willie Johnsons and two school teachers helped take care of the outside guest speakers. Speakers included Bob Patterson, Nashville; Roy Moore, Anchorage; J. T. Burdine, College; and L. A. Watson, Anchorage.

Charlie Goodwin, an Eskimo Christian from Kotzebue who was eighty-two years old that spring, gave the following testimony at one of the conference periods:

> One time my wife and I have visited a sick man that was in bed and could not be walking around anymore. When we came in, there was no one in the house, so we had a good chance to talk to him about the saving grace of God.
>
> We asked him to pray, as we have seen him being an usher and a church worker before he was ill, but he told us that he have no hope of God hearing his prayers, as he told us that he too deep a sinner to be accepted.
>
> While he was young and before he goes out trapping, he used to pay a witchcraft money for some things he wanted; he asked him that he catch many furs during the season by the help of the sorcerer. He does get his wishes, so he stick to the evil habit to obtain the necessities of life by the help of the evil witchcraft.
>
> In a vision later, the man saw people walking the broad way which leads to destruction. He said there were millions and millions of them.
>
> Before a person gets sick is the time to accept Christ is the thought for these words.

L. A. Watson said, "It was a beautiful sight to see those native people gathering into our mission buildings ready to grasp as much of the teachings of the Bible as we were able to give them." He recalled two vivid experiences that occurred during one of the Arctic Bible Conferences at Kotzebue:

> We were coming to the close of the conference and the spirit had been good. One of the missionaries had just brought a message and we were praying that the Lord would do a mighty work in our midst, but the power seemed a little slow in coming. Then Willie Johnson stepped to the old pump organ and started to play "I Have Decided to Follow Jesus," and they started singing it in the Eskimo language; then heaven came down and those Eskimos began coming forward. I have no idea how many there were, but all of them came to either accept Christ or to rededicate their lives to his service.
>
> The other unique experience was in connection with our staying in the home of the missionaries, John and Callie Thomas. The living quarters were attached to the church building; this way they didn't have to shovel snow to get to the services. We had bedded down as many as we could in beds, cots, divans, and sleeping bags. Mrs. Thomas was ill, but was trying to take care of the folk. Willie Johnson and I were charged with the responsibility of cutting up the caribou, and she was getting the cooking done for everyone.

Finally, she just got down and had to go over to the hospital for a
check-up. They discovered that she had infectious hepatitis and put
her in the hospital. You should have seen the stampede when word
got back to the crowd staying at the house. All of us had been washing in the same basin, drying on the same towel, and eating out of
the same plates. Bob Patterson, who was there from the Sunday
School Board, was leader of the group rushing over to the hospital
to get a shot. He could just see the whole village quarantined and
him stuck there for six weeks. When he went to the nurse, he asked
her to give him a shot in both hips. We teased him after that, saying
that he had misunderstood and thought it was "hipititis." Fortunately,
no one else contracted the disease.

About this same time at the opposite end of the state, plans for
a camp site were taking shape. The Marion Dunhams of Ketchikan
were on the lookout for a suitable location.

Kitschk, whose uncle was chief of the eagle clan, was mighty
among the Tlingits. The valley where he hunted bore his name
when the Spanish hunted the waters of Southeastern Alaska in
1775. "Kitschk" means "thundering wings of an eagle," and "hin"
means "stream." The area where he lived was called Kitschk's-hin;
today the city of Ketchikan stands there. It is often possible to
watch a great bald eagle float lazily through the blue spaces before
settling on a snag and silhouetting itself arrogantly against the
bright sky.

Up in the northeast corner of the four-and-one-half acre patch
of grass known as Orton Ranch, a moss covered boulder heaves up
before a little knoll. A bronze plaque on the boulder reveals that
Mr. Orton is buried here and the two other plaques on the sides of
the rock tell the names of his sons who are buried beside him. A
piece of brass tubing sticks out of the ground at the head of the
father's grave, but the other mounds are unmarked. Thirty years
ago, the mother, Alda Orton, wrote about the captivating spell of
the valley, of the bear and deer, the beaver and geese, and the
fabled black wolves of Revillagigedo.

July 1961 saw some real changes in the old Orton Ranch. They
had begun at Easter with construction of the "Brotherhood House."
Next, the old barn was torn down to provide lumber to floor the
boathouse and make a cleaner dining area there. The woodshed
was made into living quarters for the ranch director and family.
The rabbit hutch and goathouse were renovated to provide additional quarters. The machine shop and chicken house were floored

to be used for dormitories. An assembly building had been added. The assembly hall was named "Ebenezer," meaning "Hitherto hath the Lord helped us." It had formerly been a construction barracks on Annette Island, but had been dismantled and hauled on a barge to Orton Ranch. Youth from the Ketchikan Baptist Church had helped get the building reassembled in a week. The rustic and historic spot, abandoned for years to the ravages of nature, was being salvaged for use in the Lord's service.

Mr. and Mrs. Marion Dunham purchased the ranch in 1960. On July 26, 1961, an eighteen-foot barge loaded with the knocked down, ninety-six foot, prefab, future Ebenezer floated through the "roaring hole" of the Naha River into the Roosevelt Lagoon by moonlight. The next day the crew of the *Willis Shank* brought the building to Naha and the young people set to work. Girls ferried rowboat loads of prefab up the river to the campsite; boys took over coolie fashion, and moved the loads in to the building site below the burial knoll. Two days later the first Orton Ranch Baptist Camp was in progress. The girls lived in the machine shop and the boys were bedded down in the chicken house.

During the first week of camp, ten juniors made professions of faith and ten intermediates consecrated their lives to God. No one who participated would ever be the same again. Added to the spiritual blessings was the fact that salmon fishing was at its best and the swimming couldn't have been better.

❊ ❊ ❊

God revealed the territory of Alaska to Louise Yarbrough, Alaska's first W.M.U. secretary, through the pages of *Royal Service* and the pen of Miss Irene Chambers, field worker for the Home Mission Board. "Before reading this article I had not given Alaska a thought; afterwards, I could not get it off my mind," Louise declared. For six months during her second year as a student at Carver School of Missions and Social Work, Louisville, Kentucky, Louise tried to convince the Home Mission Board of her growing sense of call to Alaska. She recalls the discouraging words of Dr. Courts Redford, then executive secretary of the Home Mission Board, when he said, "Miss Yarbrough, I really don't feel that Alaska is a very safe place for a single girl." Just before graduation, however, Louise heard that the Home Mission Board would let her work as a student summer missionary in Alaska in 1954 if she would pay her own way. "Pay my own way!" she exclaimed. "I'm broke!" But a sense of God's call caused Louise to go to the local bank and borrow the money for a one-way airline ticket from her home in North Carolina to Anchorage.

During her first summer in Alaska, Louise was assigned to work with Miss Valeria Sherard, who was then associational missionary for Chugach Baptist Association. Valeria was a "walking missionary," and Louise says of that summer, "We walked from one side of Anchorage to the other over dusty, unpaved streets. I wore out two pairs of shoes in three months. However, it was worth it all because it was the beginning not only of a wonderful friendship with Valeria Sherard but of the fulfillment of my dream of serving Christ in Alaska."

At the end of the summer Louise took an office job in the Anchorage area where she worked and waited for two and one-half years before God opened the way for full-time work in Baptist missions.

In February 1957 the decision was made by the state executive board to add a W.M.U. secretary to the staff. Suggestions were being offered as to who should fill this position. It was then that one of the brethren said to the board, "A bird in the hand is worth two in the bush. Sister Yarbrough is here—let's take her."

Reporting for work on April 1, 1957, Miss Yarbrough was told, "You are elected—here is your desk but we don't have money to buy a typewriter. Maybe you can buy one if you need one." Buy one she did—forty dollars down and forty dollars per month.

For more than ten years prior to the election of a state secretary, Baptist women in Alaska had organized their work and had been active in mission outreach. During the fourth annual session of the Alaska Baptist Convention (August 24, 1949), a special meeting of all women present was called for the purpose of organizing the W.M.U., auxiliary of Alaska Baptist Convention. At that time there were five missionary societies with ninety-five members. Mrs. Felton H. Griffin, Anchorage, and Mrs. B. I. Carpenter, Ketchikan, were the pioneering spirits in work in the early years.

Since these beginning days, much progress has been made. However, statistics are not very impressive to the casual reader unless they are interpreted. For instance, the membership has remained about one thousand since 1960; but this figure probably includes three to four hundred new members each year. Since the majority of members of Baptist churches in Alaska are not permanent residents of the state, it is a constant struggle to keep organizations active and membership growing.

Likewise, many who read or heard that there were three girls and two counselors who attended the first Arctic G.A. camp probably considered it a failure. However, missionary Valeria Sherard knew that it was a victorious beginning. This small beginning multiplied; in ten years an area-wide camp attracted eighty-three boys and girls from five Arctic villages.

Again, records indicate that only thirteen women attended the tenth annual state W.M.U. convention at First Baptist Church, Sitka, in 1959. But it must be understood that ten of these women drove from six hundred fifty to eight hundred miles from Fairbanks and Anchorage to Haines, Alaska. Here they boarded a small chartered boat for a twenty hour trip to Sitka. The boat docked in Sitka harbor just as the morning session of the one-day convention was to have concluded. The entire convention program had to be squeezed into one afternoon session which ended at three o'clock just before the ten weary travelers fell asleep. That year it was not the program that made the convention worthwhile; rather, it was the hours of fun and fellowship enroute that made it a memorable event.

Because of the vast distances which separate the churches of Alaska, it has always been a major operation to get members of the state executive board together for planning and evaluating. Louise recalls that first board meeting which was held at Paxson Lodge in May 1962.

I had dreamed and planned for that first meeting. I knew it had to be something special or the women would not travel the more than two hundred miles to attend one again. Bernice Elliott, W.M.U. field worker for pioneer areas, was to be our special guest for the occasion. Bernice and I had visited the church in Valdez and drove on to Paxson in time to get everything ready for the afternoon session. I had arranged for the sleeping rooms and had requested a large room for the meeting. Mr. Brown, the manager, led us through the lobby and into the cocktail lounge which was adjacent to the bar. Mr. Brown explained that this area was closed off in the winter season and that he had planned for us to use it for our meeting. When I finally caught my breath, I said, "This will be fine—but may we rearrange the furniture?" He granted us this privilege and walked away.

When the fourteen women arrived one hour later, they walked into an atmosphere appropriate for the occasion. A large Y.W.A. poster covered the glass cabinet which displayed choices of whiskey available from the bar. Devotional books for use in the private prayer sessions were displayed on tables; the chairs were arranged in a circle, and a recording of "The Lord's Prayer" was playing.

It is hard to believe, but the Grayling Room at Paxson Lodge provided a never-to-be-forgotten spiritual retreat for the members of the state W.M.U. executive board. Every year since then the annual planning meeting of the board has been held at Paxson Lodge.

Through the years Alaska women have learned to live with the challenge of the unexpected and to adjust accordingly. The year 1967 was designated as centennial year throughout Alaska in observance of the purchase of the territory. The convention committee planned to have a centennial luncheon during the annual meeting at Fairbanks. Elaborate plans had been made for the luncheon at the Fairbanks Inn. A large historical mural had been painted by Mr. C. O. Dunkin; placemats with a map of Alaska and significant Baptist dates had been made; miniature "gold panner" favors had been cut out; and money for more than one hundred reservations had been received at the state office. On the day that the W.M.U. convention was to begin, the Chena River reached flood stage and the city of Fairbanks was inundated. All convention plans were "washed up." In November of that year, an abbreviated state convention was held in Anchorage; however, no one had the nerve to plan another centennial luncheon.

Alaska W.M.U. has always operated on a very limited budget. Because funds were not available, members generously shared in the expenses. For years state officers paid all their expenses in order to attend the required meetings. These same women opened their homes to the secretary and numerous guests who were visiting in the state. Potluck dinners and luncheon meals were always prepared by the women for associational meetings. This spirit of cooperation and sharing in expenses made it possible to plan such meetings as the state-wide G.A. conventions in 1963 and 1966.

In August 1966 one hundred and thirty junior and intermediate G.A.s arrived in Fairbanks for the second state G.A. convention. Fifty girls and their counselors rode the train from Anchorage; the Juneau counselors brought their three girls by ferry to Haines and then drove the six hundred fifty miles to Fairbanks; Valeria

Sherard and Gunita Harrell brought girls from Kiana and Kobuk by plane. Everyone arrived with suitcase and sleeping bag. All one hundred and thirty girls and counselors were housed in the educational space of the Hamilton Acres church. Meals were prepared by the Fairbanks ladies under the direction of Mrs. Orland Cary and Mrs. J. T. Burdine. An Alaskan banquet was held, and the girls wore their calico parkas which their mothers had made for the occasion. During this delightful convention, the girls had daily contact with foreign missionary Lorene Tilford of Taiwan and Valeria Sherard and Gunita Harrell, Alaska missionaries. Marjorie Jones, G.A. director, W.M.U., S.B.C., added sparkle and fun to the three day event by her delightful mission stories.

Four major emphases have characterized the Alaska W.M.U. program during the first twenty years.

Missionary education was planned for the entire church family and not just for women and children. Emphases have been on church-wide mission studies and church-wide participation in weeks of prayer and special mission offerings. Joint associational W.M.U. and Brotherhood mission rallies were held when missionaries and denominational leaders were in the state. A strong emphasis was given to missions in V.B.S. and the summer camps. Since 1962, W.M.U. has provided a mission study guide for camps and has cooperated in securing missionary speakers.

Enlisting and training of leaders and members has been a second major emphasis. Alaska churches are made up of young Christians, many of whom have never served in a leadership role. However, because Alaska churches do not have a backlog of older leaders, many of the young and untrained are thrust into places of leadership for the first time. These persons have to be taught lest they be lost in discouragement and frustration. Gayle Leininger is representative of that group. Gayle and her air force husband were active members of Calvary Baptist Church, Anchorage. Gayle was asked if she would serve as G.A. director at Calvary. Immediately she said, "Sure—but what does G.A. stand for?" Gayle approached her new job with eager enthusiasm. She studied all the materials. Every few days she telephoned Louise and asked questions and discussed plans for her intermediate G.A.s. All her preparation was bathed in prayer. At the end of her three-year-tour of duty, Gayle was program chairman, intermediate G.A. leader, and was teaching English in the literacy school. Gayle was enlisted, trained, and became excited about the privilege of serving the Lord while living in Alaska.

Alaska is indebted to Miss Alma Hunt, the Birmingham staff, and personnel from several states for their assistance in the leadership training emphasis through the years.

A third emphasis underscored the supportive role of W.M.U. in the total state mission outreach. For many years, Alaska women provided prayer support for the evangelistic crusades through neighborhood prayer meetings. Since 1950, they have prepared materials for seasons of prayer for territorial and state missions and promoted a special state mission offering.

The fourth emphasis challenged members to be sensitive to special needs and provide ministries to meet those needs. For example, in 1963 Martha Johnson, missionary to Emmonak, was invited to speak at the fiftieth anniversary G.A. convention in Memphis, Tennessee. When the women heard that Martha was going, they immediately gave money for a new permanent and some new clothes for the trip. Pauline Burnett of First Baptist Church, Anchorage, served as personal shopper to help Martha select appropriate clothes for her trip Outside.

Another special need met by the W.M.U. pertained to the Arctic G.A. and R.A. camps. For years, grocery lists were distributed and the women bought and mailed the groceries to the Arctic missionaries. Later they gave money and the missionaries ordered the supplies.

Still another ministry to a group with special needs has been the literacy schools in Anchorage and Fairbanks. Anchorage ranks fifth in the nation in the number of immigrants received annually through the Immigration and Naturalization office. Many of these immigrants desire to become naturalized citizens, but they need to be taught English and citizenship. Lillian Isaacs, Friendship Mission, Fairbanks, became aware of the unique needs of the foreign born. In 1962 while serving as associational community missions chairman, Lillian led the women to begin a school where classes in English and citizenship were taught. Several years later Lillian conducted a workshop in Anchorage which led to a literacy school at Calvary Baptist Church under the sponsorship of the associational W.M.U.

The literacy outreach has been a ministry of tremendous significance in the Fairbanks and Anchorage communities. Not only have the schools met the need of the foreign born for English and citizenship, but through them scores have found the answer to a greater need as they have come to know Christ as personal Savior.

The literacy program has not been just for the foreign born but has also included the older Eskimos of Fairbanks. Grandma Tucker is one who, after the age of one hundred, studied reading and writing and also trusted Jesus as Savior and Lord. Her story goes something like this.

"He was there again today, but I didn't go," Grandma Tucker said sadly after worship services were over. When asked "Who?" she answered, "Jesus—the one who can talk to the heart."

"Why don't you go forward to let everyone know you have trusted him if you feel Jesus is speaking to your heart," questioned Lillian Isaacs, wife of the pastor of Friendship Baptist Mission.

"Too old," Grandma replied.

Indeed Grandma was old. She could remember berry ripe times when the Russians still owned Alaska. Born near Rocky Point, Natoruck (Crystals) Tucker had to learn early that life is something to deal with, not just dream through. During August even the smallest children must pick salmon berries, blueberries, cranberries and store them in sealskin bags. Very early she learned the skills of sewing skins, weaving grass, baking bread, and Eskimo picture writing. A small smile dawns at the back of her eyes as she tells that she has made enough stitches with her bone needle and caribou sinews to go around the world and back.

Grandma remembers when the first missionaries came to her village. They asked all the people in the village to join the church and be baptized. Grandma, then a young girl, was baptized with the other villagers.

Natoruck married an Englishman who mined for gold around the Council and Nome areas. Their children were taught to obey God's laws. After her husband's death, she moved to Fairbanks to live with a daughter. She often listened to radio preaching, but began to feel that she should go to church. She told her friend, Jessie Jorgensen, "I want to see real preachers preaching."

John Isaacs began to take Grandma to the Friendship Baptist Mission. After attending services for two years, Grandma became concerned about making her public profession of faith. She would feel sad during the day and cry at night. She told Mrs. Isaacs that she would promise God that if he would let her live until next Sunday she would go forward, but then she wouldn't do it when the time came.

"Too old," she would say.

Elsie Willock used to go sing and pray with Grandma and encourage her to do what Jesus told her heart to do. She promised to walk to the front of the church with her. One Sunday Mr. Isaacs preached on Matthew 10:32-33: "Whosoever therefore shall confess me before men, him will I also confess before my father which is in heaven." Elsie and Grandma spoke together in Eskimo, then Elsie stood with her hands on her hips. Grandma stood, slipped her arm through Elsie's, and they walked to the front of the church.

"I have brung my friend to Jesus," Elsie said.

Grandma told the congregation, "I want God to 'ree-co-nize' me. I hope he will 'ree-co-nize' you." She had come to make public her faith in Jesus so God would recognize her in heaven.

The Isaacs began to talk to Grandma about being baptized. But again the answer came, "Too old." However, her heart was telling her she should be baptized because she had not really known Jesus as her Savior when she had been baptized in the village. Finally, she told Mrs. Isaacs that she would come and be baptized "after the thaw." Because Grandma thought she would have to be baptized in the river, Mrs. Isaacs took her to Calvary Baptist Church to see baptism by immersion in the baptistry. Grandma felt the water and commented, "Warm just like bath." So in 1966 at about the age of one hundred and seven, Grandma Tucker was baptized.

After Grandma's baptism, Mrs. Isaacs began to talk to her about coming to the reading classes. Again Grandma's answer was, "Too old." But when Mrs. Isaacs asked her if she would like to learn to read the name "Jesus," Grandma was eager to learn. Soon she learned to read and write "Jesus Christ," her own name, and the alphabet. When visitors went to her home, they would find "Jesus" written on the wall, on the table, everywhere.

In the winter of 1967 Grandma told Mrs. Isaacs, "I learn new word." She carefully printed JOHN and asked Mrs. Isaacs what the word was.

When Mrs. Isaacs replied, "John," Grandma's usual quiet-faced composure gave way as she cried, "Holy Spirit teach it me." She had been listening to a recording of Bible passages, and when she heard the story of John's beheading, she cried and prayed for Jesus to teach her to know John's name.

Grandma told how she took her New Testament and turned the pages until "Jesus say, 'that's John.'" She had copied it, period and all, to show Mrs. Isaacs. She told Mrs. Isaacs that the Holy Spirit teaches her many things and says she sees a "light out of this world" when someone reads the Scriptures.

Grandma prays at certain times during the day for her family, her fellow church members, and the people in the city. She witnesses everywhere. When she was in the hospital, she spoke to all the nurses and doctors about "the Lord's business." When the social editor of the *Fairbanks Daily News-Miner* invited her to tea and served the usual open-faced sandwiches and fancy pastries, Grandma declared they were too pretty for her to eat. Instead, she offered to sing and pray, and sing and pray she did.

Grandma's house and belongings were damaged by the 1967 flood. One of her fellow evacuees at the University of Alaska commiserated, "Poor Grandma; I expect you lost all you had."

"No," Grandma answered. "I only lost my things."

Grandma was touched by the kindness of the men who came from the Lower 48 to help repair the church buildings. After their daytime work, a group of them came at night and repaired Grandma's home so that it was better than ever.

Grandma testifies, "I am no more sick. My feet no more round on bottom so I can't walk. Now I stand up and go to church. I am at peace with God. Everything all right now." [12]

6

" . . Out of Every Kindred, and Tongue, and People . . ."

From *Minutes Seventh Annual Session of the Alaska Baptist Convention* meeting at First Baptist Church, Ketchikan, July 29-31, 1952.

. . . The Missions Committee brought the recommendation that in the coming convention year two missions for the Natives be established. . . .

From *Minutes Twelfth Annual Session of the Alaska Baptist Convention* meeting at First Baptist Church, Anchorage, August 13-15, 1957.

Recommendation No. 3: We recommend that the name of the Native Baptist Bible Institute be changed to Native Baptist Training School. . . .

Exactly two years from the date C. O. Dunkin held the first Baptist service in Fairbanks, he and Mrs. Dunkin again traveled the highway and were welcomed by their friends at First Baptist Church. Her cancer treatments at Mayo had been successful. The Dunkins still felt called to do mission work in Alaska, this time with the natives. They met with the pastor and deacons of First Baptist, but were unable to come to an agreement about sponsorship of the mission. Mr. Dunkin wanted to use his own initiative in securing property and buildings, put the property in his name, and not have to consult a board of deacons when he felt something needed to be done. The church stood for the principle that any work done under their sponsorship should be owned by the church and done with the approval of the church. This feeling was strong because their property had originally been in Mr. Dunkin's name, and their efforts to get a loan or help from outside sources had been thwarted until the property was deeded to the church by the Dunkins.

Central Baptist Church in Luling, Texas, offered to extend an arm to a native mission when the Dunkins could get one started, so for several weeks they canvassed the city, inviting natives to join with them. On January 12, 1947, their first service was conducted in the Odd Fellows Hall which they rented for $40 per month. Despite temperatures of fifty degrees below zero, thirty-one persons were present for this service; by the third Sunday, attendance rose to forty-five and eight professions of faith had been made.

The Dunkins transported most of the natives to the services in their panel truck, often waking the families and dressing the children for Sunday school. Their great desire was to start an orphanage for the native children, but this goal was not attained. Through the years they kept many children and native girls in trouble in their home. As Mr. Dunkin's business prospered, he employed natives and helped those in financial need.

At the beginning of 1950, Mrs. Dunkin wrote, "We have bought ground for a mission building. It is not as centrally located as we would have liked, but it came nearer suiting our pocketbook. It was $2,500. We had $756 in the bank of the missions money. We took $500 of that and put our $500 with it for the down payment, and will pay the balance off within the next year, according to the contract. Of course, it will be several months before we can start on the building, due to the ground being frozen, but I hope we can get the basement and auditorium done this year." The property was a corner lot at 1465 Lacey Street. At that time the Dunkins had a native girl and her baby living with them. The baby was eight months old and "rotten just like Freddy. We have had her since she was two days old. If she lets out one sound, we have Freddy to fight if we don't pick her up."

Before the end of the year they were meeting in their new basement. They wrote to friends, "It is wonderful not to have to rent a place, and believe me, we are taking advantage of the fact that we can have services whenever we want to. We have prayer meeting and Bible study on Wednesday and work every other week-night getting the inside finished. We didn't get our glass windows in because it turned too cold for the cement. It doesn't make any difference for it is dark all the time. We will get them in early in the spring."

Felton Griffin preached two revivals which resulted in many converts. In 1950 the mission was invited to cooperate with the First Baptist Church in a revival led by Dr. C. Y. Dossey during Alaska's second simultaneous crusade. Eight Eskimos were saved, including Tom and Elsie Willock. Mrs. Dunkin wrote, "He had not been interested in the four years that his family had been coming. Now he doesn't miss a service." Mr. Willock later became the first Eskimo deacon of a church in the Alaska Baptist Convention.

A Catholic girl who was saved in the simultaneous revival moved into the new basement with the Dunkins. She had never opened a Bible until after her conversion. Mrs. Dunkin helped her with reading lessons from the Bible. On January 1, 1951, the mission had more than two Sunday school classes for the first time. For Christmas, the Dunkins had given new song books and an organ instead of individual gifts to the children, and they seemed to never grow tired of singing. Mrs. Dunkin said that pumping the organ and trying to sing was like running as fast as she could and trying to talk at the same time.

The mission building had been planned to be useful to the natives. The upstairs provided space for those who had nowhere to stay, with a day nursery and a sewing room for the women, a laundry and place to dry clothes, and a place where they could bathe. Tuberculosis was a major problem among the members of the mission. During the first part of 1950, Mr. Dunkin wrote, "We have recently lost around fifteen either directly or indirectly because of T.B. Five had it and the others were children that had to be sent to homes, five in one family going to Valdez."

In June 1951 the property was deeded to the Home Mission Board, the value of the contribution being about $13,000. A provision of the transaction was that the building be completed and the mission become an arm of the First Baptist Church, Fairbanks. The Dunkins went again to the States, and for several months Mr. Cary preached first at the Native mission, then while they were having Sunday school, he preached again at First Baptist. One of the deacons from First Baptist preached the night service at the mission. Mr. Cary began taping his radio program, feeling that preaching at nine, ten, and eleven was too difficult.

The 1950 Christmas service at the mission was planned by

the Eskimos and was their first attempt to have a program that they outlined by themselves. They told Mr. Cary when they wanted his sermon; it came after they had sung five congregational hymns and had six special numbers in the Eskimo language. Fifty-five came for the program.

Laymen from First Baptist Church worked on the building during the winter and by the spring of 1952 it was completed. In March 1952 Mr. and Mrs. John T. Dickerson, students at Southwestern Baptist Theological Seminary, were appointed as missionaries to serve the mission when they completed their seminary studies. Richard A. Miller arrived on the field in May 1952, and served as interim mission pastor until the arrival of the Dickersons in February 1953.

In September 1952 Carl Smith, mission pastor of the Mile 17 Mission, who was living at Native mission until his own quarters were ready, discovered an Eskimo boy sitting behind the boiler. He called Dick Miller, who talked to the boy and then left to talk with the young man's sister. A few minutes later the boy shot himself fatally. Just two weeks before his death, he had made a profession of faith at the mission, but had been drinking at the time of his suicide. Funeral services for him were held at the mission.

During the summer of 1953, plans were made for the constitution of the Native mission into a church. Preceding the organizational service, the group studied and adopted articles of faith and a church covenant. The week before the date for constitution, five members of the mission were involved in a tragic automobile accident near Valdez. Mrs. John Dickerson and George McDonald, Jr., fourteen-year-old son of the driver of the car, were the only survivors. Mrs. Dickerson described the wild ride down the five-mile-long hill from Thompson's Pass into Valdez in the car completely out of control, with its brakes and automatic transmission not operating. She said the vehicle reached a speed of over ninety miles per hour, but the driver kept cool and attempted to guide the car to the bottom of the hill. When almost at the bottom, it failed to make a turn and plunged over a five-hundred-foot enbankment. The car was new; it was supposed that a rock broke the brake line. Killed were Mrs. George McDonald, Mrs. Andy Hall, and Mrs. Carl Aronson. Two of the ladies were Sunday school teachers and the other acted as church clerk for the mission.

The Native Baptist Church was constituted Sunday afternoon,

August 2, 1953, with fifty-seven charter members. It was the first Baptist church to be organized in Alaska for the Eskimos. C. O. Dunkin, founder of the native work, was not able to be present because he had gone to Valdez to help make arrangements for the victims of the wreck. John Dickerson led the service with Richard Miller bringing the sermon. The new auditorium was first used in its completed state on the organizational Sunday. Memorial services for the workers who perished in the wreck were conducted the following Sunday at the Native Baptist Church, with Pastor Dickerson leading.

The Native Baptist Church sponsored the Immanuel Baptist Mission which began to meet in the Carpenters' Hall on January 17, 1954, with twenty-eight in Sunday school and twenty-two in Training Union.

In the summer of 1953 Richard Miller was appointed by the Home Mission Board to open Baptist work in Kotzebue. The beginning of this mission was due in part to the desires and prayers of members of the Native Baptist Church who spent part of their time in Kotzebue or else had members of their families living there whom they wanted to have the opportunity of hearing the gospel. In September the Home Mission Board purchased a two-story business located on a corner lot facing the beach in Kotzebue and provided $2,000 for repairs. Tom Willock assisted in the remodeling of the building. The Kotzebue Native Mission was placed under the watchcare of the Native church in Fairbanks.

In November 1953 Mr. Dickerson and one member of the Native Baptist Church went to the Indian village of Nenana in response to a request for gospel preaching among those people. Pioneer Hall in Nenana was rented and preaching services were held at 10:30 each Sunday morning, with a Gospel Songfest in the afternoons. Mike Pitner, an airman from Eielson Air Force Base, preached for the Nenana group. That winter he drove over the trail from Nenana to Fairbanks in a jeep as long as he could get through, then used a bush flight until the railroad resumed its summer schedule. In March he began a Sunday school to teach the Bible. Only a few came at first, but soon the attendance was up to forty. A Vacation Bible School was conducted in June, with an average attendance of sixty-three and three decisions for Christ. Services were also conducted for a time in the mining camps near Fairbanks where large numbers of Eskimos were employed during the summer.

After Mr. Cary asked the Home Mission Board to restrict the Native church to native members, and the Board asked Mr. Dickerson to restore the church to mission status, Dickerson resigned because of conflicting pressures and accepted work at Palmer in August 1955.

Around three o'clock on Sunday morning, December 11, 1955, the church building was completely destroyed by fire. The members refused to accept defeat and continued services in the basement of the parsonage. Mr. and Mrs. John Jeffcoat, recently appointed as the new missionaries to the Native church, immediately began negotiating for a new church plant. Mr. Ralph Luikart was appointed by the Home Mission Board to act as Superintendent of Buildings in Alaska. Blueprints for a new building were drawn up, and Mr. Luikart arrived on the grounds to begin the building on April 1, 1957. While waiting for materials to arrive, he worked clearing out the debris. Mrs. Luikart worked with her husband and was reported to be "worth two ordinary men around a building project." In spite of hardships endured during the long waiting period, Jeffcoat served faithfully as pastor and became moderator of the Tanana Valley Association.

On the last Sunday of March, just one year later, the church dedicated their beautiful new edifice. Approximately $43,000 was spent on the building, but its value was estimated at $94,000 by a Fairbanks contractor. Executive secretary L. A. Watson brought the morning message and Tom Willock preached at the evening service.

Once when Mrs. Jeffcoat was asked what a typical day was like on the mission field, she told of a day at the end of Vacation Bible School. After commencement exercises, she left a kitchenful of student summer workers and delivered the native children to their homes, using the little Volkswagen furnished for their mission. Reaching home after eleven, she dozed off while reading the book of James, only to be awakened by a pounding on the door. Answering the knock, she found seven tired and sleepy natives, five adults and two babies, who were looking for a place to sleep that night. After feeding them and helping them on their way the next morning, she showed some Baptist tourists the mission, and in the afternoon the Dick Miller family arrived from Kotzebue; later that evening the Willie Johnsons also dropped in. They had just graduated from the Training School in Anchorage and were on their way to work at Selawik. In between visits, Mrs. Jeffcoat had helped her husband and daughter Martha get off in the mission plane to a village beyond the mountain range. Martha always took a sack of goodies and was beseiged as soon as the plane landed. She was the story-teller and planner of games for the children. The adults looked forward to "Brother John's" Bible study and news from over the mountain. He usually took clothes and other necessities to the villages when he visited. Mrs. Jeffcoat was serving as president of the Alaska W.M.U. at that time and also leading all the mission organizations except Y.W.A. at the native mission.

After John and Lillian Isaacs came in 1960 to serve the native mission, the work took on an international character. While doing missionary work in Kentucky, Mrs. Isaacs had started the first literacy ministry under the sponsorship of the Home Mission Board. Literacy work proved so successful as a mission operation that she decided to use it to reach the adults in Fairbanks who were functional illiterates. Later, she also developed a course of study to assist those who were studying to become citizens and hundreds of persons have received United States citizenship as a result. Most of these have also found Christ as Savior, and many have been baptized and become members of the mission.

The first service of the Native Baptist Mission in Anchorage was held April 19, 1953. Among those attending were natives Henry Wilde and Alice Baird. This was the first direct work with native people in Anchorage. The Home Mission Board had appropriated money to purchase property at Third and Gambell in December 1952, but that transaction was not made. In January 1953, $13,000 was specified to buy the corner lot at 802 East Third Street across the street from the 400-bed Native Hospital which was to open in the summer of 1953. A house on the lot served as a chapel and living quarters for the missionaries.

The state convention, Chugach Baptist Association, and First Baptist Church, Anchorage, cooperated to sponsor the mission. Tommy Miller, an air force enlisted man, and his wife Letitia accepted the call to begin the work. The Millers had adopted two native children and were burdened for the native people. After eight months, the Millers returned to California to continue their college work. They wrote, "It's been such a privilege working with the native people. It is with heavy hearts we leave Alaska, but we feel the need for some training for this great work."

Valeria Sherard moved to the mission and carried on the regular services until a new missionary was called. Mike McKay arrived on the field in December 1953. Mike had been a vocalist and trombonist in night clubs and a territorial marshall in the Nome area. Both as a night club entertainer and policeman, he had dealt with the sordid side of life. He was a Roman Catholic when he first attended First Baptist Church in Anchorage. He was won to Christ through the music of the church and surrendered for full time service.

Mike married Virginia Krise, who also had been reared a Catholic, and they worked in the Baptist mission in Palmer before going to the States to attend Wayland Baptist College. For two summers the McKays served under the Home Mission Board in Indian work in New Mexico and were there when the call came to return to Alaska and work with the Native Baptist Mission. They worked at finishing up the interior of the chapel and in February 1954 had open house. The first convert at the mission was Mrs. Alice Kalerak.

The mission was able to reach a number of young native men, some of whom felt called to the ministry. In the simultaneous revival of 1956, Willie Johnson, then stationed with the army at Fort Richardson, surrendered to preach; in August 1956, the Chugach association requested the state convention to sponsor a Bible school for training these young natives; and in September the Native Baptist Training School began its first session. Willie and his wife Martha enrolled that first semester, completed the two-year course of study, and when graduation services were conducted May 8, 1958, they were awarded the school's first diplomas.

At first, evening classes were taught twice a week with four areas of study: music, religious education, English grammar, and Bible. The first instructors were Felton Griffin, Roger Laube, Clifford McConnell, and Mrs. Louise Hubbs. Nine students enrolled for study in the fall of 1956 and six in the spring of 1957.

The Willie Johnsons were the first Eskimos to be appointed by the Southern Baptist Home Mission Board. Selawik was their first mission field. In August 1955 Dick Miller had begun construction of a church building at Selawik and held services in an abandoned store building until the work was finished on the building. He had purchased the land rights of Andrew Skin, a reindeer herder, to a plot on which Skin's sled dogs were tied, using one of the dog stakes for a survey marker. Valeria Sherard was the first leader of the Selawik mission, and in the summer of 1956, Miller had baptized James Ramoth and Mrs. Mabel Mitchell, the first converts in Selawik.

After serving in Selawik for two years, the Johnsons made their first trip outside Alaska. They went to Florida for two weeks of Schools of Missions, then Mrs. Johnson spoke at the W.M.U. convention in Miami, where she "stole the show," according to L. A. Watson. Willie was asked to sit on the platform with Martha, and after the session, they were surrounded with press representatives, photographers, and autograph hunters. I saw them at the convention that day; dressed in their parkas and mukluks, they left an indelible impression on my heart. Martha was also invited to speak at the G.A.'s fiftieth anniversary convention at Memphis in 1962.

After the Dick Millers left Emmonak, the Willie Johnson family were appointed to serve there. In December 1962, Willie wrote, "It is really good to have fresh bread again. Martha can operate the washing machine now that the light plant arrived." Martha had been washing on a rub board and cooking on a gasoline camp stove for their family of eight.

In 1964 the Johnson's eight-month-old daughter Annette died at the Bethel hospital after an extended illness. Willie himself had been in bed in the Alaska Native Hospital for several weeks with hepatitis.

I made my first visit to the Johnsons in Emmonak in September 1969. When E. C. Chron landed his small plane on the sod strip by the river, it seemed that all the village people were there to meet us. The children liked the name *Hunke,* evidently, because after about ten minutes they all knew it and were calling, "Hunke, look here, see this, do that," etc. all the time we were there. Willie had just harpooned a four-hundred-pound oogruk, so Martha fed us this Eskimo delicacy and her special homemade bread for supper. That night at the mission service an Eskimo girl made public her profession of faith, and early the next morning some Eskimo men killed a seal in the river that runs by the mission, so I had an altogether rewarding visit.

Through the years other natives have been trained by the Native Baptist Training School and have gone into the Lord's service. On March 6, 1960, the mission dedicated a new building.

Mike McKay served as moderator, and two graduates of the training school, Ted Moses and Harry Wilde, led the singing and devotional period. The building was planned and built to accommodate the training school. Many activities and forms of services have always been carried on at the native mission. Mike has led physical education classes and activities, and Virginia has specialized in music and drama, which she adapts to the needs of the members of the mission. The name has been changed to East Third Street Baptist Mission.

❊   ❊   ❊

In addition to working with the Eskimos in the large cities, Baptists have always been aware of the spiritual needs of those in the interior and Arctic regions. Baptist denominational and church leaders who visit our work in Alaska and we who live here always look forward to an opportunity of going to Kotzebue or Fort Yukon or Emmonak or the other villages where our missionaries serve.

My first visit to the Arctic was like a quick seminar in another teacher's chosen discipline. On the little beach of shingle which ran aslant into Kotzebue Sound, countless small fishing boats were moored, most being the only valuable possession of a family. Eskimo life has always centered around boat building and fishing; their settlements disclose their dependence on fish and their movements to follow migration of fish.

The Eskimos of Kotzebue make the most of the ever increasing tourist trade brought their way by the airline companies. Dressed in beautiful handsewn parkas of sealskin, muskrat, fox, caribou, or wolf, Eskimo artisans demonstrate their crafts. One old man explains the processing of the skins and his family displays mittens, mukluks, slippers, hats, and novelties made from different skins, each article with a distinctive design.

A lady shows how the oomiak (skin boat) was made from a driftwood frame and covered with walrus hide in her younger days. Then she pantomimes for us the hunting and slaying of the white Beluga whale from this wraparound mini-whaler. With flashing smiles and good-natured comments other Eskimos do their ivory carving and jade polishing with native handmade tools. (When I visited Israel, I was fascinated to find that the olive wood carvings the Arabs specialize in are done with a handmade tool exactly like the Eskimos' ivory carving tool.)

A favorite event is the blanket toss for which huge walrus hides, dried hard as plywood sheets, are used. About a dozen adults grasp the outer edges of the hide, and then the children vie to be first. My heart flew up almost as high as the first child when he catapulted far above the roof of the house next door and came down kicking and screaming with laughter. The blanket toss originated as a means for spotting seals beyond the edge of the ice floes.

The tundra of this Arctic region freezes to a concrete-hard permafrost in winter, then thaws to a spongy, clumped-up prairie-land in summer. Dotted with shallow lakes and streams, the tundra is a thin, insulating veneer atop the permanently frozen ground underneath. When the tundra is disturbed, the permafrost gets restless. If even a small drainage ditch is dug, the warmer temperature reaching down into the permafrost will cause melting until the ditch deepens and widens and a scar results that will be visible for hundreds of years.

Heat from the floor of a building will penetrate the tundra, thaw the permafrost, and cause the building to settle at crazy angles. For this reason houses are put on pilings to allow sufficient cold space, or on gravel pads four feet thick to insulate the ground against the building heat. Heaving presents a similar problem. Water collects in pockets beneath the tundra in warm weather, then freezes and pushes upward in the winter, forming small ice mountains called pingos. Drunken forests created by pingos grow at a grotesque pitch. Objects buried in the ground may be pushed to the surface. Many superstitions have arisen around Barrow because the coffins in the graveyard have sometimes appeared above the ground several years after burial.

Rivers also may have unique problems. In the spring, giant chunks of ice break loose upstream and stack up in the canyon stretches of the largest rivers, forming ice dams. The river water is forced downward where it may scour the bottom of the river bed with great force. Changes of up to ninety feet have been recorded in the depth of river beds from one year to the next.

Missionary Harley Shield built a beautiful, white motorboat which is his summertime link with the other Arctic mission points. When he took us for a ride and I saw the long trails of spray, cutting across each other like open scissors and leaving countless rainbows scintillating in the air as the sun charged each drop with color, I thought nothing could be more desirable.

When a young Eskimo came by the Baptist mission and invited us down to see his freshly killed moose, I went along. We watched him cut up the meat, sharing some with the missionaries as well as with other families. I learned much about the dependence the people have on hunting as they talked of other years when meat was scarce. They told of the reindeer herds brought to Kotzebue from Siberia to be domesticated, of experiments being carried on to try to make possible survival of rabbits for a new source of meat. They were amused by a similar experiment with penguins brought from Anarctica. The penguins froze to death.

The Eskimo people have a delightful sense of humor. Representative Willie Hensley, Alaska's representative on the National Council on Indian Opportunity, was to leave for Washington for a meeting with the high-level policy group in the spring of 1970. When he asked to be excused from the Alaska House for the trip, Representative Richard McVeigh asked, "Are you an Indian, Willie?"

And Representative Gene Guess added, "I wonder what Spiro will call you."

"At least it won't be 'Fat Eskimo,'" said Hensley, a very slim, handsome young man, referring to Agnew's calling a Baltimore reporter a "Fat Jap."

Willie received a $250 Christmas card in 1968—written on a hotel placemat. He was going through the chow line at the Captain Cook Hotel when Representative Earl Hillstrand spotted him and announced, "Here's Hensley who's going to run against Blodgett (Senator Robert R. Blodgett, Teller)." A few minutes later, Hillstrand came over to the Hensley's table with a placemat made up like a Christmas card. The card offered Hensley $250 for his campaign if he would run against Blodgett in 1970. The mat was signed by three political conservatives. Hensley didn't comment, but he is expected to cash in the placemat any day now.

Some of Alaska's older natives tell stories of Russian cruelty to Indians, who supposedly committed suicide rather than submit to captivity, and also of Indian retaliation in wiping out several Russian forts. One old Indian woman, just recently learning that the Russians had nuclear weapons, appealed to the government for protection. She feared that descendants of slaughtered Russians would come to avenge a massacre in 1805 by bombing her tiny village.

One old Russian man, a bookkeeper for a Russian company, held on to records during his lifetime, but a storekeeper in Sleetmute bought them from his son, and they have been lost. The old man was present during the purchase of Alaska. He said the Russians sold it because they could not conquer the Indians. According to him, about 74,000 Indians lived in the state then, and the Russians would line them up on the bank of the Kuskokwim River and see how many they could kill with one shot of a muzzle-loader gun. He said that at other times the Russians would invite the Indians to the community halls in the villages and get parents drunk on whiskey. Then they would give the children tobacco leaves to eat. They killed hundreds of children in this manner.

The Native Land Claims issue remains the stickiest problem Alaska faces. The Indians argue that because the Russians knew they were waging a losing battle, they took advantage of the opportunity to unload Alaska. They contend that since they didn't conquer the Indians, the Russians never had legal right to the land. They ask how they could sell land to the United States that they had no legal title or aboriginal rights to. To the Indians it appears that the United States bought stolen land. They ask why the Russians didn't give the purchase price to them, and why the United States didn't check into the rightful ownership. They ask why all titles to the land weren't cleared up before Congress allowed statehood.

❈   ❈   ❈

In the summer of 1955 Robert and Dora Craun were baptized into the Palmer Baptist Church. Mr. Craun was already an ordained minister. The couple came to Alaska from Pennsylvania to do independent missionary work among the natives. After attending the Palmer church for two years, they became convinced that they should become Southern Baptists.

The Crauns began the first Southern Baptist work among Alaska's Indians when they moved to Fort Yukon, eight miles above the Arctic Circle, in September 1955. Mr. Craun wrote to the editor of the *Messenger*, "We are now in Fort Yukon after many difficulties. First, we had an accident and rolled our jeep over, scattering our winter's supply of food. In Fairbanks, we borrowed a truck to get to Circle City, but about 100 miles away a rod went out. We finally got to Circle City, only to find out that the boat was no longer carrying passengers. We flew to Fort Yukon and walked a mile and a half to our cabin. We hope to get the work started soon."

In 1956 Craun built a two-story log cabin in which to live. In June 1957 the Bureau of Land Management conducted a sale on lots in Fort Yukon. John Dickerson went up from Fairbanks to bid on lots. That night at the local hotel he overheard a discussion of plans to run up the price on any lots that Baptists might bid on. Because no one knew who he was or that he was bidding for Baptist lots, he was allowed to secure desirable lots across from a new school at a reasonable price. When the Crauns left Fort Yukon in June 1957 because of her health problems, they were replaced by the Oliver Marsons, formerly of Juneau. The day the Marsons arrived, the temperature was around minus twenty. No one met them at the airstrip—the mission had no members, so they thought no one was interested in their coming, but soon after they got into the house, they noticed that every window was filled with children's faces, noses pressed flat against the glass. That was disconcerting enough, but also troublesome was the fact that they had no fire, food, dishes, or bed clothes, and that their whole year's food supply, which had been barged up the Yukon, was sitting in the middle of the one downstairs room.

The moss chinks between the logs of the cabin needed replacing, and the dirt roof had mostly sifted through into the upstairs room. Everything was soon put in order, and they didn't feel nearly so crowded when they noticed that most of the people lived in one-room log cabins; with up to twenty children in every family, living conditions were almost unbearable. Baptists had put a prefabricated building on the mission lots, but in 1958 the building burned down. The mission met in the old school building and the next Sunday evening, fifty-eight came to the services.

A dedication service for Fort Yukon's new mission building was held March 20, 1960, after a week's revival services. James Rose had supervised the construction. Following the Marsons' resignation, Don and Marianne Rollins were appointed by the Home Mission Board on March 16, 1961, to serve among the Athabaskans at Fort Yukon. Two special events for the Fort Yukon mission are the Midnight Sun Revival at midnight, June 21, every year, and the summer youth camp fifteen miles up the Porcupine River in July.

In 1963 twelve leaders of Fairbanks' simultaneous revivals visited Fort Yukon on Saturday, planning to return about two in the afternoon. At one P.M. John Thomas left with the first three preachers. At two P.M. the Wien plane had arrived and reported dangerous icing conditions. The snowstorm became heavier. Mr. Cowling and C. Y. Dossey, two evangelists, left on the Wien plane. The others decided to wait for their chartered flight. By dark there was no question but that the Rollins would have eight unexpected, overnight guests, and several Fairbanks churches would be without preachers and song leaders on Sunday. Moose and noodles were served for supper, then sleeping bags and mattresses were put on the floor. All night the howls of the huskies and snores of the preachers made music. George Patterson said, "I would not take anything for this experience IF we get out of here." The weather cleared about six the next morning, and by seven their plane had come and started them to their places of service.

Seventy people live in the Indian village of Chalkyitsik, and in the village stands a Baptist mission building. The unique thing about this building is that it represents the effort of the villagers themselves, not the missionary. The man most responsible for its being there is Paul Thomas, the village chief. The village is located on the Black River, sixty air miles or 199 river miles (Don Rollins had a boat but no plane) from Fort Yukon. In 1963 he began getting requests from the people of Chalkyitsik to begin Baptist work there. He made a number of boat trips to hold services, then requested enough money from the Home Mission Board for the people to build the mission. The $1,800 was almost sufficient for their needs.

Under Paul Thomas' supervision, men of the village cut logs about six miles above the village and floated them downstream. They were paid a small amount for their labor. Windows, plywood, plastic insulation, a stove, and lumber for benches had to be brought in by boat. April 21, 1965, was dedication day. After the service, a potlatch, with moosehead stew for the main course, was served.

The second mission is in Venetie. Here also the villagers helped construct the chapel and dwelling in 1967. Phillip Templin, a summer missionary, who returned to the area four years in a row, did much of the work on the building during the summers. Don Rollins reported, "There are at present five men serving as pastors who made their decision to enter the ministry in this mission; a sixth is planning to begin his study soon and is preaching there now. The first youth camp in the Arctic was begun by the Venetie mission in 1962 with forty-eight campers. They came from as far away as one hundred thirty miles by boats."

After the Rollins family left Fort Yukon to begin the King Salmon work in 1969, Shirley Korte, missionary nurse, was called to carry on the work at Fort Yukon. Shirley had been appointed to the Selawik mission in 1966. She had formerly worked in Alaska as a nurse in the Public Health Service Department.

❖   ❖   ❖

In October 1960 Elsie and Tom Willock enrolled in the Laubach reading course taught by Mr. and Mrs. John Isaacs of the Native Baptist Mission of Fairbanks, Alaska. At the age of eighty-three, Tom accomplished something he hadn't expected to realize until he reached heaven—he learned to read the word "Jesus."

"Let me look at it again. It's the most beautiful word I'll ever read," Uncle Tom told the Isaacs. He repeated it over and over to himself and "read" his Bible by looking for the word "Jesus" on every page.

After hours of study both Tom and Elsie were able to recognize and write many simple words. At seventy-four Aunt Elsie was thrilled to be able to write her first letter to her sister in Kotzebue. Upon receiving the letter, the sister rushed to Mrs. John Thomas, wife of the pastor of First Baptist Church there, and demanded, "Teach me to read and write."

Tom Willock was born in 1877 near Nome and moved from place to place as his family hunted and fished for a living. He lived in dug-out sod igloos, made partly from moss and logs, with seal gut windows. The floor of these igloos was made of flat stones, at least around the fire area. The stones would absorb a great deal of the heat, when the fire was built for cooking, and would keep the igloo warm. The only time the Eskimos ever built a fire was to cook their food; heating the igloo was so unimportant that they would not think of building a fire for that. Tom said the igloo always stayed warm enough even in the severest cold of winter. He took pride in telling of their ability to build a fire with very little effort long before they knew about matches.

Along the streams in the northern part of Alaska a certain kind of willow grows that produces a cotton-like substance. The Eskimos gathered this willow cotton with care and took particular pains to keep it dry. When a fire was needed, two or three strokes with a simple flint rock was all that was necessary to kindle the highly inflamable material, and a roaring fire could be made in just a few moments.

When asked what happened if the cotton got wet, Tom told how they prepared for that emergency. "We always kept a round piece of dry wood, previously cut, about an inch in diameter and two or three feet long. We would take three or four turns of a thong made of animal skin around the piece of round wood. Then we placed a long pole on top and two men would put pressure on top of a smaller round pole. A third person, by twisting the round pole backwards and forwards under pressure and on top of a stone, would generate enough heat that blowing on the heated area would cause a blaze to leap up."

Once when Tom was very young, his father threatened to sew his lips together because Tom had lied about filling the snow shed with snow to be melted down for water. The older men in the village had a very definite code about right and wrong that they tried to establish in the hearts of the children. Tom remembered them talking a great deal about some kind of "living up above," as they expressed it. They never questioned the fact of life after death. When a person died in their community, the oldest man in the area was the one who officiated at the burial, and he always told the mourners that while they would not see the deceased any more in life, they would see him again in some other kind of life beyond the grave.

The Eskimos did not dig a grave for burial. Instead they often built a cache five or six feet high and placed the body in it. The body was covered with the person's own sleeping skins, and his tools and personal belongings were put beside him. Sometimes a body was simply left on top of the ground. In the summer, after the personal effects were placed around it, leaves and grasses would be heaped up into a mound. In winter only a snow cover was made. If the dead person had no close relatives, even his skin boat became a part of the mound.

During one seven-month period when Orland Cary was directing the work of the Native Baptist Mission, he visited often with the Willocks and recorded much of their conversation because Tom could remember all the way back to the days just after Alaska was purchased by the United States. He remembered many markers left by the Russians being in use when he was growing up. Their buoys were in the shipping channels to guide ships into the harbors. His first memory, however, was of his mother carrying him very quickly out of an igloo. While she was hurrying along with young Tom strapped on her back, she bumped his head on the narrow passageway leading from the igloo. He knew his mother must have been very frightened; she carried him out to a little hill in front of the sod house and stood waiting in the bitter cold. Even though he was crying because of the bump he received, she stood outside until his father came in from hunting because she was afraid to go back into the house without him. Tom later learned the cause of her terror. A drunken white man had come into the igloo and threatened his mother. It seems a strange and sad thing that the first memory of a native Christian should be of a drunken white man.

Another time a white man became the focal point in the life of Tom's family came during his first experience in working with the government. He had been working in Anchorage when he became ill and had to return to his village. He remembered the plane landing at Kotzebue and that members of his family were there to take him home. He lay very ill in a semi-conscious condition, lingering between life and death for many days. During his illness a petition was initiated, and supposedly signed by a few Eskimos who could sign their names, asking that he be moved from the village.

In earlier days the Eskimos had a custom of removing the seriously ill and leaving them in the wilderness to die. There was a taboo on any house in which a person had died; in fact, the house was abandoned immediately if a death occurred in it, and the occupants had to seek shelter elsewhere. Since housing was a problem to Eskimos, particularly in extreme winter weather, and they had to be careful to avoid a death in their houses, they had resorted to the expediency of removing the seriously ill and leaving him to his fate. In some instances the person would be sealed up in the house and left to die while the family made other living arrangements. This custom had entered into the situation when the Willock family was petitioned to take their husband and father away.

Mr. Willock remembered going out from the village to an isolated spot along a river bank and the lonely days he spent there waiting for either recovery or death. As he was leaving the village, a white man gave him a few shells, ammunition for his gun. He became very despondent because there was no prospect of food. He was not a Christian but he had heard of God, so one night he prayed that God would furnish food. The next morning he was awakened by the cries of geese. Geese were everywhere. His family had joined him at the camp, so one of the older boys went out with the gun and in a few minutes had killed enough geese to feed the family for days to come, forty in all. Eight of these were sent back to the village as a gift to the man who had given the shells. Tom began to regain his strength from the time he prayed and was soon well enough to help his son provide food. He found that the petition was mostly a fraud perpetrated by another white man, but he never felt free to live in that village again.

One day when Tom was about ten years old, word was sent up the river that a white man wanted to talk to the Eskimos. Everyone living along Fish River responded to the invitation and descended the river in their skin boats, tying them up along the beach in Kobuk. Such gatherings were conducted through the head men. After listening to the white man, who was a Swedish Covenant missionary, for about three days, many of the Eskimos responded to the invitation to believe in Jesus. Then the missionary began to tell them that followers of Jesus should be baptized. One of the older head men asked how Jesus was baptized. The missionary hesitated and seemed embarrassed by the question because the people had already seen him baptize by putting a little water on their forehead. The missionary told them that Jesus had been baptized by going down into the water and being submerged in it and then being raised back up. After the head men understood this, they stated simply that they wanted to be baptized "like Jesus was." One of them told the missionary of a little pool of water in the stream about two miles from the village. Tom was one of those who went with the missionary to see how Jesus was baptized. The baptismal scene made a deep impression on the young boy, together with John 3:16, which the missionary repeatedly quoted, and "Jesus Loves Me," which he taught the Eskimos to sing. But it was not until 1947, after the C. O. Dunkins had been witnessing to him for three years, that Tom accepted Jesus. At that time he and his wife

Elsie were baptized "like Jesus was" and became charter members
of the Native Baptist Mission in Fairbanks.

One afternoon Orland Cary had asked Tom to take the prayer
service at the mission and invited him over to study the Bible with
him. Although Tom did not learn to read for nine years after this
time, he always carried his Bible and listened attentively to reading
and interpretation of it. This time he asked Mr. Cary to study the
fourteenth chapter of John with him. By the time Cary had discussed down to the fourteenth verse, Tom interrupted to tell the
following story.

Once while his family was living at Council, Alaska, he had
a cousin living at White Mountain, about one hundred seventy-five
miles away. When the cousin became ill, he sent word to Tom to
come see him, but because of the weather and bad trail conditions,
he was unable to leave right away to make the trip. Finally growing very anxious to learn about his cousin's health, Tom loaded his
sled with provisions and started out. Arriving at White Mountain
after two days of hard sledding, he found the cousin very ill with
tuberculosis. He had brought food and supplies, and after doing all
he could to care for the sick man, Tom prepared to leave after
three days. He told the cousin, "I may not see you any more in
this world, but if you hope in Jesus, maybe I will see you in the
next world." He then told the cousin all he knew about Jesus dying
so that men's sins could be forgiven. Soon the cousin "became very
glad in his heart." The conversation took place after the dogs had
already been hitched to the sled to start the journey home. Tom
bade his cousin farewell, and the last glimpse he had of him was of
his happy expression because of the glad feeling. Tom himself had
not made a profession in Christ as Savior at this time, but his
testimony seems to have borne fruit in the heart of the needy
cousin. In just a few days the sick man died.

On the return trip the weather became very bad, and on the
first day Tom tried desperately hard to make a certain river crossing before dark. It was during the time when there was very little
daylight up beyond the Arctic Circle, and he was anxious to make
the crossing before dark because just after making it, he had to
cross a narrow strip of land, or portage, and enter another stream.
After ascending the second stream for a short distance, he had to
enter a little rivulet, up which he would travel for a long distance.
The difficulty lay at this point; two little streams came into the

stream at about the same place, one of which would take him far afield if he should get into it by mistake. As he came to the first crossing, snow began falling hard, whipped about by a strong wind. Travel became very difficult, but hoping to have enough daylight left and thinking the elements would soon slacken up, he hastened on. He entered the second river and went up it for what he thought was the correct distance, then entered a little rivulet with confidence, thinking it was the correct one. He then traveled on for about an hour before he began to sense that he must have made a mistake.

Suddenly his dogs came out of the stream bed and the only trail open to them was up on high ground that seemed to keep rising rapidly. Before he could call a halt, the dogs themselves suddenly stopped very abruptly. Even though he had intended to turn around he thought this was not the best place to make the turn, so he began talking to his lead dog which had turned crossways in the trail and started to whine. As he coaxed, the dog continued to whine and refused to budge. Losing patience and scolding the dog, Tom commanded it to "mush" in no uncertain terms, accompanied by a lash of his whip. He was surprised to see the dog seemingly just jump into the air and disappear. When he realized that the dog had fallen into a crevasse or over a cliff, he quickly applied the brake on the sled, but by the time he could get the sled stopped, five of his thirteen dogs had disappeared. The sled was loaded heavily enough that with the brake on and the eight remaining dogs pulling back, the five dogs that had gone over the edge were held suspended in air. Willock became very excited because he didn't know just how close he was to the crevasse, or whether he had been paralleling it for some distance. It was snowing too hard for him to see clearly in the twilight, so he had to feel his way along the dogs until he could reach the tow rope to which they were hitched. He managed to get in front of the dogs and pull with his full strength, but was unable to ease the fallen dogs back up. As bady as he hated it, the only thing he could do was to take out his knife and cut the rope, letting the five dogs fall. Then slowly he inched the sled backwards far enough to turn it around safely. He unhitched the remaining dogs, tied them to the sled and fed them, then took out his canvas tarp and spread it over the sled to make himself a shelter for the night.

After he had made himself some tea on a little alcohol stove, he gathered sufficient courage to try to discover what had happened to the five dogs and to see if he could do anything to recover them. Finding a pole to use as a probe, he painfully worked himself down to a distance of some one hundred and fifty feet from the top. He kept calling to the dogs, but heard no response. By feeling around on the ground, he could tell that they had fallen to the very place on which he was standing and had evidently made strenuous efforts to climb back up the cliff, but now he could neither see nor hear anything to help him locate them.

Climbing down to a second level, Tom found the dogs at last, still tied together and seemingly unhurt, but too exhausted to even whimper. He let them rest for about an hour before untangling them so they could move about freely, then he carefully and slowly led the lead dog back up the trail he had tromped down descending the steep incline. Helping each other and stopping often to rest, they gradually worked their way all the way to the top. After feeding the dogs, he got into his sleeping bag and fell into an exhausted sleep.

When he awakened the next morning and anxiously pulled back the tarp, he found it was still snowing hard, with a driving wind causing visibility to be almost zero. Very disappointed, he pulled the canvas back over his head thinking that he might have to remain where he was for several days until the weather let up. He lay there for a long time feeling very dejected. As he was thinking, something a missionary had said years before flashed into his mind. "If ye ask anything in my name, my Father will give it to you," was the way he remembered the verse; so lying in the darkness, he asked God to give him weather good enough to find his way back to the right stream. After he prayed, he lay still for about twenty minutes, then pulled the canvas back again to look out. He saw a break in the clouds which made a light place in the sky. Jumping up, Tom prepared food for himself and the dogs, then lost no time in resuming his journey.

When Tom finished telling this story to Mr. Cary, he looked at the Bible, pointed to about where the fourteenth verse was on the page, and repeated, "If ye shall ask anything in my name, I will do it."

When Elsie was born in 1888 at Kobuk, Alaska, Eskimo women followed the custom of going out alone on the tundra to have their babies. The grandmother prepared a little house of willows and

mud and left some fish for the expectant mother. An old relative
had ordered, "If the baby is a girl, put dirt in her mouth." But
Elsie's mother was determined to keep her baby even though it
should be an unwanted girl. She was left alone in the delivery
hut wearing a dirty old parka. After the baby girl was born, she
burned all the clothes she had worn because according to common
belief, if anyone used these things again, she would die.

While very young, Elsie learned to catch, clean, and strip fish,
preserve berries and greens, and sew skins for clothing. "God made
Alaska rich," she often says. "Anyone not lazy can find enough
food in the summertime in Alaska."

Elsie and Tom were married in the Swedish Covenant Mission
in Council, Alaska, on Thanksgiving Day of 1907. All fourteen of
their children were born at home without medical assistance. Often
they were utterly dependent on God. Aunt Elsie tells that when
one of her young sons severely burned his hand on a red-hot iron
and had gone into convulsions with the pain, she prayed, "Oh God,
we have no one but you. Help our little boy." The convulsive
jerking ceased. The child slept. And when he awakened, his burns
were healed and he went back to his play.

Uncle Tom had the honor of being the first ordained Eskimo
deacon. Early in 1961 the Native Baptist Church honored him with
a "This Is Your Life, Tom Willock" program. During the program
he read John 3:16 and Psalm 23. In July 1961 Uncle Tom died while
out at his fishing camp preparing the winter's supply of fish. He
was eighty-four years old. During the reading classes Uncle Tom
had trouble retaining all the words he learned, but headlines in
the *Alaska Baptist Messenger* announced his death by stating
"Uncle Tom graduates; now he has gone to the head of the class."

Aunt Elsie continues to set an example in church attendance.
She loves to sing and is an inspiration to Eskimos, Baptists, and
tourists alike. She likes to announce before she sings her special
number, "Jesus, take my song. Take to people far away from you.
Give them my joy." [13]

✿　　✿　　✿

In 1953 Charlie Sheldon was the only Christian in the village
of Kobuk. He wrote to Missionary Dick Miller at Kotzebue expressing concern to have a church in his village so that the "children
could know the right way." That winter, logs were cut and Dick

Miller, John Dickerson, Charlie Sheldon, and two young boys got the walls of a mission building up and began holding services. The first Sunday forty villagers came to both the morning and evening services. When Miller asked about the population of Kobuk, he was told it was forty.

One reason for Charlie's concern was that a few years before this a group had tried to get a native reservation at Kobuk, thinking the Eskimos wouldn't know enough to protest; but Charlie Sheldon wanted his people to be "just plain Americans," and through his efforts the reservation plans were defeated. Charlie said a man came from Washington, D. C., to be sure things went right, and when it was all over, he asked Charlie if he had anything to say. Charlie answered, "Now my little niece can be anything she wants to be." And more than anything else, Charlie wanted her to be a Christian.

After the building was finished at Kobuk in 1954, Charlie Sheldon became our first native Baptist missionary, serving with no salary or remuneration. In three years time he had led half his village to accept Christ as Savior. One convert was his mother, Ina. No one knew for sure how old Ina was, but there was a man living on the Kobuk River who said he knew her when he was a small boy, and she was already a grown woman then. The man was eighty-five years old.

Ina's husband was a reindeer herder. She never learned to speak more than a dozen words of English, but because she wanted her son Charlie to receive training, she was willing to accompany him to Anchorage so he could attend the Native Baptist Training School.

Ina was baptized in the summer of 1956 following the breakup and thaw of the Kobuk River. The water was about two degrees above freezing, but when Dick Miller asked if she would rather wait for the water to warm up, she replied, "No! I might not be here then."

Charlie trained his people to bring their offerings on Sundays, and in 1957 all but two of the families in the village brought special offerings for home missions also. The food supply that winter had been very short. Nevertheless, Charlie continued to set an example of stewardship for his people. When L. A. Watson spoke in some Texas churches about the work in Kobuk, one church sent an offering of $100 to be used for purchasing groceries for the Sheldon family. Charlie was quick to use the gift as an opportunity to teach his people that God will provide the needs of those who trust him.

One summer the Sheldons had bad news. Charlie's X-rays showed that he was a victim of tuberculosis. Sadly, he left his family and church and entered the hospital at Seward. A short time later someone discovered that the X-rays had belonged to another Charles Sheldon, and Charlie was free to go back home. Before doing so, however, he wooed and won a nurse who was employed in the hospital. Dick Miller officiated at their marriage ceremony.

When L. A. Watson visited the Kiana Mission in the summer of 1959, he was surprised to find Charlie Sheldon there instead of in Kobuk. He had brought two boatloads of young people from Kobuk and Shungnak to attend the youth camp in Kiana, and some of them had caught the measles. Charlie had to stay with them until all were recovered sufficiently to make the trip back home, some two hundred miles up the Kobuk River.

BAPTIST WORK WITH THE ESKIMOS

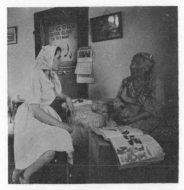
Valeria Sherard visits Nellie Baldwin in Kiana.

Sunbeam children play next to Kiana Mission building.

Wilson Tickett rings bell for worship at Kobuk Mission.

Norman Harrell calls on the Henry Stockings in Kobuk.

Children play game called "fox and geese" by Shungnak Mission.

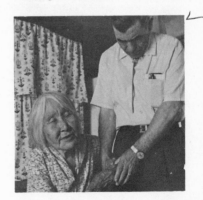
108-year-old Grandma Tucker prays with Pastor Isaacs (1967).

(All illustrations on this page are 1967 Home Board Photos.)

These children agreed to remain after church at the Anchorage East Third Street Baptist Mission to have their photograph taken (1969).

These young people rode the ferry from Mt. Edgecombe School on Japonski Island to Sitka to attend the morning services at First Baptist Church (1967).

SOME PEOPLE WHO WORKED WITH THE ALASKA NATIVES

Charlie Sheldon is pictured with his daughter in Shungnak (1957).

Charlie Sheldon's 91-year-old mother lived in Kobuk Village (1959).

Mr. and Mrs. C. O. Dunkin started Baptist work in Fairbanks (1965 photo).

The Oliver Marson family moved from Juneau to lead Fort Yukon work (1960).

Sunset Hills Church presented snow machine to Willie Johnson (1967).

Aged Tom Willock sits and listens to the story of his life (1960).

SOME BAPTIST WORK WITH THE RACES

Elsie and Tom Willock confer with John Dickerson and C. O. Dunkin at the Native Baptist Mission in Fairbanks (1953 Home Board Photo).

The charter members of the St. John Baptist Church in Fairbanks pose for an official photograph of the church beginning (1953 Home Board Photo).

The first meeting of the Jewel Lake Baptist Church of Anchorage at the Allen Meeks home attracted this group of people (August 1967).

MEETING PLACES FOR NEW CHURCHES IN ALASKA

The First Baptist Mission of Montana Creek met in this camp tent (1969).

The Hamilton Acres Baptist Church of Fairbanks met in this quonset (1954).

The First Baptist Church of Birchwood met in these two quonset huts (1959). *I visited there 1962. a Building by then.*

Charter members of Eagle River First Baptist Church used a quonset (1957).

The Sunday school and worship services at King Salmon used Katmai Club (1969).

North Kenai Faith Baptist Chapel met in this remodeled trailer home (1968).

SOME EARLY CHURCH BUILDINGS IN ALASKA

North Pole First Baptist Church was constructed with logs (1953 Home Board Photo).

Initial Soldotna First Baptist Church utilized logs (1957 Home Board Photo).

The Anchorage Potter Road (Immanuel) Mission used a quonset hut (1953 Home Board Photo).

Juneau Glacier Valley Baptist Church was made of frame materials (1967 Home Board Photo).

Anchorage East Third Street Baptist Mission portrays modern construction (1965).

The Arctic's Venetie Baptist Mission was built with logs (1968).

ANCHORAGE AREA CHURCHES
DRAPED WITH WINTER'S SPLENDOR (1970)

The Potter Road Baptist Mission (1954) is now the Immanuel Baptist Church.

The Eastchester Baptist Mission (1951) is now the Fairview Baptist Church.

The Muldoon Road Baptist Church (1960) now reports over a thousand members.

The Greater Friendship Baptist Church (1951) is one of three Negro congregations.

The Faith Baptist Church (1949) now reports over four hundred members.

The Tudor Road Baptist Church (1959) changed name to University Baptist Church.

SOUTHERN BAPTIST CONVENTION LEADERS
VISIT ALASKA

Dowis and Garrison of HMB visit Craun at the Fort Yukon Mission (1957).

I toured this Place 1963

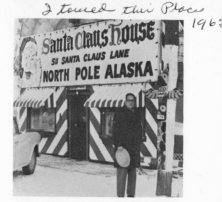

Brotherhood executive secretary George Schroeder visits Santa Claus (1968).

ABC president Edward Wolfe welcomes Mississippi mission leaders (1968).

WMU executive secretary Alma Hunt goes back for seconds on moose meat (1968).

Chron, Rice, and Dawson of HMB meet during Alaska mission conference (1968).

Seminary president Harold Graves basks in the Alaska sunshine in November (1968).

SPREADING THE GOSPEL IN ALASKA

Anchorage Jewel Lake Baptist Church conducted tent VBS and revival (1968).

Pastor Marion Dunham of Ketchikan preaches on "Bible Break" (1967).

Missionary Harley Shield uses short wave radio to maintain contact (1969).

The Anchorage New Hope Baptist Church choir sang at building dedication (1968).

Hunke and lay missionary Leonard Everman talk by Kiana's drying fish (1969).

Missionary Don Wright initiated new Baptist mission work in Petersburg (1969).

BAPTIST CAMPING IN THE ALASKA BUSH

Young people travel to Orton Ranch by a motor cruiser and barge.

Boys line up for chow in densely forested assembly on banks of Naha River.

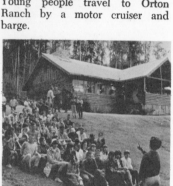

Fairbanks and Interior Alaska youth meet in rented Harding Lake Assembly.

Anchorage area young people camp in tents at Baptist Lake on Talkeetna Highway (1968).

Arctic young people sometimes fly to attend the Far North camps.

Valeria Sherard loads up boat for camp on a sandbar in the Kobuk River. *Serves in Anchorage now*

(All illustrations except right center are 1967 Home Board Photos.)

Dee Johnson (r) shows Naomi Hunke site of Connie Thomas tragedy (1970 photo). *author of this book*

Hunke and **Belew** visited Murdock, on his homestead near Soldotna (1967 Home Board Photo).

Pastors Moore, Dickson, and Midkiff met to plan mission advance (1968).

First officers of Tustumena Baptist Association at organizational meeting, (1968).

Leo Josey (1) leads a prayer during revival prayer breakfast (1968).

Rollins baptized Sgt. Paul Nichols as first candidate in King Salmon (1969).

AMONG THE MISSIONARIES IN ALASKA

The Harley Shield family arrives in Kotzebue for new assignment (1966). *Great hearted family*

Ruth Meeks (l) and Willie Johnson (r) welcome US-2 Virgie and Mike Brown (1968).

Tennessee student work team worked on the Shungnak mission building (1966).

Baptist students gather in College for a November BSU convention (1963).

Miller, Marson, the pilot, Mrs. Fling, Rollins and Hunke travel the bush (1967).

Athabascan Indian children welcome the Baptist visitors to their village (1967).

7

". . . Care of All the Churches"

2 Corinthians 11:28

Alaska means
granite-capped mountains donning purple robes in
    early evening
deep canyons winding along their meandering way
myriads of lakes carved into the face of the land
    like the initials of God
a magnificent Persian rug of tundra unrolled over
    endless acres
gold mining towns touched with the hoary gray of
    old age
the glory of heaven exploding in the cold brittle
    dome of a winter night sky
ridge after ridge of spruce and aspen-clad hills
    rolled back like waves
miles and miles of nothing but miles and miles
intoxication from carbonated air while watching the
    "Greatest Snow on Earth."
"Great Land," full of wonder and splendor, fitting reflection
    of majesty, the quaking of your earth and the shaking of
        your mountains, the blackness of your nights and
            the lashing of the oceans against your shores
only bear witness to the greatness of my God.

James Cook, son of a Yorkshire farmer and apprentice of a Whitby haberdasher, sought more adventure than the English isle could offer, so he joined the royal navy. His first command was the *Grampas;* his last, the *Discovery.* The name *Discovery* was symbolic, for from the time he was appointed to conduct an expedition of exploration in 1768 until the Hawaiian natives stabbed him in the back in 1779, his discoveries were endless.

Cook was on his third voyage, trying to settle the question of the Northwest Passage, when he entered Alaskan waters. After sailing up the coast from Vancouver and naming many mountains and bays in the Prince William Sound area, he commanded James King to go ashore and take possession of the country at Cook Inlet. He thought he had located a mighty river, though when the giant twenty-seven foot tides swept in and his command rang out, "Turn and turn again," he was amazed and at a loss to understand what was happening. Visitors who go in for gold panning in Alaska often think of looking for a bottle containing English shillings that Captain Cook recorded burying at the entrance to Chickaloon Bay of Turnagain Arm on a rise at Point Possession.

When Cook sailed up the Inlet, the navigating master of his flagship, the *Resolution*, was William Bligh, later to become famous because of the mutiny on the *Bounty*, led by Fletcher Christian. These troubles occurred some years after Bligh's trip to the Anchorage area.

So far as Cook was concerned, the most important discovery he made in Alaska was the virgin whaling fields of the Arctic waters. For almost one hundred years following his coming, sailing ships battled the grinding polar ice and vicious gales. Many ships were caught when the ice moved in early. In 1871 trapped ships left twelve hundred men stranded on the ice. They were able to make their way to five other vessels still standing free, and although the ships were dangerously crowded far beyond capacity, they arrived in Honolulu a month later with all hands safe. At Point Barrow in 1897 eight ships became caught in treacherous ice. The crews cautiously crawled along the perilous floes to the shore. The two hundred sixty-five men had very short rations, and survival in the barren wilderness until the next spring seemed impossible. George Tilton, mate of the *Belvedere*, volunteered to go for help. He traveled three thousand miles by foot, dog sled, and small boat, and was finally successful in his pleas to find help for his stranded friends. The rescue party drove a herd of reindeer to Point Barrow to provide food for the men until the next year when breakup brought relief ships.

Baptists, too, are an heroic people. The nineteen fifties and sixties found them going everywhere, starting churches, seeking that which was more valuable than "gold which perisheth." E. W. Hunke gives this testimony to the value of this kind of venture:

> Some years ago a missionary's comment changed the course of my personal ministry. He said, "The greatest work one can accom-

plish in life is to be used of God in initiating a new church." I countered with a question regarding the value of one soul.

He answered, "Winning one soul to Christ is good, and great, and wonderful. I do not depreciate this fact. Soul-winning is the imperative of the great commission; but the establishment of a soul-saving station which will ultimately win thousands of souls over a period of several lifetimes is the greater work." I have found that the Apostle Paul emphasized soulwinning, but his crushing burden was the establishment and care of the churches.

The September 1947 mimeographed issue of the *Alaska Baptist Messenger* carried an article stating that Mr. and Mrs. E. N. Sullivan arrived September 10 to work toward establishing a Baptist church in Palmer. They drove up the Alcan from Brandon, Mississippi, where Mr. Sullivan had been pastoring. The church there had helped the Sullivans purchase a house trailer for the trip. The Sullivans only stayed a short while in Alaska, according to a letter written by Orland Cary, and the work at Palmer did not have a continuing ministry at that time.

In June 1949 Mike McKay and his wife Virginia started a mission work at Palmer, first meeting in homes and later renting the Seventh Day Adventist Church for Sunday worship services. Felton Griffin preached a revival in the fall, which resulted in many decisions, and the mission seemed to take on new life. Dr. James Morgan came to preach for them in October 1950, and the church was "packed to the walls." Dr. Morgan took motion pictures that were shown in Baptist churches all over the States. He led the small group to make plans for organizing, buying property, and starting a mission fund. He promised to lead his church in Fort Worth to raise the first $5,000 toward the Baptist church building. After the revival, he flew to Atlanta to try to get the Home Mission Board to raise additional funds for the church.

After Mike and Virginia left Palmer to attend Wayland College, Charles LeClair, a serviceman stationed at Anchorage and a member of First Baptist Church, began going to Palmer and was called to be the next pastor. From November 1950, until the summer of 1951, the group met in the home of Mr. and Mrs. G. A. Krise, Virginia McKay's parents. The organization service was held in May 1951 with fifty people attending. Charles LeClair rotated out that summer, after securing the Carpenters' Hall for the new church to rent for Sunday services.

Dr. Morgan and Dr. Cal Guy were instrumental in bringing the Avery Richeys as the next pastor. The Home Mission Board bought a home for a parsonage and three lots on the corner of Matanuska and Gulcana, and a large concrete block building was constructed. The church reached a pinnacle during the ministry of Clifford McConnell, but later ceased to meet. In 1969 the work was reopened by Grandview in Anchorage where McConnell pastored. In 1970, after a year of Bible home fellowships led by James Akin, the Eagle River church is reinitiating the Palmer mission. Don Smith, one former pastor, is serving as a foreign missionary in East Africa.

Easter Sunday 1951 was just another day to many, but to a small group of people assembled in the Eastchester Community Hall in Anchorage, it was the birthdate of the Eastchester Baptist Church. Twelve charter members united together to spread the gospel in the churchless community of 7,000 people.

In August of 1950 several servicemen from First Baptist Church, Anchorage, discussed the possibilities and need of a church in the Eastchester area. They decided to hold a revival and get off to a good start, so Mike McKay preached one week and Felton Griffin a second week in August, with no visible results. The young men, three of them preachers, found out "that the Gravy Train didn't run through Eastchester,"—it was going to take hard work to start a Baptist church.

They went ahead with their plans and selected Velton Walker to be pastor of the church, as well as Sunday school teacher and pianist; Fred Chapman as Sunday school superintendent, Training Union director, and song leader; Claude Burke as secretary and treasurer; with Charles LeClair, Mrs. Patton, and Carl Rylander as other Sunday school teachers.

The first Sunday school met in Carr's Department Store with fifteen present. Eight weeks later there were forty-four present. Through the winter months a combination of bad weather and no heat presented a problem. Charles LeClair left to pastor the Palmer Baptist Church and Mrs. Patton went Outside for the winter, but God provided other workers.

As the mission grew, the group felt the need to organize, so on March 25, 1951, approximately seventy-five Baptists from Anchorage Baptist churches assembled to witness the birth of the church.

Dr. Arthur Hinson, Calvary Baptist, acted as moderator and led the church in the adoption of the church covenant and declaration of faith. Felton Griffin preached the message. The church had already purchased a lot in the community and planned to build during the summer.

On December 23, 1951, the Eastchester Baptist Church held its first service in the new building. Constructed of concrete blocks with blue cathedral glass windows, the building was almost complete. After five years of growth and progress, a name change to Fairview Baptist Church, and another building program, the church gathered on July 16, 1955, for a dedication and ground-breaking ceremony. John C. Denton, pastor of Fairview, officiated at the service. Mr. and Mrs. Mike McKay provided the music, and Felton Griffin presented a summary of Baptists in Alaska. John DeFoore of Calvary Baptist brought the inspirational message. The new building would be used for educational purposes, with the first building being converted into a sanctuary.

One pastor, Ray Hustead, served the Fairview church twice, first in 1957 when he was stationed at Elmendorf Air Force Base. Following his release from the service, Hustead entered Howard Payne College, graduating in 1961, and in September of that year he entered Southwestern Seminary, receiving the B.D. degree in 1964. At that time he received a call to again become pastor of the Fairview church, and with his wife and daughter, he arrived in Anchorage in mid August. He left the church to pastor the Frontier Baptist Church in Kodiak in 1968. Frank Bullock accepted Fairview's call and is the present pastor.

The Greater Friendship Baptist Church of Anchorage started with a revival conducted at First Baptist with Clarence Kennedy, pastor of the Negro congregation, and Felton Griffin, pastor at First Baptist, jointly conducting the services. During the revival, twenty-nine persons expressed willingness to join a new Negro Baptist church if one were organized. Seventeen of these were present and became charter members when the group met on Sunday afternoon, June 24, 1951, at First Baptist Church to organize. Within three weeks the new church had one hundred members.

During 1952 the congregation built their auditorium in the Eastchester division of Anchorage. In spite of zero weather, which did not make for comfort or ease and success in pouring concrete, the construction work went on. Each small section of concrete had to be covered and heated until it was dry, making a long, slow, and tedious job. Materials salvaged from the fire at First Baptist helped supply the needs of the Negro church.

Early in 1952 the Chugach association, through their missions committee, determined that the Grandview community needed a preaching station. The committee found a lot owned by Janet Ames, a member of First Baptist, who offered the lot at a very reasonable price to the group. Property in Mountain View, owned by the convention, was sold in order to buy the Grandview land. John DeFoore led in the building of a church on the lot. The associational W.M.U. made contributions; churches also responded with gifts, and, with volunteer labor from the association, a usable building was erected by summer.

In 1964, James A. Boney, who had helped in the construction of three other churches in Alaska, came to act as building superintendent for the three-story combination unit which would replace the old building. Clifford S. McConnell, the present pastor, stated at that time, "More educational space in the new unit will enable the church to meet the challenge of unreached people in the community."

McConnell almost brought back home an Eskimo baby when he made his first trip to the Arctic in 1966. After he boarded the plane in Kotzebue, an Eskimo man came up to him with a baby in his arms.

"You hold?" he inquired.

"Sure," replied McConnell, thinking that the woman standing behind the man waiting for a seat reservation was the baby's mother.

After they boarded the plane, the woman paid no attention to the child. When the plane made a stop before it arrived at the preacher's destination, the woman deboarded, without the child. It did not belong to her.

McConnell spent the next few minutes wondering what he was going to do with the tiny Eskimo baby. How could he ever explain this new addition to his wife? When he arrived at Shungnak, the grateful parents were waiting to claim their travelling infant from McConnell, but their gratitude was far surpassed by his.

The Valdez church first met in August 1952, in the old Congregational church building. James Rose was the founder and the first pastor. Calvary Baptist of Anchorage sponsored the work and Pastor DeFoore helped get the meeting place repaired and in a fit condition for worship services.

The first winter, however, the city building inspector condemned the building as being unstable, but allowed the church to continue meeting there until they could build a new building. Now, seventeen years later, the Congregational building is still standing staunchly.

The church decided to build a log cabin church in the shape of a "T." Southern Baptist W.M.U. members gave the church a $10,000 grant, and they borrowed $10,000 more from the Home Mission Board. They also conducted a "Buy a Log" sale, with logs costing $3 each, for the building fund. Mr. Rose, a carpenter, did most of the work. The first service in the new building was a Christmas program in 1954. By this time the mission had organized into a church.

After Mr. Rose resigned in 1956, young servicemen from Anchorage came down to preach for the Valdez church. Mr. Stewart came from New Orleans to pastor, but stayed only a few months. Dr. William Hansen wrote expressing interest in the work, and the church invited him to come. L. A. Watson met the Hansens at the Anchorage airport at two A.M. when they arrived enroute to Valdez. They got to Valdez on the last day of 1960, and he preached his first sermon on New Year's Day. Mr. Hansen wrote, "Everyone seemed happy. Things went along for about three weeks this way. Then after the service one Sunday morning, Dick Shafer, who had been serving as moderator, requested that I ask the congregation to stay after the service. I did so, and Dick got up and said, 'Today we are going to vote on Brother Hansen as pastor.' I was flabbergasted—thinking we had already been called months before. Fortunately, the church extended a call and we stayed at Valdez."

Early in the morning of Dr. Hansen's second Sunday in Valdez, a fire gutted the home of one of the members and took the life of a thirteen-year-old boy, Danny. Mrs. Kennedy, church clerk, said, "How thankful we were that God had sent us a pastor to see us through this terrible sorrow."

After Dr. Hansen resigned, Mr. Rose was again called by the church. He was pastoring it when the earthquake hit in 1964, but was on a trip Outside. He drove without stopping until he got back to Valdez because of the reports he heard about the damage Valdez sustained. During the weeks after the quake, because their building was destroyed, the church banded together with the Assembly of God people, who had a building left but no pastor. After about six weeks the Baptist group decided they would rather meet separately in their pastor's home. Rose resigned in July. When Frank Sisson arrived, the task of building a new building was urgent. He stayed until 1967 when the building was nearing completion. The Seventh Day Adventist group was using the church as a meeting place at that time, and together the two groups finished up the interior, even to installing wall-to-wall carpeting.

Lester Bonner, a service man stationed at Fort Wainwright at Fairbanks, came to preach for the Valdez church and felt led to pastor them. He tried to get a transfer to be supervisor of the army recreation camp at Valdez. For three months he drove from Fairbanks, then the transfer came through, and he was able to move his family down permanently.

While Jimmy Rose was at Valdez, he sponsored a Boat Mission, and ministered to the needs of people up and down the coast and on nearby islands. This met a long felt need.

When Vitus Bering sailed from Siberia in 1741, he was searching for Gamaland, a nebulous area east of Japan that appeared on a map drawn by a French astronomer named Delisle. Actually, "Gamaland" was a map-selling gimmick devised by Delisle. Because his map looked so empty from Japan all the way across to Hudson Bay, he drew in "Gamaland" and described it as a land of gold, silver, gems, and wealth beyond belief.

Bering wasted many days searching for the non-existant land before sailing east and discovering Alaska. As a result of his voyage, the Russians drew up a new map of the North Pacific area. While searching for the Northwest Passage, Captain James Cook did such a thorough job of mapping the coastline of Alaska that his map published in 1785 was used by all navigators until after the purchase of Alaska by the United States.

Although the riches of Gamaland proved fanciful, at least one man in the United States firmly believed in the riches of Alaska. In 1867 the Russian diplomat, Baron de Stoeckl, was sent to Washington with orders from the Czar, "Get rid of Alaska; get the best possible price." William H. Seward, Secretary of State, met repeatedly with the Russian until the price was agreed on—$7,200,000. "This is the greatest land bargain in history!" Seward exclaimed.

The night the Civil War was over, Seward was ill and alone. An assassin crashed into his bedroom and slashed at him with a knife. Seward rolled between the bed and wall and warded off the attack until the would-be killer was overpowered. Because he hovered between life and death for days, he was not told of Lincoln's death. He related that when he saw the flags at half mast and knew the President was dead, he felt that life had nothing more to offer. One cannot help wondering what would have happened to Alaska if Seward had been killed or had given up his political career.

But Seward was not given to taking defeat. As a young lawyer, against the advice of all of his friends, Seward had defended a Negro accused of lynching. He was beaten when he first ran for governor of New York. When it seemed certain that he would be the Republican candidate for the Presidency, Abraham Lincoln came out of Illinois and defeated him.

So when the buyer of Alaska was severely criticized for paying two cents an acre for a chunk of ice, "Seward's Folly," they called it, or "Seward's Icebox," he was not dismayed. However, Seward once voiced the doubt that his friends would long remember him after his death. "I hope," he said, "that some wandering stranger, some lone exile, some Indian, some Negro, may erect over my humble grave a stone, and write thereon this epitaph, 'He was faithful.' "

Seward got his wish, for on his marble monument those words are carved. But also carved in the hearts of those who live in the 49th state are the words "Father of Alaska." [14]

Both a northern peninsula and a city on the Kenai peninsula bear the name "Seward" today. The city lies at the southern terminus of the Alaska Railroad, where the grandeur of the Kenai Mountain glaciers meets the scenic fiords of the coastline. B. I. Carpenter left Ketchikan January 11, 1953, to begin work in Seward and the Kenai Peninsula. His wife and daughter joined him at the close of the school term. On January 25 Carpenter held the first services in a rented hall. Four attended the morning service and five the evening service. Mrs. Carpenter told about the change in their place of service in the December 1964 *Home Missions:*

"Daddy, do we have to leave Ketchikan?" This was the question Helen Ruth anxiously asked her father, B. I. Carpenter.

He explained that after much prayer and meditation, he felt that the Lord wanted him to go to Seward, Alaska, to begin work in that port city.

"But, Daddy, we've just got things going good here. Why do we have to leave it? . . . If we go to Seward, we'll just have to start all over again." [15]

And Helen Ruth was right; they did have to start all over again. Seward at that time was a town of 3,500 people where the bars and saloons outnumbered all other businesses put together. One night after months of meetings in the labor union hall, a young couple slipped into the services. The girl was a Baptist, but Bob Biggs' only interest was to please the girl. They attended regularly until the girl's job was finished in Alaska, then to the surprise of everyone, Bob continued to come. Finally, Bob walked the aisle, making a public profession of faith in Christ.

He later told Mrs. Carpenter, "You know, I was determined not to be talked into anything. But this is the happiest experience of my life and I am at a loss to know just what happened." He went on to reveal that the only time he had ever attended church services was when he had gone to chapel services in the army in order to skip work. "None of that made any impression on me. It was not until I came in contact with this little group that I was impressed. I wanted the same kind of happiness and peace that seemed to possess the lives of these Christians."

When asked why he had come to Alaska, Bob laughed. "This is a believe-it-or-not. I baby-sat all the way from Memphis, Tennessee, to Seward, Alaska. When I was seventeen and just out of high school, a young couple from my home town had come to Seward, leaving their fourteen-month-old baby with her grandparents. They paid my traveling expense, and I was elected to take Donna to them. I was young and brave then because, frankly, I don't believe I'd have the courage to do it now."

Bob, a senior warehouseman for Standard Oil Company, expressed his determination to win the girl and make a Christian home in Seward.

The First Baptist Church of Seward was organized on Saturday night, October 24, 1953, in a climactic service of their revival meeting, a part of the simultaneous evangelistic campaign in the

Territory. The church, constituted with twenty-three members, called B. I. Carpenter as pastor, and elected Oliver Ogle as treasurer and Mrs. Ila Rustad as church clerk. Until the organization of the church, this group operated as a mission of the Calvary Baptist Church of Anchorage. During the month of November, their average Sunday school attendance was forty-five. The Home Mission Board had allocated $25,000 for a building which was under construction. The church hoped to be in the basement for the Christmas service; they made it by Thanksgiving.

When Seward First Baptist Church celebrated its first anniversary in 1954, eighty-two were present in Sunday school, with classes and teaching staff reaching all age groups. Following a noon meal together, Pastor Carpenter showed slides of their building progress. Nine of the charter members were present; these testified to their feeling of gratitude to God for his bountiful blessings in their first year as a church. Don Freimuth presented an ivory-handled carving set to the Carpenters in appreciation of their work of leading the church. The basement was completed to the extent that the church was using it for classrooms. Plans for completing the interior of the upper auditorium were discussed at the anniversary gathering. The first worship services held in the main auditorium were on April 10, 1955.

After B. I. Carpenter resigned in May 1956, A. C. Maxwell from Fort Worth became pastor at Seward. He was just out of seminary. Seward was his first pastorate, and he was ordained by the church.

James Akin was the next pastor. When Akin resigned the Trinity Baptist Church, he stated that he and Mrs. Akin came to Alaska to do mission work, and since Trinity was moving forward, they felt they should make themselves available for service in an area of greater need. T. W. Craighead from Oklahoma and Frank Bullock from Missouri next served the church. After a year with the church, Bullock reported, "By the end of the year we have gained back to the attendance level we had before the earthquake. . . . Last summr we encouraged members to each pay for a storm window for the church. We now have storm windows which are adding comfort to the building as well as reducing the fuel bill. . . . A year ago when the earthquake hit, there was no insurance for the church building; now we have insurance. . . . We have emphasized missions this year. Thirteen percent is being given. . . . Our W.M.U. has been reorganized and is doing a good work."

James Rose pastored the church in 1969; Joe Fallon from Anchorage followed him and is the present pastor. The church clerk wrote, "Since his coming, the attendance has more than doubled. Glory be to God."

Ernest F. Lilley, of Nachitoches, Louisiana, wrote the following letter, telling about the beginning of the Anchorage, Immanuel Baptist Church:

> During the evangelistic crusade of 1953, under the direction of Dr. C. E. Autrey, I worked with Brother C. H. Thurmond, who was then the pastor of Potter Mission which later became the Immanuel Church.
>
> Brother Thurmond was located at the air base in Anchorage, and was ordained during our revival campaign there. As I remember, the service was held at the Calvary Baptist Church, with the pastors and evangelists making up the ordaining council.
>
> It was during this evangelistic campaign that we were able to get the mission ready to become a church. Services were started in a quonset hut which had been used for a garage. We began with seven people in our first service, and in the last service, we had sixty-eight people, some standing. The Spirit of God moved in a mighty way, resulting in many being saved, and one young man surrendering to preach. To God be the glory, and credit to Brother and Mrs. Thurmond for their fine work.
>
> On a Saturday evening, Brother Thurmond and I drove over to Seward and helped to organize the First Baptist Church of Seward. These were great days, and great experiences, in a great campaign of evangelism.

The Immanuel Baptist Church was organized July 18, 1954, with twenty-three charter members. The church called C. H. Thurmond as pastor. Harry Skaggs sang, "My Wonderful Lord"; Mrs. Thurmond reported that while he was singing, "Truly we felt that of all people on earth, we were the most blessed of God." John Denton, pastor of Eastchester, acted as moderator, and John DeFoore of Calvary brought the charge to the church to preach the gospel "in our homes, church, and on our jobs." Ed Schmetekopf, student summer worker, led the music and helped to prepare the program. Ed was the preacher for the next revival the church conducted August 1-8.

By the end of their first year as a church, the membership had increased 145%; Sunday school enrollment climbed from thirty-eight to eighty-four; three new classes had been organized; thirty training awards had been earned; a fully organized W.M.U. was in operation, and the Brotherhood had begun functioning. The quonset hut had been outgrown, and the church had received a loan from the Home Mission Board and laid the foundation of a new church building. When the debt for the first building loan was paid off, Pastor Johnny Newton led the church in remodeling the basement and adding an entryway. In 1970 the church faces its period of greatest potential because a housing area has grown up around it.

The Mountain View Mission met first in September 1954, in a building located at Parsons and Bragaw Street in Anchorage. Felton Griffin was chairman of the associational missions committee that secured the building. Later the mission moved to a new location in the old post office building on Taylor Street. Wyatt Flowers was called by the associational executive board in October 1954 to pastor the mission.

On July 17, 1955, the mission met to organize into the First Southern Baptist Church in Mountain View. In 1956 two lots with a building were purchased, and additional lots on which to build a new sanctuary were obtained in 1962.

J. E. Akin came from Vernal, Utah, to be the second pastor. He led in establishing a building fund and changing the name of the church to Trinity Baptist Church.

John Jeffcoat came in 1960 and led the church to begin the new auditorium. On Labor Day, 1963, the next pastor, Donald E. Wright, arrived to find the members of Trinity church out in full force at work on their new building. He saw the building brought to completion before he went to Southeastern Alaska to work in missions. Tommy Pitman was interim pastor until the present pastor, Dupre Gowan, came in April 1969. During the past year the Sunday school attendance has doubled and the church has had forty-six additions.

The Eagle River First Baptist Church, sponsored by Grandview Baptist Church, began as Trinity Baptist Mission in May 1957. The first Sunday school had nine present. It met in a quonset hut. James L. Vanderford served as pastor until he resigned because of military obligations. Marcus Price was called by the church in January 1958, and the church was constituted the following month with fifty-two members. T. F. Moore was the first ordained deacon. Mr. Price had to rotate in July, and until E. C. Chron was called in September 1958, James C. Morgan served as interim pastor.

E. C. Chron surrendered to preach while he was in the used car business in Anchorage, shortly before he was called to the Eagle River church. During the next two years the church received support from the Home Mission Board and the state convention. A bond issue made possible a new basement and repair of the old building. The church fostered two missions. Birchwood started during the summer of 1958 in the home of Ruby Jones. The mission's official beginning was in a quonset hut in April 1959. The Muldoon mission started in 1960. Mr. Chron resigned in 1960 to attend Wayland College. James Henderson and John Camp pastored the Eagle River church during Chron's college years, then the church called him again. The new building was constructed during his ministry.

Rawls Pierce has served the church since June 1967. William Konesky and Dennis Klein are the only charter members still at Eagle River.

The mission which was started in Birchwood in 1958 had to cease meeting because of lack of a place to meet. Lots were bought and two quonset huts purchased and moved in time for the first service to reopen the work in April 1959. Ben Hill, general missionary, met with the mission in its beginning weeks.

In October 1964, the mission was constituted into the First Baptist Church of Birchwood with twenty-four charter members. The new church called Frank Miller of Chugiak as pastor. He had worked with them during the formative period.

Robert Chadwick, the present pastor, went to Afognak Island as an independent Baptist missionary, supporting himself by working as a big game guide when he first came to Alaska. The island community was never rebuilt after the 1964 earthquake. Chadwick moved into Anchorage and began attending First Baptist Church. He became convinced that he could do a more lasting work for the Lord as a Southern Baptist. Since going to Birchwood, he has led in remodeling the building and in securing a new location just three hundred feet off the new freeway on North Birchwood Loop Road. Construction of a beautiful new sanctuary is beginning during the summer of 1970.

Tudor Baptist Church was constituted March 22, 1959. E. A. Ragland, the mission pastor and first pastor of the church, wrote recently from Billings, Montana, where he pastors the Southside Baptist Church, recounting the beginning of that work:

I went to Alaska with missions in mind in 1955. We moved from Fairbanks to Spenard in the fall of 1956 and joined Faith church. In the winter of 1958 I was traveling on the train to Fairbanks with the ministers of Chugach association, going to the evangelistic conference. Ed Evans was pastor of Grandview church at that time. He asked me if I would pastor a mission if Grandview were to start one. I had surrendered to preach about a month before. I said I would. When we came back home, we surveyed the community and found a Baptist family who was not active. They became active in the mission when we got it started, and since they had a quonset hut almost in their back door, they let us use it. Men from Grandview came over and moved the building materials stored in it to one end and put in a partition. We hung lights, put in a stove and some chairs; someone even built a pulpit. As I look back, those were wonderful days, although I preached at times with my overcoat on. The first Sunday we had fourteen in Sunday school, and that afternoon Evans came and brought some others from Grandview; James Dotson came from Faith; James Akin, L. A. Watson, and others came, and we had a wonderful time worshipping.

At a business meeting at the Tudor church in 1960, a hush had fallen. The group had just voted to set the Lottie Moon offering goal at $200, twice the goal set for the state mission offering and $192.50 more than the last year's Lottie Moon offering. As the moderator called for discussion, a hand went up. All eyes turned toward eight-year-old Glenn Burch, who stated, "I think it should be $300." The total received by the end of the first week was $244.35.

By 1963 Tudor church had received a new name and a new look. The name had been changed to University Baptist and the building had been completely remodeled. Volunteer labor kept the cost down to only $285. The church has one of the largest sites in the state. They have twelve lots, an entire city block. Its location is strategic and its potential great. After Pastor Gus Hayworth resigned the pastorate of the church in 1969, they were pastorless for many months. Keith Foster is the present pastor.

Mr. William Lyons, pastor of the New Hope Baptist Church of Anchorage, wrote the story of his church as follows:

At three o'clock in the afternoon on May 8, 1960, the New Hope
Baptist Mission became the New Hope Baptist Church with all the
rights and privileges pertaining thereunto. The formal ceremony of
organizing the mission into a Baptist church was solemnly performed
by Chaplain A. J. Harkness, Elmendorf Air Force Base. The services
were very impressive. Chaplain Harkness spoke from the topic, "Some
Things Are Worth What They Cost." The meaning of a Baptist
church and the Church Covenant were administered by Chaplain
Harkness also.

After receiving the title of Baptist Church, the church elected as
pastor the Reverend Earnest Smith (S/Sgt., EAFB). The church
officials elected included Frank Miller, Dan Hawkins, Robert Brooks,
James Williams, Mrs. R. Dockery, Mrs. Bessie Higgins, Mrs. Ann
Davis, Mrs. Bettie Williams, and Pfc. Paul Sharpe, Jr.

Curtis G. Miller and Dudley A. Gittens served as associate
ministers.

The church moved to the present site November 25, 1962. June
25, 1963, the pastor, Earnest Smith, was deceased. Soon thereafter
Reverend Boyd Rogers came to serve and remained for three years.

Under the leadership of the present pastor, the building was
completed and the church moved upstairs into their beautiful chapel
in September 1968.

E. W. Hunke wrote in the *Messenger*, "Pastor Bill Lyons and
his people are to be congratulated on completion of one of the
most beautiful sanctuaries in Anchorage." For years they met in a
crowded, partially-finished basement. In 1967 Home Mission Board
loan officer Roy Lewis, architect Roland Lane, contractor Les
Peterson, and Alaska Baptist Convention's state workers met with
New Hope church leaders to find a way to complete the building.
The day their dream became a reality the Governor of Alaska,
Wally Hickel, and a group of state officials came to offer the church
their congratulations. The church choir presented several special
numbers during the September 22 dedication service.

First Baptist Church, Kenai, petitioned for admittance into the
Alaska Baptist Convention in 1960. The group had begun meeting
when Stephen Barnes, a serviceman from Faith, and Jerry Harris,
a summer missionary, worked in the area in the summer of 1956.
Bruce Bowden, member of First Baptist, Anchorage, preached for
the mission after Jerry returned to school. Later the mission ceased
to meet.

On April 25, 1965, the Kenai church reorganized and began
functioning under the leadership of Kelly Dickson, a young, hard-

working pastor. When Dr. William Hansen visited the church in January 1966, he brought back the following report:

In 1964 I had gone to Kenai to try to strengthen the hand of Rev. Dave Morris over the Lord's Day. Our Friday evening was spent in pleasant fellowship and mutual spiritual encouragement. Then came Saturday. Brother Morris had to work, but I spent the day in visitation of prospects, as he had done all week. The temperature dropped to twenty below Saturday night; the inside of the quonset hut in which Brother Davis lived was not much warmer than the outside. At breakfast Sunday morning, the preacher warned: "Don't be too disappointed if no one comes; it is not unusual." No one came.

The Sunday of January 23, 1966, was quite different. The hour for Sunday school came, and twenty-seven persons attended the orderly Sunday school in the new building. The spirited morning service had thirty-four in attendance. In the afternoon the church baptized two girls in a service at the neighboring Baptist church in Soldotna. That evening there were twenty-one in Training Union.

There were signs of life. The members planned a survey in January. A layman's witnessing institute was coming later in January. A revival was to begin the last of February. A new building had been built, a split-level house. The Dicksons lived upstairs and the church met in the daylight basement. . . . Kelly Dickson seemed determined to plant an evangelical church in this strategic, developing area. In some ways his presence and the healthy growth of the church to its present thirty-six active resident members seems to be an answer to the prayer of the deeply burdened soul of earnest David Morris.

Under Mr. Dickson's leadership the church progressed to the point of obtaining new property and building another beautiful, new building. In the May 1969 *Messenger* E. W. Hunke wrote:

Pastor Kelly Dickson, his wife Mickey, and the capable leadership at First Baptist Church, Kenai, are to be commended for wise long-range planning in the construction of the new church plant. The strategically located, renewable fifty-five year leased land on the main highway is adjacent to the finest housing project in Kenai. The new prefabricated building is ninety percent complete.

Kenai's building was financed with a $50,000 bond issue, the first issue of the Alaska Baptist Convention-backed bonds. The bond program is a joint venture with the Broadway Bond Company of Houston, Texas, and the convention. Another $15,000 issue in 1970 will pay for completing and furnishing the building.

In November 1967 Sunset Hills dedicated its $179,295 church building during weeklong dedication activities. E. W. Hunke led in a study of Nehemiah during the week. Pastor Roy Young led the dedication. Allen Meeks, state religious education director, whose family, together with the Carlson family, began the work in 1960, participated on the program. Building committee chairman Frank Stockstill reviewed the church's history and presented the church's long range building plans for the future. Chugach association moderator Leo Josey extended congratulations to the congregation.

The church is located on a three acre site eight miles south of Anchorage on Seward Highway. The new 7,280 square foot first unit accommodates two hundred people.

August 1, 1969, Thomas L. Kilpatrick began his ministry with the Sunset Hills church. Mr. Kilpatrick had held many denominational offices in the California convention. Mrs. Kilpatrick had served four years as state president of the California Baptist W.M.U. The church presently is building a new parsonage on the church site, and is experiencing a period of accelerated growth because of new housing projects springing up in the area.

When old buildings were being taken down to make space for a new edifice at the Muldoon Road Baptist Church in the spring of 1970, June Chron said in the "Moose Call":

> I have mixed emotions about the old barracks going. Lots of memories are bound up with its low ceilings, cold floors and poor plumbing. Then, years ago, the kids, four daughters from five through thirteen years old, weren't at all happy, when upon organizing, we found ourselves on the building committee.

Virgil Chron explained, "We started with seven members, six of them Chrons, in July 1960, in a renovated barracks. It looked futile, but we knew God had led us. I, as pastor, called a business meeting in my living room. Our seventh member couldn't attend; he was out firefighting. After I called the business to order, I suggested we elect me as treasurer and June as clerk for the time being. Our youngest, Jill, rose to a point of order and said, 'I think this meeting is rigged,' and started to leave. Another child grudgingly made a motion; another seconded, and June and I were barely elected."

Virgil went on to explain that the girls had not forgotten the services they conducted on the highway coming up to Alaska, in which he, as pastor, extracted a half-hearted tithe from money given them by Daddy Jim, their grandfather. Nevertheless, the new mission had twenty dollars in the treasury when they landed in Anchorage.

June said, "One thing about being on a building committee at Muldoon, it means *you* get to build. For the next few weeks we had paint brushes stuck to our right hands and in our left were buckets filled with paint and tears. I just knew that nobody would ever come to the church even though the barracks was soon set off with a preacher-made, seven-sided, pink steeple and an inside paint job, including a brown floor with June Bug's footprints from the corner of the room through the door and down the stairs. She forgot that Jana was painting too. Our first Sunday we were bowled over when twenty-three came to the service. And attendance has steadily increased ever since."

The property for the Muldoon church was acquired by the Eagle River church to be used for a mission. The Muldoon church was constituted in July 1960 with fifty charter members. Two Texas churches, First Baptist, Lorenzo, and First Baptist, Crosbyton, helped finance the new church.

By 1965 the church had enrolled six hundred in Sunday school with an average attendance of three hundred and fifty. By that time they were completing their fourth building program. Their new auditorium could seat up to one thousand with Sunday school space to match. The entire program had been financed with bonds. When asked how they did it at Muldoon, Pastor Chron's answer was, "Our Lord is the one who works through his people, using good commonsense methods in order to get the message out to the world. He blesses honest effort, prayer, sweat, and tears more than wishful thinking. . . . We have maintained a constant, year around evangelistic approach. We expect revival every Sunday. We strive earnestly for a warm, Spirit-filled service every time we meet. And we have stressed the Sunday school organization as the basic tool for reaching out into the community and bringing in the people."

In 1970, when the church embarked on another building program, their membership had climbed to one thousand and thirty with gifts reaching $91,012.00, exceeding the budget in 1969. A two-hundred-thousand dollar bond issue is financing the new program, which is well under way. Bill and Wanda Shough came in 1969 to help with the music and educational programs of the church.

In 1970, Good Friday fell on the same date as in 1964 when the big quake occurred. June Chron was looking through old bulletins and found an incident related involving one of Muldoon's faithful couples who lived in a trailer. A woman they had been trying to win to faith in Christ was visiting in their trailer at the time. As was true of many others, this woman thought that the end of the world had come. She thought the Bible said that when Jesus comes, two will be talking, and one will be taken and the other left. Knowing that her hosts were saved people, she expected to see them going up at any minute, so she tried to keep her eyes glued on them so she would know for sure if this were the second coming. A crash behind her caused her to look around momentarily. At the same time the man, who had been standing in a doorway, stepped just inside the other room to catch some falling object. When she turned back around to find him gone from sight, she became wildly hysterical. Before many weeks passed, she made her profession of faith.

Work at Soldotna was initiated under the leadership of two summer missionaries in the summer of 1961. Members of the Chugach association youth rally donated labor, and the foundation for a building was completed. Work to erect the log superstructure began in 1963.

The first service was the beginning of the 1963 simultaneous revival. The church was organized in November of that year. It had been a mission of First Baptist, Anchorage, but was the result of cooperative effort of many friends. The convention donated $1,000 for the building; the Chugach association donated $500 for the water well. Muldoon Road gave chairs, mimeograph machine, and hymnals. Eagle River gave chairs, and First Baptist gave hymnals and offering plates. Lumber companies gave a discount; logs and rough timber were donated; more summer workers and some youth from the Turnagain Children's Home worked to fell, trim, haul, and saw the logs and timber. Charles Newton donated and supplied the plumbing; Carl Rylander donated the materials and built the pulpit. Because of the donations, the total cash cost of the first building was only $3,500.

Maurice Murdock ~   be the first interim pastor.
    me up from the ranks in the
    Baptist Church in Anchorage.
    ingle-handedly declared war on
    and houses of ill repute in Anchor-
    base, and brought about changes all
    of him." Murdock also led in establish-
    in South Dakota.

W. E. Midkiff came to pastor the church in 1966 and has led in the building of a large, attractive church plant. A kindergarten program was conducted by the church from 1964 to 1969.

A rural mission approximately three years old located in the Butte community near Palmer organized into a church February 26, 1965. The mission had been sponsored by First Baptist, Anchorage. By the time of its organization the new church had almost finished paying for its lots, building, and furnishings. It had reached many young people in the area. John L. Booth was pastor.

    ❀   ❀   ❀

Going from Anchorage area churches to those in the interior is much easier to do in print than it was for early Southern Baptists to do in person. When the first annual convention met in Fairbanks in 1946, a caravan of seven cars from Anchorage drove up the road for the meeting. At one point they had to wait for a bridge to be built before they could proceed. The trip took twenty hours of driving, not including camping over-night. My first trip from Anchorage to Fairbanks on the Alaska Railroad took thirteen hours, but so many visual and emotional impressions were telescoped into such a short span that I was glad the train traveled only thirty-five miles an hour. I tried to record some of the things I observed and felt in the following lines:

As the sun pushes back night's boundaries and rises in dawn splendor,
Dew drops flash from sun-crowned berry bushes.
Mists ascend; vapor waiths gather to a fullness of thick clouds.
Pussy willows, frost-rooted, bud softly. Lichens, wet with mountain rain, embrace the sheltering rocks.
Muskeg swamp waters pattern concentric rain-splash circles.
Salmon leap cascades; moose forage on the bottom of icy mountain lakes.

The wren seeks its nest, rock-covert from the winds.

Sedge grass boldly stabs through the last thin snow-crust into a new existence.

The first spring violet throws aside dead winter's old leaf cover.

(And the righteous man, tried, comes forth triumphant, gold.)

Spruce, blue spring-tipped, stand storm sentinel over vast stretches of Alaska.

New-born aspen leaves quiver into the now of their life cycle.

Squadrons of birches (Ah, Robert Frost, so many yet untamed!), newly uniformed in hues of spring-green, proud-march up hilltops, valiant, victor over icy onslaughts.

Dandelions golden the forest fringe; wild roses climb steep trestle sides; all herbs struggle upward toward self-expression, fullfillment, their achieve of being.

Huge logs drift, pile up and clog, gather debris, shove, twist, break free, reel frantically, drawn ever onward by relentless currents.

Veins of coal etched sharply against the sides of gorges, bleakly give mute evidence of cataclysmic catastrophies untold eons ago.

(Wars rage, federations fall, missile programs abort, populations explode, consume, and cease.)

Snow geese, soul-stirring, glisten in sun rays, momentarily, high overhead, spear through air: V-flight of summer.

Dall sheep white-spot precarious crags, moving shapes, springing, searching the crevices, for root-stores, fruit of field mouse labor.

Timidly, twin caribou calves lie quietly in tall rushes, while their mother, nervous, feeds, watches.

Shadow-hidden in hollow, a black bear lurks, cruel, waiting.

Mallards zero in on ponds, plow frothy furrows of spray, proudly preen sun-burnished feathers.

Beavers, disturbed by train-noise from never-ending dam-building, peer steathily over the edge of fallen branches.

Abandoned cabins of once-hopeful prospectors, homesteaders, rot disconsolately, tumbling in upon themselves, broken by the weight of negligence and time and slow decay.

In their front yards fragile fern fronds quietly uncurl, unclasp lacy fingers, reaching up eagerly, ready to receive sun and air and rain with an attitude of unending prayer and gratitude.

("Thou, God, hast spoken: to everything there is a season, and a time to every purpose under the sun; it is the gift of God.")

Frank Miller wrote in 1965, while pastoring the church at North Pole, "At the crossroads at the top of the world stands the First Baptist Church of North Pole, Alaska. Our people love their church and most of them drive at least fifteen miles in temperatures that range from eighty degrees above to sixty below zero."

First Baptist, Fairbanks, began the work and called it "Fourteen Mile Mission." They bought two lots and built a log building with a full basement, took a census, and contacted about eight Baptist families. A summer missionary, Hunter Rentz, was the first pastor. When the mission was just getting started, Warrant Officer and Mrs. Clyde Pharris of Columbus, Georgia, united with the mission and asked to have the privilege of devoting themselves to its growth.

In September 1953 the mission had a potluck dinner after morning worship, and held their organizational service that afternoon with twenty-five charter members. Carl Elder was called as pastor, and the name of the mission was changed to First Baptist Church, North Pole. When the new church became self-supporting, they voted to pay the parent church all the money originally invested in the building.

The church obtained a loan from the Home Mission Board in 1957 to enlarge the church auditorium to a seating capacity of three hundred. In February 1970 they purchased land near the new highway, reporting, "We long ago outgrew the present building." Bill Duncan is pastor. During the summer of 1970 construction began on a new pastorium and plans were being drawn for a completely new church plant on the new location.

The Big Delta church was another of Alaska's log churches. It was built without a basement. A man who ran the local saw mill sold the church the materials at cost. Most of the construction was done after the winter snows started falling. The labor was volunteer and supplied by the servicemen from the air bases at Eielson and Big Delta. Mr. and Mrs. Paul Hilty came to continue the work started by Orland Cary and First Baptist Fairbanks church. They drove a truck over the Alcan from Oklahoma with the trip taking almost a month. They said that they had been preparing for several years to answer God's call to Alaska. Mr. Hilty had worked here before. He was a carpenter, and worked first at constructing a building to use as a church-dwelling because during their early days with the church, the Hiltys lived in a tent. He did the cooking for the men who came out to work on the building.

First services in the new building were held in October 1952. Six people responded to the invitation, two coming for salvation. The saw mill had broken down, causing a delay by halting the supply of logs and lumber, and was not repaired until just two weeks before the simultaneous revival was to begin. For a time it appeared that the building could not be readied in time for the revival. Orland Cary and Dick Miller came from Fairbanks, bringing a tent to the church site, and camped there during the two weeks to save the 180 mile drive to Fairbanks. After they got the rafters and ceiling joists in place, a strong wind toppled them down again, leaving a pile of jumbled lumber. They were re-erected and the building was ready in time. The climax came when Floyd Newby, who furnished the lumber, and his wife were converted in the first service. The day after the Hiltys moved in, the temperature dropped to minus nineteen degrees.

For several years the church met in the log structure a few miles north of Delta Junction. In the fall of 1964, it purchased a lot closer to the heart of the business activity of the area and erected a ~~...~~ the old location

~~...~~ in the community of Clearwater asked Pastor James Akin to help them try to reach the thirty-five families living in their area. It is a homesteading community ten miles from the Delta church. Work started with a Vacation Bible School in 1962 which had an average attendance of twenty-two. It was conducted in a one room quonset hut rented from the Clearwater Stumpjumpers Four-H Club. That fall, the quonset hut was again rented, and weekly services were begun on Saturday evenings. Soon afterwards four Sunday school classes were provided with workers from the mother church. James Akin served as mission pastor. Paul Spriggs of Clearwater donated a two acre site, and the group bought a quonset of their own. In November 1964, they held an afternoon dedication service with sixty-five people in attendance. Harold Rhodes, an Alaska Communications System employee at Delta Junction, had been called as pastor. In October 1965, Rhodes became pastor of the Delta Junction church. At that time persons from eight different Baptist backgrounds and six different racial and ethnic groups were attending the church. Could this be a record for a church of this size?

The St. John's Baptist Church, a Negro congregation in Fairbanks, started as a mission of Fairbanks First Baptist Church. It was organized in February 1954. First Baptist helped buy the lot and put a Jamesway hut on it to serve as their first place of worship. The church organized with thirty-two charter members. Orland Cary wrote, "It was forty degrees below zero on the day they organized, and there was not room for even one more person to stand in the little building." In less than eleven months after the church organized, its membership had grown to one hundred and fifty. The members built a concrete block basement the first year, at their own expense. Charlie Alston, who was in the air force, was the first pastor. Roberts Seals, a later pastor wrote, "I was the first white pastor of a Negro church in Alaska." David Thomas is the present pastor of the church.

God put us here to serve him by ministering to others. How can we ignore the oppressed when he is waiting to speak to his loveless, dispossessed children through us? He gives us gifts to relay, entrusts us with tasks beyond our strength, then enables us to carry them out, for we have been destined since before earth's earliest ages to accomplish his purposes.

In 1953 as Ruth Smith was teaching her second grade class in the new grade school in the Hamilton Acres subdivision of Fairbanks, she kept wondering how many of the children attended Sunday school. As she came to know the children better, she asked each one which church his family attended. Many had never attended at all and others had been Baptists before moving to Alaska, but because there was not a Baptist church in their area, were not going anywhere. Mrs. Smith visited in the homes of those who seemed to be prospects and later that winter a Sunday school was begun in the Smith home. Her husband Carl, a minister, taught an adult Bible class and conducted worship service in the living room; Ruth taught juniors and primaries in daughter Carleta's bedroom, and a neighbor, Lois Moore, taught beginners in the kitchen.

Hamilton Acres adjoined one of the gates of Ladd Air Force Base which later became Ft. Wainwright Army Base. It had been a wooded area, homesteaded by a pioneer named Hamilton, which was later divided into lots for homesites. In the winter of 1953 many buyers had moved house trailers onto their lots and were waiting for summer to build. Some had wanagans attached; others head thrown up make-shift hovels or were living in basements or partially completed houses. All dreamed of summer's twenty-four hours of daylight and its night time lullaby of skill saws and electric motors.

A dentist friend of the Smiths down in the Lower 48 sent some money to be used in the Lord's work, so Carl used it to purchase a surplus Jamesway hut which he moved onto a lot near his home. The lot was not for sale because the owner had buried a pet dog there and did not want the grave disturbed, but he agreed to let Carl rent it for $10 per month.

Jerry Ellis and Seth Moore joined Carl in building pews, and the three families bought a piano, rejoicing as they worked together and planned the future of their mission. Visitors had begun coming from the air base and from other nearby communities. Before many months passed, a second Jamesway hut was added to provide addi-

through the nuts, never really sufficiently chasing the chill during the sub-zero weather.

On May 30, 1954, Carl Smith called a meeting to order for the purpose of organizing a Southern Baptist church in Hamilton Acres. Seth Moore made the motion to organize; Jerry Ellis seconded the motion. Mr. Smith read the Scripture, explained the meaning and purpose of a Baptist church and the obligation of its members. After the church covenant was read, Jerry and Nancy Ellis; Seth, Lois, and Ronnie Moore; Carl, Ruth, and Carleta Smith signed it. Carl Smith was called as pastor; trustees and a treasurer were elected. On June 16 a second business meeting was called. At this meeting the church adopted their constitution and the New Hampshire Confession of Faith, voted to unite with the Tanana Baptist Association, elected messengers to attend the annual state convention, subscribed to the *Alaska Baptist Messenger*, designated 10% of their church income to the Cooperative Program, and invited James Whisenhant to serve as guest Training Union director.

John Dickerson preached the church's first revival in September 1954. Among those coming for membership at this time were Jack and Dorothy Lane who helped for many years in the progress of the building program and growth of the church. Dorothy was the first W.M.U. president. In 1955 the Home Mission Board loaned the church $10,000 and made a $5,000 grant to them, and four lots were bought about two blocks from the Jamesway huts. Early in 1956 excavation began for the basement, but permafrost was encountered almost immediately. Each day Nate Matlock dug a few feet, then waited for the ground to thaw so he could dig some more. The men drilled a water well 55 feet deep, 20 feet through solid ice. Carl Herning donated cement blocks for the footing and foundation of the church, doing without a foundation he had planned for his ranch home in order to help the building program. After the walls of the basement started up and supplies had been bought and stacked on the ground, disagreements developed, resulting in some leaving the job of building. Carl Smith resigned in August and the work became discouraging.

The church elected Harold Brooks, James Raguse, and Roscoe Wells as their first deacons with the responsibility of holding the church together and getting the basement finished and roofed in before winter became too severe. With six inches of snow on the ground, Seth Moore took charge of the building program, and as a proof of their faith, the church ordered two new collection plates. John R. Smith, an air force man, agreed to serve the church as part-time pastor and was ordained at an associational meeting on September 18 with John Jeffcoat presiding. Smith and about forty members, mostly from the air force and army bases, spent all their spare hours, weekends, and holidays racing against winter, installing sewer lines, wiring, laying brick, putting on insulation and ceilings, and finally setting up Nelson heaters inside for enough heat to pour the cement flooring for the basement. Seth Moore was overcome by fumes from the heaters, but revived, and they beat their deadline with the weather and had their first service in the basement just after Armistice Day of 1956. Everything went smoothly until the spring thaw came, then water started running in, ruining the sheet rock and creating more expense and hard work.

In July 1957 John Smith returned to the Lower 48 to resume his seminary studies. At that time Carl Elder of Argyle, Texas, accepted the call to be pastor of Hamilton Acres. After paying his own moving expenses, he assumed a $400 fuel bill and borrowed $1,000 to have a heating system installed in the building. He continued to work part time to support his family for a year and a half until the church was able to pay a full-time salary. He introduced a strong visitation program that resulted in bringing many faithful families into the church and gave it needed stability. Some of these families continued sending their tithes to Hamilton Acres for ten years after they moved on. Mr. Elder was the first Hamilton Acres pastor to be elected president of the Alaska Baptist Convention. He resigned in 1959 to return to Southwestern Baptist Theological Seminary.

Aubrey Short was the fourth pastor of Hamilton Acres. After the spring revival the year he arrived in Fairbanks, the church built an auditorium on top of their basement. After a year with the church, the membership had doubled, and the financial picture improved. Then the air base closed and 135 members moved away almost overnight. The church was not able to build back up quite so high again, but soon the army moved in, and they reached many new families for membership.

Dr. William Hansen came as pastor in September 1962. He led

reports from building committees, discussions on needed buildings, discussion of loans, or of applications for additional loans. The church was not meant to stand still, and once more they had chosen the best pastor they knew of, but because their standards were so high, when leaders were needed elsewhere, people looked to Hamilton Acres. This time the pastor was elected executive secretary of the Alaska Baptist Convention. When he left in August 1963, Dr. Hansen wrote, "As I review the time mentally, it was a happy and God-blessed year, with a good deal of growth on my part and happy relationships with you saints of the Lord."

Robert Buchanan came next, and falling in line with the other pastors, he put on his overalls and went to work on the building. After just six months he had to leave because his wife Sammy developed cancer requiring extensive surgery not available in Alaska. A time of discouragement swept down on the church which didn't lift until Edward E. Wolfe came from Woodward, Oklahoma, in November 1964, reorganized the church, and brought a new time of vitality and progress. When Faith Baptist Church, Anchorage, called Mr. Wolfe in September 1966, the bottom seemed to drop out because of the spiritual peaks the church had attained during his ministry.

The church contacted Bill Duncan of Las Vegas, Nevada; the big flood hit, and when Mr. Duncan came in view of a call, he found the basement flooded and all the classrooms, kitchen, nursery, restrooms, furnace, and supplies wiped out. The sewer system had backed up into the rest of the mess, and the whole thing smelled. Everyone in Fairbanks was in desperate condition and members were working at home trying to salvage personal belongings. But deacons Jack Hansen and Ross Covington, who had worked during the year without a pastor to keep the Sunday services and jail services going, were determined not to be defeated by a little muddy water. They began at once to pump water and haul debris from the church. When help arrived from the Home Mission Board, Lower 48 volunteer workers reconstructed the plumbing, the wiring, put in new partitions, walls, furnaces, and did everything that needed to be done except some painting, and even helped on the new addition that lay unfinished. Mr. Duncan cleared out the pastorium to provide a home for his family, but plenty of work was left when they arrived. He pastored the church until February 1968, then accepted a call to North Pole, Alaska.

Hugh Hamilton came as pastor in March 1968. Since then a new pastorium has been purchased and the new educational wing completed. In December 1968, Mr. Hamilton wrote, "Our mountain-top experiences began with our work here. Our hearts have overflowed with spiritual blessings. Since March we have had 91 additions." Writing about their trip up the Alcan, he continued, "The highway is just like the Christian life—up, down, and around, with few smooth places in between. We came 5,400 miles without an accident, then just 120 miles from Fairbanks our trailer caught a crosswind and overturned on the icy road. The car also went over, but we were able to right it quickly. We were in deep snow, which proved a blessing, but we had to wait five hours for help to come. . . . Living in Fairbanks is like living right in the middle of a Christmas card scene."

After sixteen years and nine pastors with 940 members accepted, and despite setbacks and hardships, Hamilton Acres Baptist Church expects to remain because it was built by God on faith and blessings. Four ex-pastors have served as president of the Alaska Baptist Convention: Carl Elder, Aubrey Short, Edward Wolfe, and Bill Duncan. One ex-pastor served as executive-secretary: Dr. William Hansen. The church has licensed the following men to preach: Dave Steele, Edwin Cook, Ross Covington, Norman Noble, Art Webb, Ron Jordan, Ronnie Moore, and John Smith.

In December 1969 the church set up the Cary Scholarship Fund to assist young people who want to attend a Christian college. Ruth Jeannine Cary was the first recipient of the scholarship. Her father, the late Orland Cary, was one of the first Fairbanks pastors and her mother is a member of the church. Doris Elder, a devoted nursery worker, is another long-time member. Two of her sons and one step-son are Baptist preachers. One son, Jack, gave much financial help to building Hamilton Acres; another son, Carl, was the church's third pastor. Mr. and Mrs. Robert Hamilton and Robert, Jr. are the members holding the longest continuous membership, having joined in 1956. Mrs. Alma Matlock, who has served as church clerk for nine years, is also a talented artist whose baptistry scene of Alaska's mountains, streams, and birch trees enhances the beauty of the church.

In 1954 two Immanuel Baptist churches, one in Fairbanks and in Anchorage, organized and petitioned for admittance into the Alaska Baptist Convention. R. W. Deadman, Immanuel Baptist Church, Fairbanks, reported on the beginnings of their work:

A group of Christians started praying for a solution to a difficult situation; we prayed from about Thanksgiving until January of last year. Through prayer we were led to the Native Baptist Church of Fairbanks with the sole intention of forming a mission and becoming a Southern Baptist church. We moved our letters January 10 when we met and organized the mission. We held Sunday school January 17 with ten persons present. May 9 we organized the Immanuel Baptist Church with seventeen charter members. We had, when I left home (to attend the state convention), and I hope it is more now, thirty-three members. We are still praying and have unlimited faith. God has answered our prayers, and we haven't wanted for a single thing, including money. . . .

We purchased a lot, one hundred fifty by two hundred feet, and, by the way, we have the best church site in Fairbanks. Last Tuesday morning a bulldozer went in there and started digging a hole for the foundation of our building. You might say we are silly, but we are building a church there the first thing, the main auditorium of which will accommodate five hundred thirty-six people. You might hear from us, and it might be a plea to send us some money, but right now the Lord has given us so many things. We have been given a building which we hope to set on a foundation. We have been given the forms for that foundation, and finishers up there have said they will finish the floor. We have carpenter friends that are going to work. . . . It is a Southern Baptist church, and with the Lord's help we'll keep it that way.

If we holler for help, do the best you can for us.

John Thomas, his wife, and four children, came from Fort Worth to be the first permanent pastor of Immanuel. The church held its first service in the basement of the new building on Thanksgiving Day, 1954. The service was led by John Thomas and attended by all the charter members. Because of the extreme cold weather, the service was short, with prayers and thanks expressed by the members.

The Immanuel church later merged with the Native church to form Calvary Baptist Church of Fairbanks.

In the *Anchorage Daily News* for March 6, 1970, the following article appeared under the heading "Mace in the Churchyard!":

> Law'n order fans, cheer up! The bulls are still busting in Fairbanks!
>
> Last Sunday Hez Ray—member of the State Athletic Commission, Fairbanks Sports Co-ordinator for the Arctic Winter Games, and creator of the highly successful Fairbanks recreation program as city recreation director—was accompanying his wife and five kids to the Calvary Baptist Church, when he noticed a lady churchgoer, noticeably upset, being talked to by a police officer in the parking lot. Inside the church someone mentioned that the officer had been there an awfully long time.
>
> "I'll go see what's the matter," said Ray.
>
> It turned out that the lady was being ticketed for out-of-state license plates, but she couldn't understand what was happening. "Everything's gone wrong," she said. Ray, finding what the charges were, started to comfort the lady. He also questioned the officer on the need for whipping a U-turn off the freeway in order to chase down the violator in the church parking lot.
>
> "Why, I could ticket that car, too," said the policeman, pointing to a car with Louisiana tags.
>
> "There's one with Texas plates, too," agreed Ray. "You could have a ball in the church parking lot, but wouldn't it be better to spend your time fighting crime on Second Avenue than bothering little ladies on their way to church?"
>
> While Hez was escorting the lady to his car, the officer shoved the ticket at her, saying, "Sign this, lady, or I'm gonna take you down and arrest you!" which sent the gal into tears again.
>
> "For Pete's sake, officer, she'll sign it," said Ray.
>
> "You shut up. Say another word, and I'll have you arrested."
>
> "It's a free country."
>
> At this, the officer set out to drag Ray across the parking lot to

his squad car, with Ray trying to make himself understood, avoid being beaten, and still hang onto his Bible.

"Now, listen," he said, overcome with the absurdity of the situation, "you can't put me into that car."

"Why not?"

"Well, to begin with, I'm bigger than you are."

After another tug of war, the officer said, "I'm calling for help."

"Go right ahead," said Ray. "I'm not going anywhere."

The second gendarme arrived in proper broadsliding fashion, bursting from his car in fine Chicago style. Number one burst out of his car and collared Ray again, while Ray tried frantically to signal Number two with his free arm.

No such luck. "SHUTUP!" hollered Number two, and both set upon Ray, becoming winded in short order.

Finally, Number two whipped out his can of Mace. "You know what this is?" he snarled.

"Yes," said Ray and ducked. Number two let Number one have a fine blast of Mace in the eyes, finally managed to get Ray with the second squirt, and off they went to the station. Ray was booked, and they took away his ring, his glasses, his Bible, and his belt. "I like to lost my pants," said Ray.

Of course, once the officials figured out who Ray was, he was hastily released, but not before he overheard Number one, who was trying to get the Mace out of his eyes, mutter about Number two, "That's the second time that blankety-blank has shot me!"

"I never did abuse those officers," said Ray. "If I'd known they were going to try to nail me to the wall, I should have gotten in a few licks."

The important issue, according to Ray, who resigned his $20,232 job as city recreation director in a bid for a vote of confidence from the city manager's office, is that the whole absurd affair could have happened to anybody, and people without the stature of Hez Ray might not be so promptly released.

"Why," he said, "if I were Joe Doe, I'd still be in there for assaulting those goofy officers."

The original ticket for out-of-state plates was torn up, since the police are discouraged from bothering people in private parking lots.

Mr. Ray was offered his job back with an increase in salary and he went back to work. His family have been longtime members of Calvary church. The issue was finally settled outside of court.

Elizabeth Whisenhant wrote from College, Alaska, describing the beginning of the University Baptist Church. She said that on a cold Sunday in December 1958 a group of about seventeen people gathered to form the University Baptist Mission's first congregation. "An inefficient space heater first nearly drove us out with an over supply of heat; then we nearly froze." All the adults, the group included five young children, joined the mission that first Sunday, one as a candidate for baptism.

"A little Thomas organ was at the front," she recalled. "Since I was the only one who had musical experience (piano), I was asked to perform on the organ; it was the first time I had played such an instrument for congregational singing."

For several Sundays they had only worship services, then began an adult Bible class taught in the church with a children's class in the parsonage, which had been opened to mothers with small children. When an addition was added to the back of the garage, it was divided into nursery, beginner, primary, and junior classrooms—all except the nursery were "mini-size." The intermediates met in the parsonage, and any young people who came had to join the adult group.

The mission became University Baptist Church in December 1959. Charter members who are still with the church are John and Ann Shilling and James and Elizabeth Whisenhant. Because of "bursting seams," the garage at the parsonage was converted into Sunday school space, which relieved the situation temporarily, but everyone knew they had to build a larger facility.

One day James Whisenhant saw a model of the university's plans for future roads, and housing, and led the church to acquire property on University Avenue. Members of University had ground breaking ceremonies with Dr. A. B. Cash of the Home Mission Board as special guest speaker.

"To me, the most impressive evangelists we have had in our church were Dr. Daley, editor of the Kentucky Baptist paper, and Beryl Compton, who at one time was a member of the vice squad of the Atlanta, Georgia, police force. He was very much aware of the meaning of sin and preached positively against it. He also made everyone feel that it's a Christian's privilege to witness, and it did not enter his mind that anyone would refuse to go visiting with him," Mrs. Whisenhant remembered.

John Dickerson was the first pastor of University Baptist Church. The first meeting place was a garage that had been moved from the Native Baptist Church in the summer of 1958. The basement on University Avenue was started in 1964, and the church met in it until the auditorium was ready late in 1969.

Dr. J. T. Burdine from Kentucky was called to pastor the church on January 1, 1961. He worked with students at the university and developed a B.S.U. program at the church. In 1966, Fred Mosely recommended to the Home Mission Board that a student facility be provided in the basement of University church. The board gave the church $35,000 to assist in their building program in order to make this center possible.

A letter from Pete Beard, B.S.U. Director of the University of Tennessee, to Dr. Wendell W. Wolfe of the University Baptist Church, reveals the kinds of contacts Dr. Burdine made for student work:

> The Tennessee Baptist Convention Student Department responded to a request made to the Home Mission Board by the pastor of University Baptist Church (Dr. J. T. Burdine) for a student work project to construct a Baptist Student Center and church auditorium adjacent to the University of Alaska campus in the summer of 1967. Since Tennessee, Kentucky, and Texas had previously shared in student projects, in order to provide variety in projects and in team personnel, other states were permitted to send a few selected students. Final composition of the team included nine boys, three girls, and the director with his wife and two children. There was one from Florida, one from Texas, three from Kentucky, and remainder from Tennessee.

> This was to be a joint project among the Baptist Student Unions of these states and the Home Mission Board. The states provided their proportionate share of the work team expenses in transportation, food, and personal items. Tennessee provided the director, vehicles for transportation, camping equipment, and tools for working. These items and expenses came from the regular Student Summer Mission funds accumulated by the voluntary gifts of students in the states represented. Because of the high food cost in Alaska, the Home Mission Board provided $1,500 for camp expenses. . . .

> The work team gathered in Nashville on June 11 and began the drive to Alaska on June 12 in a V.W. bus, a double cab pickup, and a Chevy van which was being delivered to the pastor of the church. We camped in tents but ate in restaurants in order to conserve time. Every possible kind of weather was confronted enroute to Fairbanks. It rained some every day. We drove through a tornado watch, actually seeing one, two hail storms, and snow. On two nights we were completely soaked. We arrived in Fairbanks on June 22 in time to experience one of the strongest earth tremors in some time. We began work the next day. Mr. James Boney, who supervised construction, endeared himself to all the work crew, as did the people of the church. We left on August 12, just prior to the flood and a week

earlier than planned because funds were depleted. The interior and heating unit were not completed.

The group experience, together in a common cause, was both frustrating and rewarding because of diversity of experience, maturity, and insight. Through abrasive joking, tiring hours, heated discussions, and moments of inspiration, a deep sense of Christian community was born. We left Alaska, the "cold spot" to the north, with a profound appreciation for its people. Though we did not journey far from our destination, Alaska-67 provided opportunity to experience a larger Alaska from the past and present. In short, we enjoyed the people's individualism, their rough reality, and admired their adventuresome attitude.

Holland and Mary Butler have served two tours of duty in Alaska, the first at Ladd Field in 1953; then after an eight-year-tour in Alabama, they returned to Eielson AFB and joined University Baptist Church. Mary wrote about their experiences in two churches in Alaska. They joined the Native Baptist Church in 1953. At that time all the Training Unions except the nursery and beginner departments were meeting together. Neither she nor Holland had ever attended Training Union, but they went that first night and Mary was assigned a part for the next week. She got cold feet, so Holland took the part for her, but said he would never attend Training Union again. That night the pastor, John Dickerson, talked about the importance of Training Union and how badly they needed leaders for the other departments. The following Sunday the Hollands were back again and volunteered to take a junior union. "We felt this was the Lord's leading, because two other military couples volunteered for the other unions, neither of us choosing the same group. Since then junior union has been a great part of our lives."

Holland was ordained as a deacon by the Native Baptist Church. Mary wrote, "We are very thankful for the Baptist work in Alaska for this was the beginning of our dedicated work for God."

One interesting activity at the Native church was transportation. "Holland was on the transportation committee and at this time we had an army surplus bus with a big wood stove in the rear; the stove pipe was out the back window. In the coldest part of winter Holland or Harry would go over an hour before time to leave and build a big fire in the bus to have it warm for the native passengers. Later the bus started giving problems, and we would go by in our station wagon and bring as many as sixteen natives to church on

Sunday nights. Many nights we would go early and have coffee with the Tom Willocks," Mary continued.

After returning to Alaska in 1964 and uniting with the University church, Holland served on the missions committee. The church purchased a mobile chapel for the Anderson Mission, which was delivered in March of 1966. The drivers arrived in Fairbanks with the chapel on a Saturday afternoon, very discouraged, cold, and hungry. They had abandoned the trailer and truck twice when they spun out on the Alcan, and had a number of flat tires. It was around minus thirty degrees, and they were not properly dressed. "We managed to get some extra parkas for them, gave them a big, hot meal, and Holland told them he would go with them on to Clear."

About thirty miles out, the tong of the trailer collapsed and the front of the trailer landed on the highway. They came back to Fairbanks, rented an electric welder, acetylene torch, and bought plate steel to make the I-beams for the new tong since there were none to be found in town. They did not get the trailer ready for towing until late afternoon the next day. "When they reached the Tanana River at Nenana, one of the drivers was very hesitant to cross the river on ice, but since there was no other way to get across, he had no great choice!" After they left the main road at Clear, the roads were very narrow with some "great curves." The trailer had to be backed up in order to get around the sharpest of them. Finally, they delivered the trailer at its destination and arrived back in Fairbanks about 11:30 P.M. The drivers agreed that they would never again deliver a trailer to Alaska in the winter.

Mary wrote, "On the dedication day of the chapel, we headed for Clear early in the morning. It had been snowing for several days and the snow plow had not been over the road. Our little VW made a good snowplow, and we made our way slowly along. Most of the way we couldn't tell the road from the ditch, and I had such little faith that I kept insisting that we turn back. Holland had greater faith, and we made it to Clear in time for the morning worship service. The service was very good and the dedication service in the afternoon was rewarding."

Vern Baker's first Sunday with the University church was Easter 1968 when he came before them in view of a call. He had been minister of education for eleven years, but had never before pastored a church, so he faced the congregation that morning "with fear and trembling." His first Sunday as pastor was June 16, 1968. The church still met in their basement. He decided that his first major task was to find some funds to complete the auditorium.

In July, Vern wrote Jack Gulledge, pastor of Emmanuel Baptist Church, Tucson, Arizona, telling of the church and its need. "I even suggested the possibility of bringing a crew of builders up here to help us complete the job, the idea coming from the great experience the men had who came up following the flood of 1967."

In a letter dated July 30, 1968, Jack Gulledge wrote, "If I had any sense, I'd tell you that what you are attempting is impossible. Too many ingredients will have to work together. But for some crazy reason I think you may be just the man to do it. It's worth a try. We both know the odds."

Baker reported, "It is a miracle of God the way things worked. Following much prayer, we were able to get almost $20,000 for a piece of property on College Road, the old church property. By March Jack Gulledge had lined up nineteen men, all builders, who were coming to help." Two high school seniors, Claire Huhn and Deborah Betts, from Shreveport, Louisiana, worked at odd jobs all year long to earn money to come to Alaska and cook for the work crew, help in Vacation Bible School, paint, and do whatever was needed.

Dr. Charles Wood, pastor of First Baptist Church, Tucson, took over the coordination of the project when Jack Gulledge moved to another work. Nearly $7,000 was collected to pay for the expenses of all the men. First Baptist, Tucson, sent five of the men; First Baptist, Muskogee, Oklahoma, Vern's home church, paid for three; University Baptist in Fort Worth, Hillcrest Baptist in Dallas, and Emmanuel Baptist in Tucson also sent men. Other gifts came from many sources. Project Alaska was well-launched.

Vern wrote:

Well, the crew arrived right on time, Saturday, June 14. A group of our own folk met them at the airport with a large banner. The picture-taking started at that point and never did quit. Everyone got off in reasonable shape—after such a long trip. Everyone acted as if he were an old traveler by the time he got to Fairbanks, but I noted that George, Pat, Mrs. Hickey, Mr. Honeycutt, and few others looked back at the Alaskan Airline jet and then looked up into the sky as if to thank Someone for bringing them through. I don't think Mrs. Hickey ever thought it would fly at all.

AND THEN THE WORK STARTED, well, almost then. We did worship on Sunday, and I got to preach at them. Our get-acquainted supper was a huge success. Mrs. Whisenhant had done a great job of planning times of fun and fellowship—from the first supper on Sunday to the *Discovery* riverboat trip on the Chena River, to the picnic at the University of Alaska picnic grounds, to the wild game banquet on the last Friday night.

AND THEN THE WORK STARTED, and it really started, twelve days of hard work . . . until we spent all our money and had to quit.

The work wasn't finished, but much had been accomplished. Baker wrote to the Project Alaska crew and friends of the project at Thanksgiving time with a progress report:

God still answers prayer. In September we had come to a complete standstill. We had actually spent more money than we had, just trying to get in for the winter. We had discussed closing up the windows with boards and forgetting using it this year. Out of the blue a gift from Dallas got us into the building, then a check arrived from Muskogee for $5,000; a letter from the pastor told that it was a gift from a man in Arkansas who was interested in missions, and it allowed us to take other steps. This provided the windows, the carpet, and maybe some for lighting. It was just a plain answer to prayer. We had gone just as far as we could go. . . . We moved into the new auditorium the first Sunday in October. It looked pretty rough, but it was great. Since that time we have had over twenty additions. The spirit of the church has been just great. We have renewed hope that we may be able to complete the auditorium by March or April.

Baker stated that the support received from the Home Mission Board in getting the property and the first phase of the present building, then the Tennessee B.S.U. group, the work done by the Project Alaska crew, and the constant sacrificial labors of the men and women of the church have made possible the place of worship they enjoy today.

In Alaska the concept of homesteading is as common as bread and butter. The community of Salcha, located thirty-five miles south of Fairbanks, is dotted with homesteads of pioneers who dreamed dreams of contentment and quietness and have made their dreams a way of life. The area is bordered on one side by the Salcha River and on the other by intermittent bluffs and bottom land: fertile soil for agriculture, and also, to others who had a different vision, for the planting of a New Testament church.

A Presbyterian minister, Mr. Bingle, began conducting services in Salcha in 1948, meeting sometimes at the church camp at Harding Lake, in homes, or at the Salcha Store in a quonset hut. By March 1960, the attendance had dropped so low that the Presbyterians decided to close their mission. Two charter families of the Salcha Baptist Church had attended their service.

In April 1960 the William Wyser family, members of First Baptist Church, North Pole, Alaska, dedicated their efforts to starting a Baptist mission in the Salcha community. Mr. Del Shultz and son Aggie, of Mile 48, and Mrs. W. J. Haven and family of Eielson Air Force Base, agreed to meet with the Wysers and to pick up children enroute. General missionary Ben Hill and the pastor at North Pole asked for permission to assume the work when the Presbyterians closed; a mutual agreement ensued and the three families met regularly, together with the Joe Balch family who lived on the premises of the mission. During the severe cold their custom was to meet whenever the temperature was warmer than thirty below zero.

The North Pole church licensed Bill Wyser, age seventeen, who served the mission as acting pastor. The quonset hut, with a cross on its front, nestled at the foot of a bluff on the Richardson Highway, served as a meeting place. The first work project was the digging of a basement and installation of a Yukon heater. A construction shack donated by Roy Harness of Anchorage was added to the rear of the quonset to provide two small Sunday school rooms, and an old school bus provided by Joe Balch made up the rest of the existing classroom space.

John Warner came from Atmore, Alabama, to preach a revival in October 1960, and provided a needed spiritual thrust. The coming of the Ray Penfield family and Ben Post gave support to the growing membership. After the Wyser family rotated to the Lower 48, prayers were answered, as Robert Paquette, who had just surrendered to the ministry, came to fill the pulpit. His wife, Carolyn, replaced Carol Rollison, who rotated out, as pianist. Soon afterward, the Morris family, also instrumental in helping the mission become a church, joined.

The winter of 1960 was characterized by its bitter cold, but the mission members carried on an active visitation program. On the Sunday before Christmas the temperature dropped to sixty-two below, but sixty-three persons attended the Christmas program that evening. Early in 1961 the need for a larger building faced the ever increasing congregation, which numbered 116 on Easter morning.

The Salcha Baptist Mission officially became the Salcha Baptist Church on September 17, 1961, with forty-five charter members. Robert Paquette was called as pastor; Ray Penfield was elected as deacon. On November 19, 1961, Benjamin Post and Bill Arnette were ordained as deacons.

In March 1962, the church successfully bid for and received a two-story war surplus building which was dismantled and re-erected into an attractive church building on a one and one-half acre tract of land donated by Joe Balch. Construction of the building continued during the summer months. The new building was dedicated on October 1, 1962, simultaneously with the opening of the fall revival preached by Charles Padgett of Birmingham, Alabama. The Alaska Baptist Convention contributed to the building program through the state mission offering; the balance was raised and the work was done by the members and friends of the church. The day the building was dedicated, ninety attended Sunday school, and the new building was too small to seat the crowd for the worship service.

During its first year the Salcha church led the association in baptisms per capita. They baptized one for three, which was one for every two resident church members.

After the Paquettes rotated back to the South, Frank Miller of Anchorage accepted the call as pastor in June 1963. In September 1963 the Salcha Baptist Church voted to start the Eielson Park Baptist Mission at Mile 24 Richardson Highway with George Wilkinson as acting pastor and Ray Penfield assisting in organization. On September 29, 1963, the church licensed George Wilkinson, Ray Penfield, and Lawrence Manning to preach. In October 1963 a new fellowship room was started as an addition to the building, and this was completed in March 1964. On March 22, 1964, Eielson Park Baptist Mission was organized into a church.

When Frank Miller resigned the pastorate, Ray Penfield was called as pastor of the Salcha church. On April 5, 1964, Mr. Penfield was ordained to the ministry and a five day revival began with Bob Buchanan preaching. Mr. Buchanan organized a junior choir and the juniors won fourteen of their friends to profess faith in Christ during the revival.

Family Night, the first Saturday of each month, featuring a

covered dish dinner, singing, and fellowship, was a unique feature of the Salcha Baptist Church which provided opportunity to reach many who would not attend regular church services. The informal meeting of neighbors and the friendly atmosphere that prevailed frequently proved the open door for reaching into hearts and homes in the community.

September 27, 1964, promotion day activities included the awarding of two- and three-year attendance pins to Salcha Baptist families. Recipients of three-year pins were the Balch children—Nancy, Lynx, and Janice, and the Jones family—Mr. and Mrs. Sanford Jones and their four sons, the Comeau boys, Myles, Roland, Patrick, and Sanford. Cynthia Jones, five years old, received her two-year pin.

The following excerpt was taken from our 1967 Christmas letter from the Jones family:

> August was another very eventful month. Fairbanks experienced quite a jolting earthquake followed by many tremors. Strawberries ripened and then it rained and rained some more. Every chance between showers, we picked strawberries, but most of the lovely berries were lost. On August 12 the big flood hit. Daddy, forseeing the possibility of trouble, had left home on Sunday afternoon to return to work at A-67; an hour after he left, the Salcha River took out about ½ mile of roadway just north of us and isolated our family from Eielson and Fairbanks. News started filtering in later that night that Fairbanks was in danger. Mama and the children spent three anxious days during reports wondering if Daddy were safe. Patrick was up on Mt. McKinley hunting with our interim pastor and knew nothing of what was happening. Mama could not go to work and little could be done at home because the electricity had gone off; the water was contaminated—so she had no cooking facility, no washing no sewing, no ironing, etc. Thanks goodness for battery radio—we listened all day long. On Wednesday the report came that Daddy was okay; on Thursday the road was repaired and Mama went back to work. Saturday about 5 P.M. Daddy came home. He had Patrick with him; Patrick had a caribou. Everyone was talking a mile a minute to catch up, meat was being prepared for the freezer, tension was gradually released, knowing that all were safe and once again within the shelter of their home, and then the telephone rang—the first time in over a week. Mama answered it, only to receive the message that Wayne was reported missing in action in Vietnam; telling Daddy was the hardest thing Mama has ever done. Prayers went up immediately; the others were notified. Daddy and Pat went back to work on Monday because Fairbanks was crying for help in cleanup. . . . On Sept. 10, just as the family was about to sit down

to dinner, the phone rang and news came that Wayne's body had been found and positively identified. . . .

The Sanford Jones family, Mile 41½, Richardson Highway

The December 1967 *Alaska Baptist Messenger* carried the statement: "Mrs. Betty Dee Jones of Salcha is to be congratulated for having earned the 'outstanding award' in the Southern Baptist annual associational minutes contest. Betty is the very efficient clerk of Tanana Baptist Association and her 'contest' performance is typical of the way she does all her work. Thank you, Mrs. Jones, for bringing another recognition to Alaska and commendations to you, Tanana Association, for having selected such an outstanding clerk."

Rayburn P. Moore served the Salcha church from August 1964, until June 1966, with John Thomas serving from November 1966, until May 1967. In May of 1967, land was purchased for a parsonage at Mile 37 Richardson Highway. Keith Foster came as pastor in June and was able to move his family into the completed parsonage by November 1967. When Foster left to pastor the University Baptist Church of Anchorage in the spring of 1970, the church called Rayburn Moore to serve a second time. Present plans are to relocate the church building in the same area as the parsonage.

In March 1970 Betty Jones wrote, "Jim Penfield, former member of Salcha church, attended revival services recently. All were greatly pleased to see him once again with his bright, cheery smile. He is back in Alaska on TDY from New York state, where he is stationed in the air force. The last time Jim was here was in August 1964; his father at that time was our pastor, and Jim was one of the young boys who helped build the church."

The Salcha Baptist Church started a mission in the trailer court at Mile 24 on the Richardson Highway, close to the main entrance of the air force base, in November 1963. The first services were prayer meetings held in homes. The Salcha church purchased a lot in the court and moved a house trailer from its church to the site. In addition, a wanigan was already there and the church made arrangements to secure a quonset hut as a meeting place.

By February 1964 a report to the *Alaska Baptist Messenger* stated that "people packed like sardines" described the situation of the Eielson Park mission on February 2. The trailer, wanigan, and connector which the mission was using were crowded to capacity with seventy-three in Sunday school. When a visitor expressed surprise at the attendance, a nine-year-old responded, "We always have lots here."

When the song leader announced that the next hymn would be "Bring Them In," he noticed people glancing furtively around, probably wondering where they would sit if they were brought in. George Wilkerson, ordained March 18, 1964, pastored the new mission.

The April *Messenger* reported, "A daughter mission grew up and severed its ties to the mother church on March 22. Eielson Park Baptist Church came into existence on Sunday afternoon." Ray Moore, Sunday school superintendent said, "I have never seen a Sunday school grow so large in such a short time. We have an average of sixty-six in Sunday school and seventy-three in church."

After the 1967 flood, volunteer flood workers assisted in the construction of the Eielson Park church. Joe Fallon, a preacher, one of the flood workers, was later called as pastor and led in finishing the building.

James and Fern Akin came to Tok from Delta Junction to hold the first Baptist services in the Tok Lions' Hall on June 7, 1964. Mrs. Bertha Huff, mission clerk, who ran a trade post in Northway from 1949 to 1958, related the following incident that occurred at the first meeting:

> The Lions' Club was also used by the Lions to show movies to the community, hence right by the door sat a high stand used to collect the movie fee or sell tickets. The first Sunday while Bro. Akin was arranging his portable pulpit and unpacking hymnals, a small, smartly dressed little girl in a fluffy dress came skipping in the door. She cast an eye up at the usual ticket seller's seat. Seeing no one, she hastened forward to Bro. Akin and said, "Where do we pay to get in?"
>
> I saw him struggle against a laugh as he explained to her that no one ever had to pay to attend the Lord's service, but each one gave what was on his heart.

For years our Christmas mail included greetings from James and Fern Akin, usually with a picture of the two of them peering out through a veil of icicles dangling from their parkas, or of a mission building with only its roof visible because of the high snowdrifts. A note always accompanied the picture telling us that the temperature was 63 degrees below zero when it was taken. One winter, however, when the temperature went down to 76 degrees below zero, they decided that it was too cold even for people who are prone to brag.

That was the winter of 1964-65 when the Akins were serving the Tok Baptist Mission and living in a three-room dwelling which consisted of three construction cabins moved together, attached by tar paper and insulation. Their home site was about five miles from the center of the community where the Lions' Club building in which they were holding services was located.

On December 10, 1964, a cold front swept down from the Tanana Valley and lasted four weeks. Because the borrowed, pot-bellied woodstove installed in their living room was cracked and would not hold heat, they moved their bed into the kitchen-dining room area, hoping to keep warm in the one room heated by an oil cookstove. But during the first Saturday night after the beginning of the sub-zero weather, the cookstove refused to burn because the oil had become too thick to run from the barrels to the house through the three-quarter inch pipe. James used a portable propane gas heater to thaw the oil, but it soon froze again.

After a cold, sleepless night, they were invited by their nearest neighbors, the John Summars, to stay with the eleven of them in their two-bedroom log cabin. The Akins accepted the warm invitation and lived in the Summar home until the weather warmed up enough for the oil to flow again.

Because their new Chevy II could not start in such weather to get them into town for Sunday services, they invited another neighbor family to join with them in the Summar home for Bible study and worship. With the temperature 70 degrees below and no transportation, they felt an attendance of eighteen was commendable.

The next day James went back home to check on things and found their water supply frozen solid and the plastic containers broken. An automobile battery sitting behind the oil stove had burst. The radiator of the Chevy II, checked to 50 degrees below, contained slushy ice, and the pure anti-freeze in the can had frozen solid. He learned later that it had to be mixed with water in order to remain liquid in extremely cold weather.

Mrs. Bertha Huff did not become a Baptist until November of 1964. Her husband Louis was on shift work, making it impossible for him to come two Sundays out of three, so Mrs. Huff drove the fifty-six miles from their home in Northway so she and their son Johnny could be in the services. She wrote, "There are many small things that bothered me at the time that later became very important as I watched. Remember, I was a new Baptist." She went on to tell how the Akins began driving ninety miles to Scotty Creek and the fifty-six miles to Northway once a week to have Bible study in the homes. "As I watched this couple year in and year out go about this grueling schedule, my heart was full of mixed feelings. Sometimes, and mostly, I rejoiced with them."

Then Fern began making doughnuts to supplement their personal income, and Mrs. Huff asked herself, "Does God expect this much of them?" After a year of doughnut making from dawn until time to travel up the road so they would be fresh for delivery after the Bible studies, Akin figured out their books for income tax purposes. James teased Fern that she "almost broke even," and Mrs. Huff related, "My heart almost broke. Fern is badly crippled, not just in one leg but both. But as I looked back at that time, I've praised God over and over."

Mr. and Mrs. Les Reeves, the couple who ran Scotty Creek Lodge, had three children. Mrs. Reeves taught them, using the Calvert Correspondance Course. Then Mrs. Reeves learned that she was dying of cancer. It was a slow, lingering, painful death; she stayed with the Akins in Palmer during her last weeks. "I kept asking myself if it would have been too much for them to bear if the Akins had not ministered to them. Would Mrs. Reeves have gone home to the Father victorious? Would Mr. Reeves and the children have been able to bear the passing of their wife and mother with that same victory? Would they have been able to see the mother go with peace in her soul?" Mrs. Huff answered her own questions by stating, "Thank God for his love and grace! Thank God for his servants, Brother and Sister Akin, and that I have known them and seen God's work manifest in their lives."

In July 1965 the Tok mission obtained a loan from the Home Mission Board and purchased three and one-half acres in Tok with two houses on the property. The Akins moved into the smaller, unfinished building, and he completed it. No water was available on the site, but electricity was brought in. Not until the summer of 1969 was the mission able to get a ninety foot well drilled and paid for. During the summer of each year a Vacation Bible School was conducted.

One Sunday morning in the summer of 1966, while James Akin was preparing for morning services, he heard a knock on the door of the mission. Opening the door, he found Andrew Nakarak, a short Eskimo man, whose bloodshot eyes intensified the look of distress on his face. Dissatisfied with a life of drinking, Andrew indicated that he had come for help.

That night Andrew was the only one who came to the mission service, so James and Fern had Bible study just for him. In this service he prayed for forgiveness and asked the Lord to save him. He continued attending the mission services while he worked on a construction job near Tok. He had a wife and nine children back home at Shaktoolak, Alaska, a small village about ninety miles east of Nome. He began to be concerned about them.

Just before Andrew left Tok, the Akins invited him for dinner. During the meal they found that he was the mayor of his village. He was determined to go back and show by his life and attitudes that Christ had given him new life. The last time the Akins heard of Andrew, he was witnessing to men in Fairbanks who have drinking problems.

February 2, 1968, the Akins left Tok to serve as missionaries in the Matanuska and Susitna Valleys. Captain Jerry Douglas came for a while from North Pole Baptist Church to hold Sunday morning services. Mrs. Carol Thurneau had Sunday evening and Wednesday night services in her home. Finally, only three families were left attending the services, and Mrs. Huff wrote, "These were the events that had our three families in despair. None of us could play the piano, and we had no pastor nor long-standing lay member. Carol had made her decision for Christ in January 1967. We just didn't know how to lead our mission forward. Personally, I know I could never worship in another church as long as there was a Baptist church closed in this town." But they did close down the mission. Carol and Lewis went to Glennallen for a while, but were not happy there. Carol's children pleaded with her to stay at home and teach them Sunday school; they kept up their prayer meetings on Wednesday night at her home.

Mrs. Huff decided to write the Akins for help. She said, "We loved them too much to have someone else tell them the mission was closed. I had literally wept for a week over its closing." In January 1969 the Akins and Pastor Don Davis of the sponsoring church, First Baptist, Fairbanks, came to meet with the mission group at the Huff's home. They encouraged the group and helped them to reorganize. Akin promised to come from Palmer once a month, weather permitting, to preach for them. Davis promised to try to find them a pastor.

The very next week Louis Huff went to the Greely base barber for a haircut. Huel Waddell, pastor of the Delta Junction church, was the barber. He recognized Louis from seeing him at a youth rally, and asked him about the work at Tok. When he heard of the need at Tok, Waddell offered to come each Saturday to hold Saturday evening services. Mrs. Huff wrote:

Mrs. Hunke, there are no words to describe what they have done for this mission with the Lord as their sponsor and director. Every week, regardless of temperatures, they loaded their car with Bro. Glover and servicemen and came with the portable organ and Daisy Waddell to play. That month without our mission had seemed years and years long. Now to have not only a pastor, but music and the house swelling with male voices and young lives full of enthusiasm—there are no words for the uplifting and joy we felt! Always in the background was Bro. Glover; later he began loading his car with his sons and more servicemen, so that two carloads came, and always there was music and Bro. Waddell's sermons that reached out and said if you want a church for your community, you'll have to do the work. He taught us to move without a shepherd. By spring we'd learned to act. We took a survey; we moved back into our mission building with warmer weather; we asked for a revival and got it with Bro. King of South Carolina coming to preach. Bro. Waddell still came on Saturday, and we filled our car and sometimes another one, and worshipped Sunday in Delta with Bro. Waddell.

Then came the determination to have Sunday school on Sunday. We'd start with the coming of the summer workers. We were told we were not going to get any summer workers. Still we determined to grow and advance, and work must be done on Sunday. We, with God helping, would not only try, but would do it. Then came word we were getting summer workers just as we were to open. So with John and Cathy Dillman, the Sunday school was opened and we also had John to bring the services. (The Waddells had gone out on vacation.)

We prayed and we hunted all these weeks for a pastor, but none could be found. Now summer was coming to an end, and with it John and Cathy. We wanted a Training Union for our young people. We wanted them never to be so unprepared and helpless as we. John and Cathy agreed to help start one. Everything was smooth all summer. Even before we had any idea of a summer worker, with our determination, pastor or no pastor, we'd have Sunday school on Sunday, came a determination for a two week Bible school, something we'd never done before. All others had been one week. We had a huge success; God blessed beyond our imagination. (I put the length of the highway on my car as I was hauling workers and youngsters.)

Timidly, we'd written Bro. Davis and asked if one of the other two summer workers for Fairbanks district wasn't busy, could she come play the piano for Bible school. It wasn't a necessity, but would help. Sister Davis drove down with not just one but both girls, and how we worked for our Lord those weeks, and how those girls and the Dillmans blessed and strengthened us! The girls had young people's services every evening after Bible school in front of the church fireplace. . . .

We still had no pastor, but we were still determined. Not only would we have Sunday school, but we would have all the others (organizations) too. I would take Sunday evening for Bible study. Carol and I would take turns for Training Union. She'd keep on with the Wednesday night service, and that left Louis for Sunday morning. He didn't say he'd bring a message, but he'd do something. Then we went off to the convention in Sitka. He was so inspired that he told me there in Sitka that he knew he was going to do the work right and bring a Sunday message.

After he'd committed himself, Bro. Davis arrived in Sitka telling us he'd just had a Baptist minister join his church, and he would talk with him about Sunday morning services for us. The Dillmans left before we got back to Tok, but Bro. Billy Baxter and family arrived from Fairbanks and had Sunday school and worship services with us. I took the Training Union and Robert H. Conner of St. Louis, Mo., arrived with five high school boys (they'd been touring Alaska). Bro. Conner brought the evening message and those boys rocked the mission with music. This then was the first Sunday. We'd thought we'd expect a let down when we found ourselves responsible for leading God's work in the mission alone. All we could do was stand amazed and thank God for his continued blessings. . . .

Was ever a mission more blessed? Bro. Baxter still comes every Saturday evening and leaves after Sunday morning worship. Louis brings the Sunday evening message—he is improving with the Lord's help and our prayers. . . . Last Wednesday night we had seventeen juniors and intermediates for Bible study.

Last month we had revival with Bro. Keith Wilkerson of Chickasha, Okla. He knew our pastor, Brother Baxter, in Oklahoma. When two spirit-filled Okie pastors get together with a few God-fearing Christians, the Lord blesses. We now have six juniors awaiting baptism and two adults have come by letter.

Note, this is my blessing: every time our group determined we could and would do something to lead our church, the Lord honored that bending of our selfish will and help was sent. How marvelous that Bro. Baxter is here so we have a pastor to turn to! The joys of having this man in our home every Sunday for dinner before he returns are beyond any measure. The fellowship and love of Christians is so wonderful, I sometimes wonder how heaven can be more sweet. . . . When things were at the lowest, God sent us not a pastor only, but a pastor, a pianist, a congregation from Delta—servicemen hungry for home cooking and a home. We gave a little and God blessed by the tons. Then youth rallies, hot dog roasts, and always Bro. Glover with his Bible in his hand.

Mrs. Huff reported later that the six juniors were baptized in a service at Delta Junction. Billy Baxter had an automobile accident in the winter of 1969 during one of his trips to the Tok mission. His neck was hurt, but he was able to be back with the church after a few weeks. Carol Thurneau "carried on almost single-handed. I have never before been so privileged as with knowing Carol. She is really a wonderful person; perhaps someday you will meet her. The hours she has spent cleaning, starting fires, hauling water, etc., for the church and its responsibilities over all these years are immense. She is truly God's servant and enjoys doing it all."

Baptist work in Glennallen started in June 1965 when Roy Moore, former religious education secretary for the Alaska convention, came from the New Orleans seminary to begin services. By the end of July seventeen Baptist families had been located and four Sunday services held. The work had no sponsoring church at first; the state executive board authorized initial funds to begin.

At the August 10, 1965, meeting the board voted to purchase a new $10,750 mobile chapel for use at Glennallen, to be used later at other new mission points in the state. The board also voted to make Glennallen the second Pioneer 2000 Club project. The money was used for property on which to set the trailer. By October the 2000 Club had contributed $560 toward the project; the trailer chapel had been set up, winterized, and was being used for services.

Calvary Baptist Church, Anchorage, agreed to sponsor the Glennallen mission and called Frank Burger to serve as pastor. Burger was stationed at Ft. Richardson and made the round trip to the mission field each week. After serving the church for about a year, Burger was succeeded in the pastorate of the mission by Donald Swafford, a recent graduate of New Orleans Seminary, a classmate of Roy Moore. Swafford began full time work on the field in July 1966. During the winter of 1967 the Calvary church sent a team of voluntary laborers every week who made the 375 mile round trip and gave more than 1,000 hours to building a twelve by twenty-four foot extension to the pastor's home. The builders encountered permafrost only one foot beneath the surface of the earth and had to struggle against the frozen ground for three months in order to install disposal facilities.

Swafford left the work after a few months, but returned to resume the pastorate in February 1968. He reported excellent response by the community in his efforts to work with youth.

❖   ❖   ❖

In Alaska we wait all winter for May and green leaves and robins. Last spring I was amused to find the first birds of the season in the back yard, furiously chasing the snow flakes of a late May flurry. I felt like joining them with a broom to sweep away all evidence of the eight months of winter just past. For days I had watched the birch trees, my eyes following each limb to where it terminated in a little corymb of smaller branches, which then ended in a cluster of tiny twigs. I had waited and watched the blue sky through this lattice work of living wood. This May morning I was rewarded by flushes of green buds bursting forth at the end of each twig. This was what I had been waiting for, but I found more; I found the face of God in green. Awareness often lifts the veil from the holy presence in unlikely places, especially in Alaska.

In winter the landscape brims over with new snow. Frothy ice fog clings to every twig, clothing even the lowliest weed with the glitter of jeweled diadems. But underneath, the shrivelling cold has long since killed the tender growth, for death is always the price for kingly crowns. The withering fingers of fall frost touch the leaves of our spruce and birch and aspen forests by early September, turning them to gold and dropping them off one by one onto the ground, like gold coins in a temple's coffer. Though spring always seems long in coming, our eagerness is finally rewarded with a swaddling of green gauze around the tree tops by the last of May. Quickly, then, the wild roses open their first petals wide to the sun and fill the air with sweet fragrance as they give their essence to us. Ferns first lift filigree fingers, then whole palms of praise toward heaven. Summer days are for wandering along the inlet beach in search of wild strawberries or walking in woods deeply carpeted with velvet mosses or slushing through cranberry bogs where satin leaves stiffly display clusters of berries like shed blood.

Putting Alaska into words is hard; putting Southeastern Alaska into words is practically impossible. E. W. Hunke has described in the *Messenger* trips to Juneau, Sitka and Ketchikan:

The brisk Taku wind rushing down between the massive snow-capped Juneau mountains caused our skilled pilot to slip the big 720 jet sideways into position for landing. Outside my window, the stately, turquoise-toned Mendenhall Glacier stood like a sentry guarding gold. A pastel, baby-blue sky enhanced the scene. The heavily coated ground crew with face masks and fogging breath served as a grim reminder that Juneau was cold. The forty-three mile per hour wind and minus thirteen degree temperature combined to produce a minus seventy-four degree chill factor. Alaskans talk about "chill factor" rather than comfort index. . . .

The huge, American bald eagle perched atop the rocky island in Sitka Sound was a beautiful sight. Dick Miller motor-boated me along the Baranof Island coast on a clear, sunny day. The warmth of the Japanese current provides a mildness for Sitka's climate. Vast forests cover the glacier-rounded slopes of Southeastern Alaska. The Tongass National Forest is filled with deer. The limit is four deer, and many sections remain yet to be hunted. The churches in Tongass Association are located in Ketchikan, Sitka and Juneau. No roads connect these towns, so one travels between these towns by ferry or plane. The distance and expense prevents these churches from fellowshiping together. . . .

The towering spruce trees on a multitude of inlet islands crowded down to the shoreline, which was broken by the glacial curves of the magnificent mountains. Snow covered peaks of indescribable beauty in the background silhouetted the scene before us. Three pair of killer whales had returned to calve in the placid waters of a small bay in Carroll Inlet on Revillagegedo Island. Sea gulls carefully observed our movements as well as the whales' splashing and spewing geysers. Squadrons of geese and ducks with heads stretched forward in flight skimmed low across the waters as if on a secret military mission. The solitude and beauty of this unspoiled plenitude of nature makes the problems of life seem unreal. Orton Ranch on the Naha River near here represents more than ten years of dreaming and working in the lives of Pastor and Mrs. Marion Dunham. In November 1967, the Alaska Baptist Convention accepted Orton Ranch as a gift from them.

All the way up the Inland Passage the sparkling sapphire water was dotted with green-forested islands. When the *Malaspina* docked at Sitka, the first thing I saw was an old derelict which

lay like a dead water rat at the edge of the pier with its hull
rotting and paint chipping. The town showed that it had survived
a series of seiges. In the Indian village in the heart of Sitka,
sagging timbers shored up with unweathered braces, characterized
the houses. The roofs had been patched until they resembled the
geometric designs of the Indian basket work on sale in the shops.
Weird Tlinglit ceremonial masks; Chilkat blankets in patterns of
turquoise, black and yellow; war canoes; and totem poles combined
with gleaming icons and steaming samovars left over from Russian
days welcome the visitor and announce the diverse cultures that
come together in Sitka.

The Sitka Chamber of Commerce folder calls Sitka "an island
of beauty in the heart of the Alexander Archipelago." It does not
overstate the facts when it says that Sitka's rooftops are "shingled
with gulls, her harbors confettied with boats; driftwood gnarling
in the summer sun with a backdrop of snow-peaked mountains
sloping to greet the emerald green isles in a meringue of whitecaps
offshore" adds to the conclusion that Sitka is scenery personified.

During the 1700's Russian traders and explorers were establishing outposts in Alaska, planning to occupy it for Russia. In 1799,
the southernmost Russian outpost was established near Sitka. "This
stake in the heart of fierce Tlinglit Indian territory was to prove
a formidable challenge to both the Russians and their enemies
for the next half century." Finally, the day came when all Alaska
became United States territory, with Sitka, long known as "the
Paris of the Pacific," its capital.

Herb Hilscher, in one of his pamphlets called *The Heritage of
Alaska*, tells the story of the first Alaska Day, October 18, 1867.
It is one full of drama and pathos. The ceremony of the transfer
of Alaska from Russian sovereignity to that of the United States
took place on Castle Hill in front of Baranof's Castle in Sitka.
Captain Alexeii Pestchouroff of the Russian navy represented the
Czar. General Lovell H. Rousseau represented the United States
and wrote the following official report of the transfer:

> At precisely half past three o'clock, the troops were brought to
> present arms. A signal was given to the USS *Ossipee* to start firing
> the salute. The ceremony was begun by slowly lowering the Russian
> flag.
> Suddenly, the exercises were interrupted! The Russian flag had
> caught in the ropes attached to the flag pole. The soldier who was

lowering the flag continued to pull at it, and tore off the border by which it was attached, leaving the flag entwined tightly around the ropes.

The flag pole was perhaps ninety feet in height. Several Russian soldiers attempted to ascend to the flag, but could not make their way more than halfway up the pole. Finally a boatswain's chair was made with a rope, and a Russian soldier was hoisted upward. The soldier detached the flag from the ropes, but, not hearing the command from Captain Pestchouroff to bring it down, he tossed it down. In its descent, the Imperial Flag fluttered open and fell on the bayonets of the Russian soldiers.

The United States flag was then properly attached and began its ascent, hoisted by my private secretary (the general's son) and again the salutes were fired.

Captain Pestchouroff stepped up to me and said: "General Rousseau, by authority from His Majesty, the Emperor of Russia, I transfer to the United States the Territory of Alaska."

In a few words I acknowledged the acceptance of the transfer, and the ceremony was at an end.

The laceration of the double-eagle emblem must have been a heart-rending sight to the Russians present. Princess Maksutove, wife of the governor, fainted and had to be carried away. The Russians and Creoles wept. That day in history was an ignominious finale to the Russian occupation of North America.

Because of the prayers and interest of the First Baptist Church of Juneau, Nancy Hill, Ray Huff, the E. B. Gurleys of Mt. Edgecumbe, and others in the state convention, a Sunday school was established at Sitka. On August 5, 1956, the First Baptist Church of Sitka was constituted. Twenty-five entered the new organization as charter members. Leroy Stringfield, summer student missionary, served as mission pastor. The church voted to give 25 percent to the cooperative program, saying, "We don't want others to have to wait as long as we did for the gospel."

Sitka then had a population of 3,500; Mt. Edgecumbe, a five minute ferry ride from Sitka, had a population of 2,500. The people from Mt. Edgecumbe come to Sitka to worship, a number of them being members of the church.

The church met for three years in the Women's Club Building. Dale Proctor served as the first pastor. The church purchased lots and started construction of their own place of worship as soon as they felt able. The Sunday School Board's plans did not call for a basement, but because of the natural lay of the land, the top story of the plans were put into a basement, and what was to have been the bottom floor became the top story. Plans for future development called for adding the top story onto the first unit, then extending out from the left side of the building with the permanent auditorium, making a T-shaped building.

At the time of the dedication of their first building early in 1959, James Samples was the pastor. He had formerly been a building contractor and was a great help in the building program.

During Dick Miller's pastorate at Sitka, he worked extensively with the students at Mt. Edgecumbe. Writing for the June 1966 *Messenger,* he shared with readers some of the opportunities and problems of that ministry:

> Religious activities among students at Mr. Edgecumbe High School, like all schools operated by the Bureau of Indian Affairs, are controlled by regulations of the federal government. Upon admission of a child to the school, his parents express a church preference for the child which cannot be changed by the child until he is eighteen years old.
>
> In the past, religious activities of the students have been limited to Sunday morning services and one hour on Tuesday night when on-campus religious instruction was permitted. In the spring of 1966, for the first time students have been allowed to attend Sunday evening services as well as other special services which do not conflict with school activities. All church attendance is voluntary, although school officials are encouraging it. . . .
>
> Our work with the students centers around the Tuesday night Religious Instruction period. Through the year, with the assistance of the Alaska Baptist Convention, our students have viewed a series of religious movies. A series on the life of Christ which had extended over from last year was conducted at mid-year. At present we are viewing a new series on the life of Paul. The religious movies are shown three nights per month. On the other nights we usually have a visitor who is interviewed about his life, his work, and Christian experience. These have been some of the best meetings of the year. Attendance varies from a dozen to 25 or 30.
>
> On selected Saturday afternoons, students come to the church basement for recreation and fellowship. Three or four students have joined our church choir which practices on Sunday afternoon.
>
> The highlight of religious activities this year was the city-wide revival with Tony Fontane. Both opening and closing services were held in the Mt. Edgecumbe Field House. A large number of students made decisions for Christ in these services. The effect on the students has continued to be manifest.
>
> In our own church services several students have made decisions. One student, Rita Ramoth, daughter of one of our members at

Selawik, was baptized on Easter Sunday. It was a privilege to see her make this decision as I had the joy of baptizing her father in Selawik in 1956. We have rejoiced to witness Christian growth in these young people. . . .

This year I have been better satisfied than any previous year with our ministry to Mt. Edgecumbe students. The relaxation of regulations to allow students to attend Sunday evening services has been a great blessing. The past Sunday we had ten girls in our evening services. It was thrilling to hear them enter the discussion in Training Union. Another indication of the quality of our students is that almost one-third of them were on the spring honor roll. Our group had the largest percentage of any religious group. . . .

It has been a joy to work with these students: Eskimos, Indians, and Aleuts, for we do have some of each race in our group. Most of these students come from non-Baptist homes. Pray for them.

Opal Miller said about their pastorate in Sitka, "We stayed there eight years and became very involved in the community as well as the church. It was hard to leave, but we felt it was the Lord's will. Our two youngest children, George and John, were born at Sitka."

William Neal Baker came to Sitka as pastor after the Millers moved to Anchorage in 1969. In 1970 the Sitka church voted to assist in sponsoring a mission and began home fellowship classes at Biorka.

In March 1965 the Tongass Baptist Association, which had been a "paper association" for years, became a reality. Mr. and Mrs. Dick Miller of Sitka, Joe Patterson of Juneau, and Mr. and Mrs. Marion Dunham met in Ketchikan for a three day associational meeting. The Glacier Valley Baptist Church of Juneau was received into the association, making a total of four churches. The group made plans for a summer camp at Orton Ranch and invited the Baptist churches in Prince Rupert and Terrace, British Columbia. The Tongass churches voted to include associational missions as a budgeted item, and considered how to make possible future meetings in which more church members could be involved.

Twelve miles north of the limits of Juneau lies Mendenhall Valley. Rimmed by mountains, streaked by streams, and covered with spruce, the valley contains two thousand homes, and in the center of the valley, a mile from the face of great Mendenhall Glacier, stands Glacier Valley Baptist Church.

The story of the church began in Room 422 of the Baranof

Hotel in Juneau. In July 1963 the Clay McDole and Frank Lescallette families met there and discussed the need for a mission in the area surrounding the airport. After discussion and prayer, they shared their conviction about the mission need with Richard Moore, interim pastor of Juneau's First Baptist Church. He suggested they take a survey of the area to discover prospects. The following covenant was drawn up and circulated in the community:

> There is a need for a Baptist church in the vicinity of the Juneau airport. The population of that area is rapidly growing and the churches of the city are not able to effectively minister to the spiritual needs of such a large number of people, located so far away from the geographical center of their activities. In view of this fact, we, the undersigned, do hereby covenant under what we believe to be the guidance of the Holy Spirit, to form a Southern Baptist mission in that area, with a view of establishing a self-supporting church at the earliest possible date. We will support this mission with our time, talents, and money.

After two nights of visiting in the area, they had sixteen signatures. The rest of the week was given to prayer, then a general meeting for all those interested in the new work was held in the basement of First Baptist Church on August 4, 1963.

On August 11, 1963, the group that was to become Glacier Valley Baptist Church had their first worship service in the home of Mr. and Mrs. Melvin Gaines at Thane, Alaska. Thane is four miles south of Juneau. Twenty-three attended, most driving sixteen miles from the valley where the church would be located. With no sponsoring church and no promise of support, the group organized into a church and called Richard Moore as pastor.

The first month was filled with heartwarming and uplifting experiences and tiring and burdensome details. Several meetings a week were held at the home of Glynn Estes at Lemon Creek to write a constitution and by-laws, select teachers and officers, and make plans for a dedication service. The dedication service was on September 1, 1963, at the Open Bible Church building, the only building available in the vicinity of the new work. Roy Moore, Alaska Baptist Convention religious education secretary, preached the sermon of dedication. The church was constituted with twenty-three members.

Within a few days a property committee was selected and the tedious task of locating a site began. The need for more spacious quarters than the Estes' living room because acute as the congregation grew.

Two months after their organization, the church joined other churches across the convention in plans for simultaneous revivals. They received word that Ed Wolfe of First Baptist Church, Woodward, Oklahoma, would preach for them. Plans for the evangelistic effort included duplicating song sheets, for they had no hymnals or instruments. The lack of a building further tested their faith, then on October 9, as they met for prayer in the pastor's trailer, the answer came.

Mr. Estes, chairman of the property committee, arrived late, but with a smile. He announced, "We've found it," and described 2.77 acres along the highway just a few hundred yards from where they sat. The land had a small frame house already on it. Mr. Estes had put down $100 earnest money because he was convinced that this was the place the Lord wanted the church.

The questions persisted, "How can we buy it with our income? Where will the down payment come from?" Discussion was lively and feelings were strong that this was the right property, but the enormity of the $4,000 down payment threw the group into indecision. The pastor called the group to prayer concerning the need, and after prayer, a new spirit of faith prevailed. The vote to purchase the property was unanimous. "The Lord will provide" became a watchword for the pioneering church.

When the property committee contacted the owners of the land again and explained the circumstances of the small church and their deep desire for the land, the owners lowered the down payment to $1,500. The trustees made up that amount themselves from savings or borrowed funds. The property was purchased on Friday before the scheduled revival. They worked the next day, felling the trees and pulling stumps for a parking lot; the evangelist arrived while they were cleaning the building. They met Mr. Wolfe at the airport wearing their workclothes, took him to the home where he would be staying, let him borrow some coveralls, then together they finished the work in time for a fellowship prayer meeting that night.

The house had been used as a summer home, so had no restrooms, running water, or heat except for a fireplace that had to be kindled three hours ahead to get the temperature up to about 40°, then the back door had to be left open because of the smoke.

Mr. Wolfe tells, "The room was so full of smoke from the fireplace that I had to memorize the Scripture since I was unable to see my Bible." Because they had no church furniture, the members brought dining room chairs for the first Sunday services.

The next day they borrowed some metal folding chairs from the Episcopal church and rented a piano, but on Tuesday the Episcopal pastor remembered that they needed the chairs back for a meeting on Wednesday. The Baptist mission on Douglas Island, just across the Gastineau Channel, had been closed for some time, but when the Glacier Valley group had approached the state convention board about using or buying the pews from the mission, they were told they could not. The board objected to a clause in the Glacier Valley constitution which left the question of baptism in doubt, so would not approve pastoral aid nor offer any help to the group. Tuesday night Mr. Wolfe preached on the "Church and Its Ordinances," and at a business meeting following the service, the church voted to strike out the offending clause from their constitution.

Late that night, Mr. Wolfe called Aubrey Short, president of the convention, telling him of the church's action, and asking again for the use of the pews. Mr. Short told him to go get them, so on Wednesday the men borrowed a pickup to bring the pews and pulpit stand from the Douglas Island mission. The house began to look more like a church. During the revival, two members joined by profession of faith, and they recorded a high attendance of thirty-five. Also, Alaska got a grip on the Oklahoma pastor's heart so that he later returned to serve as pastor of the Hamilton Acres Baptist Church, Fairbanks.

Mr. Moore returned to California in February 1964, and for ten months Frank Lescallette, a young coast guardsman, filled the pulpit. After the spring thaw in 1964, the members added two Sunday school rooms, restrooms, and a furnace room. The building remained unsealed and without permanent light fixtures for several years. A fall revival was preached in October 1964 by Dr. Ray P. Rust of First Baptist Church, Bastrop, Louisiana, and the church was strengthened numerically and spiritually.

Edward Owens of Osprey, Florida, with his wife Lois and two sons, accepted the call as pastor and arrived on the field January 16, 1965. He stayed just one year and returned to Florida.

The church wrote Stanley File of their need for a pastor in

April 1966. Under doctors' care for years for leukemia, Mr. File had been told he could not work in cold or mountainous areas, but the same week he received the letter from the Glacier Valley Church, the doctors at Ochsner Clinic in New Orleans told Mr. File that his health had so improved that the latest test showed "negative on all counts," and that he could serve wherever he wished. He wished to return to mission work, so he and his wife and two children arrived at the Juneau ferry terminal on July 13, 1966.

When Frank Lescallette left to enter college in Pineville, Louisiana, to study for the ministry, the church purchased his home, located just behind the church building, for the parsonage. It, together with two other nearby homes, were used for Sunday school space, replacing the cars that had served for many classes. By November 1967 the church had forty-six members from fourteen families, eighty-five in Sunday school, thirty-five in Training Union, $4,000 in the building fund and $3,000 in the general fund. They had an organ, piano, sufficient Baptist hymnals, furnishings, and graded literature.

By this time also the Alaska Baptist Convention had contributed one-third of its mission offering ($600) to help with the purchase of property. The Home Mission Board gave the pews from the mission at Douglas and $200 a month operating expenses. The First Baptist Church of Ketchikan contributed a pulpit. A friend of the church gave a wall furnace. The Bell Forest Baptist Church of Bel Air, Maryland, contributed $25 a month for two years. The Oldham Little Church Foundation of Texas granted money toward the next unit.

The church welcomed Olyn F. Roberts from Mississippi as pastor in September 1969.

The story of the beginnings of Christianity and of Baptist work in Alaska is always a story of individual courage. A man or a woman had a vision of the need and felt the call of God to come, usually starting with nothing and staying to build a congregation and a building. Such a story could also be told about a Father Duncan sent by the Church of England to a tribe of Indians in British Columbia. He found that the Indians had cannibalistic tendencies and decided to omit from his ritual all references to blood because they found in those references an approval of their way of life. His church officials recalled him, but he went to Washington, D.C., and asked permission to settle his people in Alaska. He was given Annette Island, just south of Ketchikan. Like Moses, he led an exodus down the long trail, then traveled by boat, to the new land. Starting with nothing, the people built a thriving community, today called Metlakatla; they had their own salmon cannery and later an electric power plant.

Later the federal government leased a part of the land from the Indians and put in a Coast Guard installation and Weather Bureau station. It was to this part of the island that B. I. Carpenter went for Bible study in homes during the early years of the work in Ketchikan.

During the summer of 1965 Marion Dunham of Ketchikan reported that extension services had been started again on Annette Island. On October 10 Dunham went to the island to launch a new Sunday school schedule. The Sunday school began with seven classes and thirty-five persons in attendance. The morning offering was $140 and the mission asked that ten percent should go for the Cooperative Program. The next Sunday C. S. Hodge, educational missionary of the convention, was present to assist with the newly-organized program. He reported "a great time with 48 in Sunday school and 53 in the worship service."

The mission began as a Friday evening fellowship in a home. The home services have continued.

In 1968 the Annette Baptist Mission constructed a new building from two trailers by joining the units with a peaked roof and a foyer. The location was selected by Lt. Com. David J. Bain, who was later killed in an accident. The deceased's wife, parents and home church in New York joined with the mission and sponsoring church in establishing the David J. Bain Memorial Fund for the purpose of building a place of worship for the Coast Guard and FAA families on Annette. Dan Hill pastors the mission.

8

". . . Think It Not Strange . . ."

1 Peter 4:12

From *Minutes of the Seventh Annual Session of the Alaska Baptist Convention,* July 29-31, 1952, in Ketchikan, Alaska.

> A request was presented to the Convention that prayer be had that the fire then raging near the Standard Oil Company in Ketchikan be brought under control. The Convention held a short prayer service until word was received that the firemen were getting the fire under control.
>
> The report of the Sunday school was dispensed with until another time inasmuch as Mrs. B. I. Carpenter, the Sunday school superintendent at Ketchikan, was at the fire.

Fiery trials, both literal flames and the searing pain of tragedy, have been the portion of Alaska Baptists. Many buildings have burned. Both Negro churches in Anchorage, Shiloh and Greater Friendship, caught fire and sustained damages during the same week in February 1956. Greater Friendship was partially constructed with salvaged materials from First Baptist Church, Anchorage, which was gutted with fire early in 1953.

Late on the night of February 13, 1960, Pastor Don Davis of Fairbanks First Baptist Church called the convention office to tell about the total destruction of their building. The fire was discovered at six P.M.; the cause was an explosion in the furnace. At eight P.M. about two hundred persons were expected to attend a wedding at the church. Earlier that afternoon several pastors and missionaries had been at the church for a fellowship meeting of the evangelistic conference in session that week. Mr. Davis lost all his books when the pastor's study was destroyed. The church had the oldest existing Southern Baptist church building in Alaska.

Fire burned the inside out of Faith Baptist Church of Anchorage in February, 1963. Both the police and insurance company agreed that the fire was an act of arson. The fire started in three different places. It was detected in the basement by a passerby who called the fire department about four A.M. The damages were estimated at from forty-five to seventy thousand dollars. The church had recently voted and applied for double the amount of insurance to go into effect when their policy was renewed. In just twelve more days, they would have had $100,000, instead of the $50,000 worth of insurance with which to repair the building.

Joe Patterson, pastor of First Baptist Church, Juneau, was attending a borough meeting at the high school directly across the street from his home on April 26, 1967, when he heard the fire sirens screaming. As the meeting continued, so did the sirens, and soon Joe could tell that the fire must be in the immediate vicinity. He and his wife had often referred to the house where they lived as the "fire-trap," but within the next month they were planning to move into the new $70,000 parsonage the Juneau church had purchased.

Someone interrupted the meeting saying that the house on fire was just across the street, but by the time Joe could rush home, hope for saving all the family had faded. The youngest child, Steward, age two, had been taken to the hospital. Two neighbors, E. T. Nygard and Pat Ingram, had caught him when someone had tossed him from an upstairs window, but when they had climbed up to rescue whoever was there, they were driven back by the smoke. Making one last frantic search, they had felt a body beneath the window sill, and had brought down Susan, age thirteen, who was also treated for smoke inhalation. Mrs. Nina Patterson, Sara (Susan's twin), and Mark, age seven, perished in the conflagration.

All the furniture and personal belongings of the family were destroyed. They carried no insurance.

Memorial services conducted by E. W. Hunke, Mark Boesser, Episcopalian rector, and W. E. Beyers, pastor of Juneau Presbyterian Church, were attended by over five hundred persons. Throughout the ordeal, Patterson's faith did not falter.

Later that same year Mr. Hunke went to Sitka to preach a revival. The day he arrived in town, a call went out for a party to search for the Sitka church's Training Union director and two children who had gone out in a boat. They were never found; only their boat, discovered with a huge hole ripped from its bottom, was recovered. The life jackets were still in the boat. That Christmas we received the following letter from Merl Lynn Hutchins, the wife and mother of the drowning victims:

> I'm not sending Christmas cards this year; my heart is too heavy for frivolous cheer. The one I loved most and our two darling children have gone on to be with our Father in heaven. It's not that I begrudge them their place up there, but it is so very lonesome for us left down here. As much as we loved them, I wouldn't ask God to send them back down to this world full of sin. I'm thankful to know that they all loved the Lord and are safe with Him now. The privilege of knowing Hutch, Beverly, and Bruce is a wonderous memory time will not loose. I'm thankful these precious three were loaned to me for a short time. I know He doesn't love my dear Elaine less, but knew my heart needed one left. We trust the Lord to care and not give us more than He helps us bear.

The end of 1968 brought tragedy into many Alaska Baptist homes and churches. Tom LaFollete, a Sunday school teacher at Anchorage First Baptist, died in a Point Barrow plane crash, which also claimed the lives of seven top state officials. Kotzebue school superintendent James Wolverton, member of the Baptist mission and charter member of Sitka First Baptist Church, passed away with a heart attack. Joe Chron, brother of E. C. and Virgil Chron, was lost in a boat accident. A Wien Consolidated airliner crash killed thirty-nine people, including two Christian missionaries who planned to help start a Dillingham Baptist mission. Both Pamela Pettis, twenty-one-year-old daughter of the Chuck Smiths of Anchorage Sunset Hills Baptist Church, and her husband died in a broadside automobile accident near their Willow homestead. E. W. Hunke conducted their funeral.

James Whisenhant, former Alaska Baptist Convention president, a member of University Baptist Church in College, seriously injured his knee on a ski trail and dragged himself several miles in sub-zero temperatures. A special prayer request was mailed out to the churches when it was feared he would lose his life or limb. After a few weeks "Whizzy" wrote to the convention office, "I want to thank you and all Alaska Baptists for your prayers for me after my recent skiing accident. This very meaningful experience influenced my life in many ways; it was the most dramatic experience of answered prayer in my life. With such a severe and painful injury, I should have lost consciousness or gone into shock. I prayed as never before; if I had fainted, I knew I would awaken with frozen hands and feet. God answered that prayer, and I can remember every minute of the agonizing eight hours of struggling up that mountain. It is unfortunate that one must have such experiences to learn the real meaning of prayer, but I thank God for it."

"The blood-red sun seemed aflame with wrath as it cast a long, brilliant trail of reflected crimson down the length of the rippling Salcha River. The lingering haze from the smoke of raging forest and timber fires filtered out the glare until we looked directly at the sun," thus Mr. Hunke described the scene that cut short our mission survey trip in the summer of 1969. For a time, news reports sounded as though all of northern Alaska would go up in smoke. After our small plane was grounded, we had to wait several days before we could fly home. Mr. and Mrs. Don Rounsaville, teachers from California, spent that summer at our mission in Fort Yukon. They volunteered to help with fire fighting. Because they were willing to let the firefighters use the Home Mission Board truck from the mission when the fires became fierce in the area, the fire crew returned the favor when the Porcupine River campsite was threatened. They bulldozed a circle around the camp, cutting a wide swath so that the fires would not leap over; the young people will still have their trees when they arrive at camp this year.

*   *   *

Connie Thomas, the talented and consecrated daughter of John and Callie Thomas, worked hard the summer of 1958 in order to attain the Queen step in G.A. and be ready for the coronation scheduled for August 31. Her father had resigned the pastorate of Calvary Baptist Church of Fairbanks in order to succeed Dick Miller as missionary at Kotzebue. The family planned to move to the new mission field the first part of September.

Connie was thirteen that summer, and it was a trying time for her. She was an excellent student—always making top grades—and had a personality that had won her many friends, but she was having an inner struggle, asking herself, "Do I remain the obedient child and do what my parents expect, or do I rebel against having to go off to the wilds and leave my friends and miss out on everything I've looked forward to?"

Everything seemed to be going wrong. When her friend, Deoley Shofner, had arrived back in Fairbanks with a short haircut, Connie decided to have her beautiful, long hair cut too. Her mother took her to a beauty shop, and the operator literally whacked it off. Connie was just crushed; she cried and cried. Mrs. Shofner had gone with her back to the beauty shop to have it styled so that it looked nice, but the experience had not been a pleasant one. Connie wanted to lose some weight so her coronation formal would look nice on her, so without making a sensible plan of dieting, she had quit eating properly. Her parents knew she was losing some weight, but didn't think anything about it at the time. But worst of all, Connie did not want to go to Kotzebue, and she felt tied in knots just thinking about it.

John had planned a goat hunt before they moved, and Connie had been eagerly anticipating going with him. She had gone on many hunts before, even during the winter, and because she was such a good sport and could keep up with him, John enjoyed having her accompany him. Her four younger brothers, aged two through ten, still weren't old enough to go on the longer hunts, but Connie's friend, Deoley, and her parents, Nuell and Goldie Shofner, planned to go on the goat hunt.

Deoley, now Mrs. Dee Johnson, Western Airlines sales representative in Anchorage and member of Faith Baptist Church, told the following story of the hunt:

> We had planned on doing several hunts on this trip, so Callie and the younger children had stayed in Fairbanks. John Thomas, Connie, and their oldest boy, John Charles—with my parents and me and my little brother, who was only four, made up the party. We had driven in two cars down to Kenai Lake. There were several lodges there at the lake's edge, so Mother, John Charles, and my little brother stayed in a lodge while the rest of us went on the first hunt. We had planned to get back and let me stay with my brother while the others went on the next hunt.
>
> After we got all our gear together, the bush pilot had to make three trips to get it all up to the area where we wanted to hunt. We took off from the lake, flew over a glacier at its end, then off to the side of the glacier where there was a little valley with a lake in it and mountains on both sides that were good for goat hunting. At the end of the valley two little slits revealed two more glaciers perched up above us; they fed the lake we landed on up there. Another man from the Lower 48 had joined us; I don't remember his name. We set up camp at the edge of the lake and were eager to start out the next day, the first day of hunting season.
>
> When morning came, Daddy and I decided to go up the moun-

tain at one place, and John, Connie, and the other hunter went up
at another point. Daddy and I beat them to the top. Daddy had
served in Germany during World War II and had a great deal of
mountain climbing experience, so he could figure out the best ways
to go up. The incline was so steep that our original plan for me to
carry the gun while Daddy carried the pack didn't last long. Pretty
soon he had both the pack and the gun, and I just barely got up the
mountain. We saw the others a few times during the day.

Though Daddy dearly wanted to get a goat, he made sure that
I had the first chance at one, so I got my goat about noon. After he
skinned it out, he left me with the meat in an open, level, grassy
place where no animals would be likely to bother me, and I took
a nap that afternoon while Daddy went back out looking for another
goat. He didn't find one. We thought we were starting back in plenty
of time to reach camp before dark, but we hadn't been able to judge
the mountain properly, so by the time we finally got back, it had
been dark for about an hour and a half. We had expected to have
everyone ask what took us so long, but when we got there, John
and Connie still hadn't come in. The other hunter was there. He
had separated from them and had been in about thirty minutes.

Daddy fixed us some supper and waited around a while and
when they still didn't show up, he fired off his gun a couple of times,
and we thought we heard them shooting back. As I recall, John said
later that he heard Daddy's shots and shot back.

They had gone on over the top to the other side of the mountain
we climbed to get their goat. They had also killed one, but John
knew that they couldn't take it back to camp by dark because the
mountain was too steep with too many slides, and had decided not
to take the risk. They had their rain gear along, so he found a little
nook and they had fitted themselves into it and wrapped the goat
skin around them to help keep themselves warm. It rained a little
during the night, but when they started out the next morning as soon
as it began to get light, the weather was pretty good. John knew
we would be frantic because they hadn't shown up, but they had
eaten some K-rations, so were in good spirits as they set out. Just
as they reached the top of the mountain and started down the other
side, the weather began to close in on them. Actually, a willawaw,
a freak, sudden storm that strikes without warning, had hit. The
weather kept getting worse until John had to leave the goat meat
that he had been trying to pack out on his back.

He said that Connie was following along behind him. The wind
kept getting stronger and made it exceptionally cold because of the
sleety rain. They had begun to get wet, but still weren't too un-
comfortable, and he hadn't realized how tired Connie was until he
made a turn and she didn't make it with him. He noticed immediately that she didn't turn, so he turned around and called her.
That seemed to wake her up, so she just stepped in right behind
him again until they came to a place where they had to sit down and

slide down a slick place. When they got to the bottom of the slide, Connie couldn't get up again.

He carried her for a long way, but about two-thirds of the way down, he couldn't carry her any further, and she wasn't able to go on. About that time Daddy found them. He and the other hunter had gotten up that morning and started looking for them. It was such a big mountain with so much area to cover that they had walked for hours and still not nearly covered it when the other hunter got sick and had to come back to camp about mid-morning. Because of the cold rain, Daddy wouldn't even let me get out of my sleeping bag. Before long everything in camp was soaked. The water had even blown into the plastic cover around my sleeping bag and was sloshing around inside.

Daddy found John and Connie about the middle of the afternoon. Connie had collapsed shortly before he reached them. John had been doing all he could for her and was trying to slide her slowly down the mountain without hurting her, so he was almost in a state of collapse himself. Because of the severity of the storm, Daddy was almost dead on his feet by the time he got to them. The other hunter had gone back out to search again, and when Daddy spotted him, he shot to get his attention. Even though he was quite ill, the hunter went on up to where they were, so everyone was there except me. By that time John had rested long enough to get a second wind, and he was the only one capable of trying to get back to camp. He came down, and when I first heard him coming, I got out of the sleeping bag and ran a few steps toward him. My first thought, when I saw him coming back without Connie or Daddy, was that something had happened to Daddy. I cried out, "Have you seen Daddy?"

He shook his head "Yes," but was too exhausted to say anything but "Connie's bad." Then he gasped, "Take sleeping bag up there." I grabbed up the first one at hand, but it was too big for me to carry, so he made a motion with his hand to the one that I should take. He sat there with his head drooping down, without being able to say anything more.

By the time I got up to the place where he had pointed, Daddy could see me coming and direct me on up to where they were. I was completely soaked through when I reached them. The first thing Daddy did was to strip Connie's wet clothes off and put her in the sleeping bag. He and the other man kept trying to rub her arms to get some circulation started so she would warm up, but she didn't have enough body heat left to warm up any at all. Daddy had me to take off my wet clothes and get into the bag with her. She moaned a few times, but never did make any real response to my questions.

I told Daddy how bad John was, so he started back down because he knew they couldn't stay out there without sleeping bags that night, and it had begun to get dark. Daddy was tired out when he got down to camp, and he and John were both trying to rest up enough so they could take the bags up in order to stay with Connie. Connie wasn't doing anything, so I became frightened and begged the other man to go toward camp to see why they hadn't come back. Because he wasn't able to do anything for us, he did start back and got there just as John started up to us. After John got back up, he checked Connie before getting into his sleeping bag and discovered that she wasn't breathing, so he tried to give her artificial respiration. He couldn't do much because he knew she would freeze if he took her out of the bag. He decided that maybe I could do it easier. I had never done it before, but he told me how. It was a one person bag, and I was behind and down so that the top of my head came about to her shoulder, but I did the best I could. I have no idea how long we worked; time seemed endless at that point, but finally John made the decision to quit. He offered me his sleeping bag, but I couldn't see making the change and taking his bag, so I stayed with Connie. I heard him praying after that. I don't remember the words, but all the emotion of a father who had lost his precious daughter was in his voice.

As soon as daylight came, I got back into my clothes and went down to tell Daddy. Even though he had gone through the war and had seen many people killed in different ways, he found this hard to accept. He said later that when he first found them on the mountain, he knew it was inevitable, but his mind refused to comprehend it. He and the other man went back up to John. They closed up the bag and dragged Connie's body almost back to camp, but since they were all so tired that the three of them together couldn't get her over a little stream, they had to leave her there that night.

The next morning we could hear the bush pilot circling. About noon the clouds opened up enough for him to land. He yelled for us to leave everything, that he'd be lucky to get us out without worrying about any belongings. He was struck completely numb when we told him all that had happened.

Daddy put John and me on the first flight. We had to take off our coats to save the extra weight. When we landed, the pilot pushed us out of the plane and took right back off to go for the others. Daddy and the hunter had managed to get Connie's body over to the place where the plane would land, so on the next trip the pilot was able to bring them and her body. Daddy said that as they were flying out of the valley, he could see the clouds closing in behind them; it was really by God's grace that any of us got out. The storm was located only on that one mountain and remained so long that it was about six weeks later that the wildlife service was able to go in to get our equipment out. They even climbed up and got all the goat meat and skins we had left high on the peak.

When the plane landed the second time, we had already told the hunter's wife what was wrong, so she had called the police and ambulance. John had just sat down inside the cabin and wouldn't move. I kept asking him if he wanted anything, but he couldn't even hear me. I even shook him to try to snap him out of it and get his attention. When Daddy came in, he was too tired to even reach down to untie his boot laces. I asked him if I could do anything for him, and I remember his asking me if I would mind taking off his boots for him.

I got them unlaced, then had to cut the socks off. I'll never forget how his feet looked—completely white and horribly wrinkled. The police were afraid that both John and Daddy were on the verge of a heart attack, if they hadn't already had one. The ambulance hadn't shown up yet, so they borrowed some quilts and put both of them in the back of the police station wagon to get them on to the hospital. Years afterwards Daddy said that the ride was the most harrowing thing imaginable, swaying around those curves on the Seward Highway with the sirens shrieking. The doctor kept them both in the hospital in Seward for three days. I didn't even get a cold from all the exposure.

A family who went to the Baptist church in Seward had an apartment in their basement, and they took us in while Mother and I were waiting for Daddy to get out of the hospital. A man in Fairbanks who had previously lived with the Thomases drove Callie down to Seward. She arrived while I was having my first long sleep, and when I woke up, I thought, "What will Connie's mother feel when I walk in, one of the two girls on the trip; won't she resent the fact that her daughter didn't make it and I did?" I went into the room where she was sitting in a chair. She just reached out both her arms to me and gathered me in and hugged me close to her. I remember she said, "I'm glad you're here."

I thought, "No more tremendous woman could ever live." Later on she told me that she was glad I had been with Connie. I don't know whether as a mother I could ever have that much of a Christian attitude or not. She's always made me feel like a daughter ever since. She and John have kept track of me, and always let me know that they have cared about my troubles. I know they're good Christians.

When we got back to Fairbanks, crowds of people from the church were waiting at both our houses—we lived just a block down the street from the Thomases. Connie's funeral was at the Native Baptist Church. Many of their friends came up from Anchorage. L. A. Watson came to preach the funeral and Roy Moore helped officiate. Before Mother and I had come up to Fairbanks that summer, Callie had written saying that Connie was to be crowned Queen in the G.A. coronation and asking if Mother could find her a white formal in Anchorage. I hadn't planned to be in the G.A. ceremony, and since I had a white formal, Mother just put it in the suitcase for Connie to wear.

The funeral service was planned around the coronation that was to have taken place just five days later. All that summer Connie had worked hard and made sure she didn't miss a single G.A. meeting.

I wasn't that interested, so I would ride along with her to the church and sit with her while she memorized the material. She knew everything word for word, and I know how proud John was of her for carrying through with it. Some other friends of hers who were to have been in the coronation took part in the funeral. One was Carleta Smith. She had already passed the Queen step, and I remember she recited Proverbs 31, the passage that Connie had planned to give at the coronation. The girls were dressed in the white formals they had gotten to wear for the G.A. ceremony. The dress Mother had brought for Connie to wear had taken on a little ivory tinge that made it clash with the white satin in the casket, so some church members went to town and found another dress for her, and I wore the one she had intended to wear.

Each of us carried a long-stemmed red rose, and Connie had a bunch of red roses in her hands. Her crown had already been secured, and it was placed in the casket on the pillow beside her. The sermon was on the theme of life's greatest crowning glory—that being called home to heaven was the greatest honor of any person's life; even though it was wonderful for a girl to work hard and receive the G.A. Queen's crown, still the reward Connie had received was far more to be desired than any on earth.

I remember suddenly starting to cry, and that I couldn't stop until my mother came and held onto me. Although I never again felt such a rush of grief as at that moment, it was years before I could talk about Connie or the hunt without crying. I always felt as if God had a reason for my coming to Alaska. I told Mother when Connie died that I knew it had something to do with God's plan for me, but I didn't know what. I still can't understand why she was taken and I was left, but I felt God working in my life at that time.

❊   ❊   ❊

Mike Brown of Clyde, North Carolina, and his wife Virgie of Statesville, North Carolina, were assigned to replace Norman and Gunita Harrell in August 1967. They lived in Kobuk and also carried on the mission work in Shungnak.

In October as Mike was returning to Kobuk by boat, the motor froze when he was about half-way home. He started walking through the sub-zero darkness of the Arctic night, but because he was afraid to get out of sight of the river he stumbled and fell into its icy waters.

After making his way back to the top of the river bank, Mike discovered an unoccupied cabin that contained a tarpaulin and one solitary match. He did not find the match until daybreak, late the next morning.

The first thing he did was to slip out of his frozen clothes and wrap himself up in the tarpaulin. "Moisture from my breath actually froze on the inside of the tarp," he reported in a letter to the Home Mission Board. "I needed to get back to Kobuk before nightfall because the river was freezing. I needed to be there for a new Christians' class the next evening." He was so exhausted from unloading lumber for a meat shed that he fell asleep in spite of the severe cold.

Coming down stream he had stopped to cut down a pine tree to use to make new oars for the boat. Because his power saw was too dull, he chopped the tree down with an axe. "This took longer than I had planned," Mike said, "and that is when the motor froze up. I used up all my energy trying to get it going again. Then I poled the boat across the river and started walking. Autumn floods had eaten out the bank in some places, so I had a difficult time finding my way without sliding down into the water."

At one point he used up all his matches on the damp, frozen drift wood, trying to start a fire, but then decided that the best thing to do was just keep moving forward. Once, lying in the snow where he had fallen, he heard the sound of an electric motor and thought he must be getting near Kobuk. The river was carrying the sound, however. Kobuk was still five miles away.

When he found the one remaining match the next morning, he carefully gathered scraps of old newspaper and paper bags from the cabin into a heap, and nursed the flame along until the fire was blazing high enough to catch a few pieces of wood. Then he held his clothing and even his feet in the flames to thaw. "My feet were so cold that when I stuck them into the fire, I couldn't feel the heat. I kept pulling them in and out so I wouldn't burn them.

At nine A.M. he walked into Kobuk in time for the class he was to teach.

One night that winter Virgie visited the Wood's house. Their baby lay sick with a fever of 105 degrees. Virgie washed the child with ice water to try to bring down the fever, and after midnight it dropped to 102 degrees. The child had a convulsive kind of shaking periodically, but seemed so much improved that Virgie went home about 3:30 A.M., thinking she was better.

The family called for Virgie again early the next morning and asked her to accompany the little girl on a charter flight to Kotzebue Hospital. Virgie did this and remained with her until she died from meningitis, then travelled back home with the body.

In cold weather the Eskimos are in no hurry to bury their dead. An older sister in the family was away from home attending high school. She was notified and flown home, but several days passed because a plane comes to the village only every third day in good weather. The grave was hard to dig because the ground was frozen. The family discarded the hospital casket of plywood and built a new one of twelve by two inch lumber. The women made a new parka and mukluks and knitted new mittens for the body of the child.

The funeral service was held on a Saturday. Because darkness comes so early, they waited until Sunday to travel to the grave on snow machines. They first set up a tent on the site, then while the women cooked, the men cut trees and prepared the grave, using the trees to build a bonfire for warmth. Before the burial, everyone ate, then they gathered around the grave for the singing of a song, Scripture reading, and prayer.

But this sad story had a brighter side. In the revival one month later, the parents and three brothers and sisters of the deceased child professed faith in Christ.

9

". . . I Sought for a Man . . ."

Ezekiel 22:30

From *Minutes of the Tenth Annual Session of the Alaska Baptist Convention,* meeting in Valdez, Alaska, August 23-25, 1955.

The Missions Committee Report was brought by B. I. Carpenter, chairman of that committee, and recommended that L. A. Watson be called as Superintendent of Missions in Alaska, under the terms suggested by the Home Mission Board, and that the Missions Committee be authorized to work out a program of activity with the Superintendent of Missions, such programs to be approved by the Executive Board of the Alaska Baptist Convention.

Motion by James Dotson, supported by John Denton, that the Missions Committee report be adopted. MOTION CARRIED UNANIMOUSLY.

When L. A. Watson came to Alaska, he had been appointed superintendent of Southern Baptist mission work in Alaska by the Home Mission Board and jointly called by the Alaska Baptist Convention to serve as their executive secretary-treasurer. He had been working with the states of Colorado, Nebraska, Wyoming, Montana, North and South Dakota, leading them into forming their own convention. When that convention was organized in November 1955, he informed them at the last session of his decision to come to Alaska. He was the Alaska convention's first paid executive secretary.

Watson was born in Arkansas, but grew up in Oklahoma, where he pastored, graduated from Oklahoma Baptist University, and served as state missionary. He became superintendent of rural missions for the Texas Baptist Convention; from there he went to California to pastor the Truett Memorial Baptist Church of Long Beach. He was moderator of the Los Angeles Baptist Association, vice-president of the state convention, and instructor in the California Baptist College. From California, he went to Arizona to superintend the mission and stewardship work.

When Baptist work opened in Colorado and Wyoming, he went there as a superintendent of missions for the Arizona Southern Baptist Convention and developed that territory into a state convention. He had two churches to begin with. The convention was organized with ninety-two churches, fifty-six of which he personally started.

His wife, Evelyn Brooks Watson, had led the W.M.U. work of the Colorado convention. Their two grown children remained in the States; a daughter, Martha Jean, then eleven, accompanied them to Alaska.

When L. A. Watson arrived in Alaska, he began writing a feature in *The Alaska Baptist Messenger* called "Under the North Star." The following account came from his first column:

On January 2, 1956, our alarm rang at 5 A.M., and we all began to arise and dress. Every member of the family, including Larry, our grandson, was up and soon settled around the breakfast table where the meal was eaten but not particularly relished because just as soon as we were finished, the family was to be separated indefinitely. Each one kept out of sight of the others in order to hide his emotions. Don, the married son, scampered back to bed to cover up in the dark. Gayle tried to stay up until he told his daddy goodbye, and Mariette, our daughter-in-law, was left sitting in the living room feeding Larry his early morning bottle. She, poor girl, was stuck and had to weep openly as we told Larry and her goodbye.

The motor had warmed up while we were getting the last of the packing done. We checked the mileage and rolled out of the driveway, hoping for good weather all the way from Denver to Anchorage. Not much was said for a little while; we knew, if we did talk, we might turn around and go back. . . .

By the fifth day we were far enough north that we had to turn our headlights on at 3 P.M. and keep them on until 9 A.M. The weather grew much colder and I thought something was happening to the car. The brakes seemed to be sticking. We could barely make it up some of the hills. Though it was late that night when we reached Customs on the Canadian border, I inquired as to where I might secure help. The mechanic of a garage about five miles further on greased the front end of the car with airplane grease and changed the timing to suit the cold climate. He said we had come through a place 57 degrees below zero.

The next morning we watched an old trapper take off with his dog sled to carry provisions to his cabin. We had hoped to reach Anchorage by night, but we hit an area where the temperature dropped to 67 below zero, and since gas freezes at 60 below, I had to keep pumping the foot-feed in order to keep the lines from closing up. Before we reached Alaskan Customs I could hardly turn the wheels. I asked the man at the customs station what to do, and an old trapper sitting nearby said, "We put up and don't go any-where." We were told that if we stopped very long we wouldn't be able to start again, so we moved on, and in about twenty miles the temperature rose ten degrees. Leaving the motor running when we stopped for lunch warmed the steering column enough to give us easier driving when we started on again.

We encountered such a strong wind as we came down the moun-tains that we were forced to stop at Palmer, Alaska. We drove into a service station to inquire about lodging, but the wind was blowing too hard to get the car serviced. My wife was unable to stand up under the force of the wind as she got out of the car, and it was some time before she, by holding fast to the car door, could draw herself up to her feet. We dared not attempt to get any luggage out of the car.

The next morning everything was quiet when we awoke. The sun came up by mid-morning, and we soon reached our long-dreamed of destination to take our place under the North Star to do our bit to make up for the cold by contributing our lives and service to making a warm Christian fellowship.

Feeling the need to get first hand information regarding the work in Alaska, Dr. G. Frank Garrison, Associate Executive Secre-tary of the Home Mission Board, and Dr. S. F. Dowis, Secretary of Missions for the Board, made a trip up here, and L. A. Watson took them on a tour into the native villages up beyond the Arctic Circle. They went first to Fort Yukon where a lot had been pur-chased on which to erect a new building. The Pacific hut where the mission had been meeting had burned to the ground. The hut in which Crauns, the missionaries, lived had been moved from the old location onto the new lot, leaving volcano ash about "shoe-mouth deep" all over the old site. "I suppose Dr. Garrison had not been off the sidewalk in twenty years, so he was siddling about, spraddle-legged, trying to keep his shoes from getting dusty," re-lated Watson. "Finally, he wanted a drink of water and asked if he might have one. Missionary Craun went over to a barrel, dipped some water out with a stewer, then poured it in a glass for him."

While he was getting the water, Dr. Garrison asked, "Don't they have running water here?"

Watson answered, "Yes, they just run down to the river and get it and run back again."

One thing Dr. Garrison didn't know was that if he had looked into the barrel, he could have seen ice worms on its side. When they had put ice out of the river into the barrel, they had gotten some ice worms along with it, and the worms had survived in the barrel.

The men flew from Fort Yukon back to Fairbanks, then on to Nome and Kotzebue where they "bushed out" on a chartered plane to Kiana, Selawik, and Kobuk village. When they reached Selawik, they landed on the river that runs through the middle of town because the planes have pontoons during the summer months. They had to climb a slick, muskeg bank to get up to the mission building. As they were walking around, Dr. Garrison didn't seem very impressed with anything he saw. Miss Sherard was preparing to leave on her four months vacation to do more school work. Watson suggested to Dr. Garrison that he and his wife might come to Selawik and live a good, quiet life while Valeria was gone. Garrison indicated without hesitation that it wasn't his calling to serve there, and as far as he was concerned they could just transport all the people out of there to some other place where their spiritual needs could be more easily taken care of.

In Kobuk they were met by Charlie Sheldon whose father had been one of the first reindeer herders in the Arctic. Charlie had not gone to school, but his brother had been sent to school at Mt. Edgecumbe. When he finished with his textbooks, the brother had sent them home to Charlie, and Charlie learned to read and had educated himself. He had found a Bible somewhere and in reading it, had found Christ. He wanted to be baptized and began to inquire how he could be baptized "like Jesus." Finally, one year a school teacher who was doing some prospecting came through Kobuk and told Charlie that there was a preacher in Fairbanks "who baptizes like you want," and he gave Charlie the name of Dick Miller. Charlie wrote to Dick and the Native Baptist Church sent Dick over to see him. He had to fly five hundred miles into Kotzebue, then three hundred more in a bush plane to get to Kobuk. He was convinced that Charlie had found the Lord, but couldn't baptize him then because ice was four or five feet deep on the Kobuk River. He promised Charlie to come back and baptize him the next summer. He presented Charlie's name to the Native Baptist Church and the church approved him as a candidate. When he went back and baptized Charlie the next summer,

Charlie was the first Eskimo to be baptized by Baptists beyond the Arctic Circle.

After looking around in the Kobuk trading post a while, Watson suggested to Dr. Dowis that he take Dr. Garrison over to meet Charlie's mother, who was then about ninety years old, while Watson went over to get some pictures of the mission building. Watson had been in the cabin before and knew what to expect. They had a storm shed at the front of the entrance that visitors had to go through to get into the main cabin. When they killed game, they put it out in this shed to cure properly. It gave off a terrible aroma.

"When Dr. Dowis opened the door and pushed Dr. Garrison in and he got a whiff, he started backing out like a horse with the blind staggers," reported Andie Watson. "He wouldn't go in to meet the old mother, so they had to bring her out to him."

After Charlie Sheldon was saved, he would take his Bible and go from cabin to cabin, reading it to the families in English and interpreting it into the Kobuk dialect. Soon after Andie Watson arrived in Alaska, he received a request to preach a revival in Kobuk. He went in December when the days were very short. The sun came up at 11:30 A.M. and set at 12:30 P.M. He remembered making the trip in an old Norseman plane which had no heat. "We all got so cold going over there, we kept rubbing our legs and knees to keep the circulation going. When we arrived, it was so cold I sat by the fire and baked my knees, and the bones kept on aching even after they thawed out," he told his traveling companions.

When visitors came into the village, they usually stayed at the trading post. An extra cot was kept in there, so Watson had planned to sleep on it during the revival. When he arrived, he found that a traveling nurse had beaten him to the cot. He didn't know what he was going to do for a place to stay, but some of the villagers told him of an eighteen-year-old girl who lived in a cabin alone while her parents were some seventy miles up river camping and trapping that winter. He persuaded her to sleep with the nurse on the cot in the trading post so he and Dick Miller would have a place to sleep. The whole week it didn't warm up more than minus fifty. The Yukon stove, half an oil drum made into a stove, would only hold enough fuel for two and a half hours, which meant he had to get up that often to replenish the fire. He finally got so sleepy that one night he decided to just sleep it out and get up and start the fire again the next morning. The hardest thing about the experience was sticking his bare feet into his shoes when they were fifty-four below zero.

The Lord blessed the revival. People from Shungnak, fifteen miles down river, came and camped during the revival. Everybody in the village wanted to come. One night everyone was there except one old woman who was ill and two others who stayed in her cabin to keep the fire going for her. Watson described it:

> I had to preach through an interpreter. I used Charlie as my interpreter, except I called him my interrupter. I'd preach about five minutes, then he'd interpret for ten minutes. I didn't get much preaching done through him. But the Lord blessed. The people had heard Charlie read the Bible, and they were receptive to the Word. One night I was preaching without an interpreter. An old man was there who had attended every service. He was deaf; he couldn't hear the Eskimo language; he couldn't understand the English language; and he couldn't read lips. He was in a desperate way, and my heart got so burdened for him that I prayed God to break through the sound barrier and the language barrier and reach that man's heart. When I gave the invitation that night, the old man stepped out and came forward, telling Charlie that he wanted to be saved. He was nearly eighty years old and didn't live long after that. This goes to show how the Holy Spirit can work. Over half of the village made professions of faith during that time.

The people from Shungnak wanted to have services, so Watson and Dick Miller got two Eskimo dog mushers to take them down on a dogsled. The two of them plus Dick's accordian made quite a sled load. The mushers traveled only in the day time, and the days were so short that they had to "really go right along." Watson put all his clothes on and borrowed some wolfskin leggings to wear. He got two snowshoe rabbit skins to put over his socks, then put on some air force fleece-lined boots. He also wore a wolfskin parka and mittens, then he crawled down into the sled and wrapped two sleeping bags around him to try to survive the trip.

It took an hour and forty-five minutes to get to Shungnak, so it was dark by the time they arrived. Watson's feet had begun to get cold, so he went on into the building while the dogs were unhooked. He told the driver he had learned why Eskimos have short noses. "If they were as long as mine, they would all have frozen off long ago."

When he got to the trading post and peeled off his wraps, all the school children began coming in to "see the white man." They had white school teachers, but they're interested in every white person who comes there. "They came ganging in and looked at me shyly, but I had a few tricks for them, and then I sang a few choruses for them and got them to singing. After a while I told them to go tell their families to come because we were going to have church services. They started out and put what we call the 'mukluk telegraph' into operation, running from cabin to cabin to pass on news. We had forty-five people there that night. Dick played his accordian and I preached; this was the first Baptist service ever held in that community."

While at Kobuk, Dick and Andie took their meals with Charlie Sheldon. He was married to a white woman who was a nurse, but who died later of an ulcerated stomach. All Eskimos like hot cakes, so they had them every morning. Andie reported:

> We had to get by on two meals a day because that's the way they ate. I would really fill up on hot cakes in the morning because I didn't know what we might have at the next meal. We ate roast beaver, which was not too bad. Then we had fish, which they boiled, intestines, eyes, and all. I just couldn't eat that, so they gave me something else almost as bad—canned Spam. One day Charlie had gone to his fish trap in the river; they catch tom cod and stack them and have them for the dogs to eat. They take the liver out of them, and the eggs because they spawn in the winter, mix them together and cook them for their vitamins. Something had been stealing Charlie's fish so he had set a trap. When he went down that morning, he had a lynx caught in it. He beat the lynx to death with a pole and brought it in. I took pictures of it, then Charlie skinned it out. The pelt was worth about ten dollars. After he got it skinned, he began to dress it out, so I asked him what he was going to do with it and he told me "eat it."

Mrs. Watson got a letter from Andie written that day in which he told her, "We ate the beaver yesterday and we're going to eat the cat tomorrow."

A cheechako sometimes has a hard time in Alaska.

One year when Watson was in Kobuk during caribou season, the hunters from the village were bringing in caribou and "stacking them like cord wood." One man had killed forty-five. The hunters just cut the racks off, loaded them on the dog sleds, and brought them in. Everybody in the village would share and share alike—in the skinning, cleaning, and meat. He said that when they got in the Cessna 180 to fly from Kobuk to Kotzebue, they flew for almost two hundred miles without being out of sight of the caribou herd, which gives some idea of the vastness of a herd believed to number well over a million animals. When a herd swept down over an area eating the muskeg and moss, it would take from twenty to thirty years for it to grow back again because of the short growing season in the Arctic.

Natives from all over Alaska came into the Anchorage Native Hospital for treatment. Often they had tuberculosis, which meant they would stay for several months convalescing. They would look out the window of their room and see the people coming and going from the Native Baptist Mission across the street. They got to where they would spot the members of the mission who missed the meetings and would ask about them. As soon as the patients were able to be out of the hospital they would attend services, and many were saved and went back to their villages carrying the gospel with them. Afterwards there would always be an open door in those villages when Baptist leaders would go to try to have services.

L. A. Watson remembered that when Dick Miller felt the time had come to leave Kotzebue, they had planned to survey Unalakleet and other villages on the lower Yukon and Kuskokwim. Mike McKay, missionary at the Anchorage Native Mission, asked them to look up a family in Unalakleet named Ivanoff. Mrs. Ivanoff had been in the hospital and had made a profession of faith at the mission. They found the Ivanoff house, one of the few in the village with screens on the door, but when Mrs. Ivanoff came to answer their knock, she didn't seem pleased to see white men. Then Watson said, "We are friends of Brother Mike McKay down in Anchorage, and he wanted us to call on you"; she quickly unlatched the door and urged them to come in. Ivanoffs were a very refined Eskimo family. The first thing she asked was if they were going to start a Baptist church in her village. She offered to let the church meet in her house, and said her daughter would play the piano. After surveying, Miller decided that was not the place to begin new work.

Many years passed, but each time Watson's plane had to lay over in Unalakleet, he visited the Ivanoffs, and she always asked when Baptists would start a church. One time he was waiting for a plane in Nome, when a native lady came up and spoke to him. He returned the greeting without recognizing her; then she asked, "Are you on your way to start a Baptist church in Unalakleet?" He replied, "What are you doing here, Mrs. Ivanoff?"

She said, "I've been over to court. My nephew has been arrested, and his trial is being held in Nome. If we had had a Baptist church in Unalakleet, we wouldn't have to be over here at court today."

Watson related, "In my heart I knew she was so right." One of the heartaches for L. A. Watson was having to leave Alaska without getting work started in Unalakleet for Mrs. Ivanoff and her family and the many others there who need the gospel.

While serving Alaska as executive secretary, L. A. Watson traveled constantly and extensively over the territory, and every trip proved to be an adventure. Many trips were in response to urgent calls which arose up in the Arctic. In May 1960 he flew into Kotzebue and found the John Thomas family living in the dark basement of our Baptist church there, hoping and praying that somehow they might get above ground before another dark, long winter rolled around. The next day Thomas and Watson took off in the Home Mission Board's Tri-Pacer to visit Valeria Sherard in Kiana. Since the house where she lived was not insulated, when the weather was cold and windy, it was impossible to warm it up. The snow was wet and sticky when they landed in Kiana, and the Wien bush plane was already grounded there. When they were ready to take off, they were able to get their plane airborne only after a long drag on the snow.

They flew in to Kobuk and held services there the next day, then tried to land at Shungnak where a chapel was to be built during the summer. They were unable to land the plane because of crosswinds. After several attempts, they went back to Kobuk. A lady met them and said a man was taking off for Shungnak by dog team, so Thomas got on the sled, went to Shungnak and got Charlie Sheldon to come back with him. One of the ladies brought Watson some caribou steak, but he didn't have any shortening or seasoning or anything to eat with it. He stuck it in a skillet and put it in the fuel drum oven, hoping for the best. When he awoke from a nap, the steaks were just right. He found that another lady had baked bread that day, so he got a loaf and a can of

Carnation milk from her, and had the "most delightful dinner" he can ever remember.

The next day they flew to Selawik, and after making several passes, they were pointed to a place beyond the village where the wind had blown away the snow, and they made the best landing of the whole trip. Watson wrote, "I was elated over the new living quarters which Willie Johnson erected last summer. He is one of the most talented Eskimos it has been my privilege to know." After dinner with the Johnsons, they took off for Kiana where they were to pick up a passenger. When they started down to land on the river, they saw that the Wien plane was still grounded. They were caught in such a bad white-out that they couldn't tell what ground conditions were like until they were too close to the snow to go back up. About the time Watson was hoping that Thomas would give it the gas and fly on to Kotzebue, the skiis hit the snow; it balled up, and he pulled back on the stick until they came to a screeching halt. When they stepped out of the stalled plane, they found themselves in fresh snow kneedeep on top of the river ice. The Eskimos rushed out to the plane, and together they tromped down the snow, cleaned off the skiis, and pushed the plane on up to the front of the village. After dinner, Thomas wanted to collect their passenger and take off, but Watson reminded him that they had gotten stuck with the two of them, and it was pretty sure they could not make it with three. Thomas agreed, and they found a place to sleep with an old Russian gentleman who had lived in that village for more than fifty years. Thomas went on over to start the fire at the mission because whenever a missionary comes to one of the villages, regardless of what night it is, the natives expect to have services.

That night a wind came up and blew some of the snow off and crusted over the rest so that they could take off the next morning. After resting a while in Kotzebue, they decided to fly to Deering across Kotzebue Sound. This was an old mining town. The people there are crossbred with Russians and other Anglos. They had asked for Baptists to open work, so the object of the trip was to find a meeting place so that Thomas could begin services. They flew over the ice in the sound both ways. Watson stated, "If you have never flown over a frozen ocean, I can tell you that it gives you a peculiar feeling, especially when six polar bear hunters were lost north of Kotzebue and their planes had gone through the ice and the men were still being searched for. Two of them walked and crawled for sixty-four miles across the ice in order to reach a village."

After spending the night in Kotzebue, Watson was able to make plane connections and get back to Anchorage the next day. "It was really good to get home and crawl out of the heavy winter clothes and get into the first bathtub since leaving for that long Arctic jump." However, the worries of an executive secretary are not all over when he reaches home. Watson expressed the woes of others in his position when he went on to explain, "On top of finding a desk piled a foot deep with work, I found that a group of preachers had resigned their work for first one reason and another. Just about the time we think we are getting to the place where we do not have to worry about a group of pastors for our churches and missions, here comes a raft of resignations."

A superintendent of construction had been working later that year, trying to get living quarters erected for the Thomases. Because he had to leave the work, Watson went up to check on progress. When he arrived in Kotzebue this time, he found that John Thomas had arrived home just two days before from the hospital at Fairbanks, where he had undergone major surgery. His intestines had ruptured, possibly from a plane crash a few months before, and a seepage had caused inflammation and resulted in an abcess that required removing a section of the intestine where gangrene had set in. And to cap it off, the oldest son, John Charles, had broken his ankle, so was unable to help with the heavy work. All the work of trying to finish construction was left up to Mrs. Thomas, and she was bravely trying to carry on.

The Thomases served at Kotzebue for two more years. The day they were scheduled to move out, L. A. Watson arrived home in Anchorage at 6:00 P.M. to find glaring out at him from the headlines of the evening paper pictures and a report of a storm in Kotzebue which had washed the front street away, damaging most of the buildings along the shore drive. There pictured in the paper was our mission building, jutting out with all the earth washed out from under it. Watson hurriedly made arrangements that would allow him to stay in Kotzebue long enough to take care of whatever needed to be done and caught the 9:00 P.M. plane. When it stopped in Fairbanks, he learned from the Isaacs that Mrs. Thomas and John Charles were not expected in until the next day.

His plane was being held up or "wait listed," so he was thankful that he would get to see them at the Kotzebue airport before he moved in to stay at the mission.

When his plane arrived the next day, he dashed to the terminal building through a drenching rain, "all wound up to talk like a phonograph," only to discover that Mrs. Thomas had cancelled until Sunday afternoon. He was offered a ride by a businessman, a hardened sinner, who said, "You need to say a prayer for Kotzebue; we're just about ruined." He drove as near to the church as he could get, then Watson grabbed his suitcase and ran for the door. When he reached it, a sign read "Use other door." This door had blown off and was nailed up. The back door was swollen from so much rain that it took one on the inside and another on the outside to open it enough for him to squeeze in.

When he got inside, Mrs. Thomas said, "I knew when you saw the paper, you would be coming up." He entered amid boxes and mud just a "little less than wading deep" where friends had come and gone helping the family pack and bidding them goodbye. He was told how the waves came up between the buildings and water rose in the basement about eight inches. The furnace was out because water had gotten into the electric motor. Watson removed the motor and blower fan and dried them in the cooking range.

All their household goods were packed and the sleeping bags had already been sent to the airport; there was no food nor any utensils to cook it in.

The next day Sunday services were held in the living quarters where the furnace was going again. Just as worship service began Sunday night, a fellow next door rushed in and said, "There is another storm coming. We need to get the oil drums away from the beach." He referred to the drums which had been collected in an effort to save the houses on front street. The people were supposed to cut the ends out of the drums and fill them with gravel. The city had promised to provide gravel and backfill for areas that had washed away. Rain continued to fall all that week. More than half of the natives lost their boats. A floating fish cannery washed ashore near the church, and the villagers worked all week to free it. If it had not been there, the church would have sustained much greater damage.

Watson spent a busy week—repairing the roof, mopping and drying out the basement, hanging doors, filling more than fifty drums with gravel, cooking, and conducting services at night. He saw that the new missionaries' groceries did not get wet, and that locks were repaired on all the necessary doors.

In the fall of 1960, Mrs. Watson took their daughter Martha to Seattle for a physical checkup after she seemed to be losing the use of her right leg. It was discovered that she had sustained an attack of polio, leaving her entire right side partially paralyzed. Because she was not able to get around from class to class, Martha was unable to attend school that term, but had a tutor come to their home to instruct her. She recovered the use of her side through prayers and physiotherapy. The previous year Mrs. Watson had spent several months in hospitals. In January, during an operation at Providence Hospital, Anchorage, her heart had stopped. The doctors opened her chest and massaged her heart for two hours before it would go on its own again. After twenty days at Providence, she was transferred to Virginia Mason Hospital, Seattle, for further treatment. Because of unfavorable reaction to drugs used to keep her blood pressure up during the crucial days following the heart stoppage, skin grafting and plastic surgery on Mrs. Watson's legs became necessary. She fully recovered, but illness struck the Watsons again in 1963. At that time doctors told Andie that his stomach was so severely ulcerated that he would require extensive treatment and several months of rest. The doctors' verdict led to his resigning his position and leaving Alaska in June 1963.

When L. A. Watson resigned, Felton Griffin wrote the following tribute to him:

> God was good to Alaska Baptists to give us the services of Dr. L. A. Watson for a time. Prior to the time when he came to serve as our Executive Secretary here, our work was more like scrambled eggs than a functioning convention for the cause of Christ. We well remember the time when it was almost an impossibility to get our convention to launch a cooperative program on anything. Each church was going its own direction, and cooperation was talked about but rarely practiced in our country here in the North.
>
> This led to confusion on the part of those who had sincere desires to help us in Alaska. The Home Mission Board, as well as others, received continually conflicting reports from several sources. If they responded to one group, the other crowd was somewhat repulsed and felt left out.
>
> After the coming of L. A. Watson, the establishing of an office and some degree of a sane contact with the Home Mission Board,

our work began to take form and forge ahead with rapidity and poise. Brother Watson leaves the Alaska Baptist Convention well organized, with able staff members for various positions, and a sense of direction. It was not an easy task and took from him some of the finest and most productive years of his life. It leaves him poorer than when we found him in his health.

Brother Watson is a patient man. His relationship with pastors in Alaska has not been one of forcing his views on them, but of presenting a program and waiting until his co-workers could see the wisdom of his suggestions. His patience in the face of many rare difficulties here reveals a great faith in the Lord and in his fellow preachers.

He is one of God's most considerate men. His attitude toward others is indicative of a great soul. Never has he been anything but Christian in his relationship with the pastors of Alaska. It is doubtful that we could have found anywhere one so kindly considerate toward others.

When L. A. Watson came to Alaska, we had twenty-three churches and missions in the Territory; now we have forty-three. Under his leadership we have started the Baptist Foundation; provided for Ministerial Retirement; established a Department of Religious Education; and secured a secretary for W.M.U. work.

We all should thank God for the privilege of working with this man of God who has so unselfishly given of himself for the cause of Christ in our land.

Watson's response to the tribute was published in the next issue of the *Messenger:*

The last issue of the *Messenger*, edited by Dr. Felton Griffin, read as if it were paying tribute to SOMEBODY. I had made the statement that I wanted to edit the last issue because there might be need for a rebuttal to the May issue. After reading it, I have been humbled by the way my yokefellows in the cause of Christ expressed their feelings toward us and our service rendered. The wonderful praise heaped upon me reminded me of the Negro hired hand, who was wondering how he was getting along with his employer. One day when he went to town, he called his employer up on the phone. When Mr. Johnson answered, Sam asked if he did not need a hand to work on the farm. Mr. Johnson replied, "I have all the hand I need."

Sam asked, "Is he doin' his work all right?"

Mr. Johnson said, "Yes, he does such a good job I would not think of letting him go to hire another."

Sam was so carried away with delight he said, "Mistah Johnson, dis am Sam. I was jes callin' up to check on myself."

At the present time L. A. Watson is serving as missionary to the Indians of two associations in Oklahoma.

✿   ✿   ✿

Dr. William H. Hansen succeeded L. A. Watson, becoming the convention's second paid executive secretary. In his new job he supervised the cooperative work of the thirty-four churches and fourteen missions of the state convention and edited the *Alaska Baptist Messenger*. In September 1963 Hansen wrote in the *Messenger:*

> I've been in my new job for ten days, and it seems like a month! Just clearing up the material that had accumulated on the desk for the executive secretary was a task for Hercules! Press releases, letters, reports, requests for information, new supplies, and a profusion of Baptist papers and literary publications overwhelmed me. A piece of recent mail coming to our office was addressed to the "Alaska Baptist Mess." I claimed it.
>
> Nevertheless, I think I will enjoy this new task assigned me by the Lord and the Southern Baptists of Alaska. A challenging future lies out ahead of us. This great state can be claimed for Christ while it is still young. The prospect of it seizes me. Of course, it will not be easy because the devil doesn't give up his territory without a fight, but under the mighty hand of God it certainly is within the realm of possibility. I believe that our vigorous, determined, evangelistic pastors mean for it to become a reality. Our warm-hearted churches, too. God is going to bless us.
>
> A few weeks ago many of our churches were without pastors, and the outlook for some of the churches without leadership was dismal indeed. But the Lord has worked, and leaders have come forward. It's wonderful to be partners with the Lord.

In reply to queries about how God calls men to Alaska, Dr. Hansen delivered the following address in the chapel of Southeastern seminary in December 1965:

> First, I need to say what a call to Alaska is NOT.
>
> It is not a call to adventure, though a man must have an adventuresome spirit to like working for the Lord in Alaska. Many of the people who come to our state possess unusually aggressive traits which impel them to search out the far reaches of the earth, to push to the very frontiers of human existence. But the call to Alaska is not a call to adventure.
>
> God's call to Alaska is not a call to enjoy the fantasies which so many people associate with the state. Some imagine Alaska to be

a glamor world, charmingly possessed of long summer days and nearly non-existent night; beautiful Northern Lights and the midnight sun; the fascination of the Eskimos, with their log cabins, dog sleds, parkas, and umiats; the lustre of gold, and the lore of the cold. The Lord does not call his servants merely to enjoy these fantasies.

Nor is the call to Alaska a call to nature, though the 49th state is in fact one vast and beautiful outdoors. There are mountains in Alaska, more than you can count, from towering Mt. McKinley to a host of smaller peaks which loom large in any comparisons. If Minnesota has 10,000 lakes, Alaska must have a half million. There are glaciers—one, the Malaspina, larger than the state of Rhode Island; some, like the Mendenhall, beautiful beyond description. There are rivers and fjords which take your breath away. Alaska is a land of natural beauty, but God's call is not a call to the world of nature.

Rather, God's call is a call to follow people, Alaska's people, some already Christian, but often restive and searching. More often they are non-Christian, immoral, and godless people, because Alaska does have people who want to throw off the restraints of godly and orderly living. Sometimes they are materialistic people whose main object is to make money and make it fast. And then there are disappointed people—persons who come to Alaska because of deep personal problems, hoping to find a new lease on life in a youthful state. The call of God is the call to bring the gospel to these, the people of Alaska.

The Lord's call is a call to help people meet their problems constructively. Our state has five times as many alcoholics per capita as does the average state. Many Alaska families have marital difficulties because some come when problems develop, thinking they will move to a place where they will be together, just the two of them, on a homestead somewhere, and can resolve their difficulties. Too often they find their dreams do not come true and the wedge between them drives them further apart. In some who come to Alaska there is a moral destitution, a sad lowering of the level of human existence without the presence of God. Alaska's call is a call to work with men who have problems.

God's call is the call to pace the gospel to men who live aggressively and relentlessly at a break neck speed. Alaska's people are inordinately busy people, especially in the summer after months of cold. They work beyond human endurance and wisdom. To these we are called to place a hand on the shoulder and counsel: "Friend, slow down; think with me of the eternal; take time to be holy."

The call of God to Alaska is furthermore a call to plant churches in an already overchurched state. Even the smallest remote community has its missionaries; everyone sends missionaries to Alaska. God's call is not for more churches alone, but for strong, gospel-based churches filled with saved people which reflect not the independence of over-aggressive preacher-personalities, but the glory of Jesus Christ.

God's call to Alaska is a call to the preacher who has learned to be independent and self-sufficient in the grace of the Lord. Sometimes preachers write and say, "I would like to come if someone can pay my way." We are frank to say to these, "You'd better stay home because after you get to Alaska you won't have enough money to leave when the going gets rough."

Some would come if they could build a church while leaning on mission money, home ties, supplement programs, sponsoring churches, and the like, but many of Alaska's churches will never be built under these terms. God's call to Alaska is a call to make one's own way.

Finally, God calls men to Alaska to be strong in the Lord. It takes an inner spiritual strength to go it when you are alone in a far-off village. It takes a commitment to the task when prices are high and jobs are hard to find and the oil is running low. It takes a life yielded to the Holy Spirit to melt men who are too hard to yield themselves. And it takes a gospel purpose born in a gospel preacher who knows the why and wherefore of his message and the lostness of men who do not know Christ.

This is the call to Alaska.

The day dawned just like any other with no indication that before nightfall Alaska would be catapulted into screaming headlines.

About three o'clock that afternoon a rancher down on Narrow Cape, a long finger of land washed by the Gulf of Alaska south of Kodiak, noticed something strange. His cattle turned away from their low-lying grazing ground and began to move rapidly to higher land. The day was bright and sunny; the sky was blue and cloudless. The mountains stood serenely draped in their snowy shawls. A gentle wind was blowing in from the turquoise sea. Yet the cattle sensed something and seemed vaguely anxious.

In Anchorage, Don Wright, pastor of Trinity Baptist Church, parked his car in Penney's lot and looked on the first floor for a picture frame he needed. A clerk told him to try the furniture department on the third floor, but instead of doing so, he decided to try Woolworth's, three blocks away on Fourth Avenue.

Out at the Turnagain Children's Home Ed Knudson was sweeping snow off the roof. At the Baptist Building Louise Yarbrough and Bernice Gillespie were still working. Bernice was trying to get Louise to rush so they could go by Fourth Avenue Cleaners to get her suits. At the new National Bank of Alaska building Roger Laube was in the Trust Department on the second floor trying to finish up the day's work.

In Kodiak the SELIEF, an 86-foot scow, was tied to its slip

in the picturesque harbor at the foot of the mountains. Its hold contained $3,000 worth of Alaska king crabs ready to be unloaded at the cannery.

By Alaska standards the day was warm, about thirty-five degrees in Anchorage and Kodiak. Spring was coming. People were betting on when the ice would break up at Nenana. Breakup time is somehow symbolic to Alaskans. Winter isolation finally yields to spring's friendly persuasions.

But down underneath the earth's surface, something was happening. Just what, no one knows for sure; even the cows make unreliable seismologists. More than fifty miles down under the earth's crust a river of boiling pitchlike substance circles the iron core of the earth. Some think that the constant opposing currents of this huge river strain the earth's crust. Where the crust is weak, it may crack and Alaska is known to lie on a weak layer of crust. And at 5:35 P.M. the crust could no longer endure the strain. It let go.

Across more than six hundred miles of alabaster mountains and sparkling seas, of spruce forests and secluded coves, of towns and expanses of animal-tracked snow the earth shook and groaned as it cracked open in hundreds of places. It buckled bridges and toppled buildings; it snapped trees and heaved up highway pavements; it sheared avalanches of snow and stone from mountain tops and raised mighty waves in the ocean.

On Kodiak Island the clairvoyant cattle were safe on high ground. At the head of the bay long fissures opened and the bay rushed in. Then the ground snapped shut and spewing geysers shot skyward.

At the back of Woolworth's, Don Wright picked up a picture frame to look at just as the first waves of the quake struck the building. Tossing the frame back on the counter, he dashed for the front door, dodging customers and leaping railings and counters. Reaching the far side of the street, he grabbed the nearest parking meter for support and found himself swinging round and round the meter.

A lady nearby was struggling to hold onto two small children. On one of his swings, Don managed to grab the smaller child while the other child and his mother crawled forward until all four of them were hanging to the pole.

"Let's pray," the lady said to Don.

"And so we prayed!" Don reported. "The only difference was that she had her eyes closed, and I kept mine open. Looking toward the Anchorage Westward (a tall hotel nearby) and seeing it swaying over us, I started to run back across the street to a parking meter on the other side; then I noticed that Woolworth's was lunging out at us from that side, so I decided to just stay put."

Fourth Avenue suddenly sank several feet below the level of the parking meter where the four were clinging. When the quake stopped, Don could see that it had sunk more than twenty feet just a block away. He ran the three blocks back to his car and found that the year-old Penney's department store had been destroyed.

When the Turnagain Home began shaking, Ed dismissed it as just another quake. "We have them often in Anchorage," he said. "However, it didn't take long for me to realize that this one was different. I secured myself in a position astride the roof, determined to ride it out."

Ed stayed on top all through the harrowing experience. Several times he tried to climb down on the ladder, but it kept flopping away from the building, making it impossible for him to grab it. Warily he watched the building's two chimneys, expecting them to give way any minute. Both were partially destroyed. Coming down after the quake was over, Ed's wry comment was, "It was not an ideal place to sweat out an earthquake like that one."

Louise and Bernice were used to tremors, but this was no mere tremor. Bernice, remembering that people are often injured by flying glass during quakes, soon decided she should get farther away from the window. In so doing she fell to the floor and could not get up again. Louise then realized that she should get out of the way of the filing cabinets. Staggering around the desk, she fell to the floor, and there they sat out the next five minutes, watching the walls moving back and forth and the book shelves and file cabinets dumping their contents to the floor. Driving home afterwards, they found the foundation of their apartment house cracked and were warned to vacate it in the event of another quake. They did not take their clothes off that night nor the following day and night because they wanted to be ready to flee should it be necessary. There were more than forty tremors the next thirty-six hours, so many times they ran outside. They were without water, heat, electricity, and sewer during these next hours, and upon going to a supermarket to buy flashlight batteries, they found plywood boards, replacing glass windows and doors, a gas lantern or two providing the only illumination, and a quietness and state of shock prevailing.

Roger Laube was knocked to the floor of the bank and remained there praying during the quake. Then he ran down to the basement where men and women were screaming in the darkness and helped get them out and calmed down. Finding it impossible to get to his car or call home, he ran over to First Baptist Church and found it standing without a crack. Since it was just across the street from Penney's five-story department store which had collapsed, it had already been set up as an emergency station for the employees and customers. "We won't be giving that Easter Cantata tonight," he thought ruefully. But on Sunday morning the combined choirs sang beautifully and meaningfully the numbers that they didn't sing on Good Friday.

Philip Laube was on the bluff area of the Turnagain suburb shovelling snow. He threw a shovelfull of snow and landed on the ground in the shovel with the snow. Struggling to regain his feet, he heard the porch timbers cracking overhead and the ground opening up in front of him. His only thought was getting home, so he jumped over the moving crevasse and ran the four blocks, dodging cracks and miraculously staying on his feet all the way.

By the time Philip reached home, an eerie expanse of ruin lay behind him. The bluffs overlooking Cook Inlet had fallen away two hundred yards inland, taking with them more than one hundred houses snapped into pieces and plunged into deep gorges. The area was like a brown sea of motionless waves, peaked with pieces of homes and broken trees. Philip found his mother stuck in the basement where she had spent the five minutes of the quake on the waxed tile floor trying to dodge the piano which was rolling on casters and the desk which was also sliding. A neighbor who came over to check on their welfare was able to break in the heavy basement door, which had been bowed by the pressure of the heaved ground, and another interior door to get Irene Laube out.

On Fourth Avenue the pavement was billowing, cars bouncing,

people falling, and one whole block of stores, mostly bars, was sinking twenty feet into a huge crack of the quivering earth. The marquee of the Denali Theater dropped to the level of the sidewalk.

At the Mt. McKinley Apartments the elevator quivered and stopped near the eighth floor, then began bouncing up and down, causing Delphine Haley to scream in terror. When it stopped momentarily, Delphine squeezed through a small opening in the doors and climbed upward. She groggily made her way to the stairwell and hysterically pitched herself down each flight until she came to the landing. Looking back, she saw that the entire structure was streaked by zigzagging cracks.

In Turnagain Marjie Summers got her little brother out the front door, then her mother joined them and they started to run across the street to the ball park. Suddenly the street disappeared. They held onto two birch trees; two other trees beside them disappeared. Terrified, Marjie began to run. Her mother followed but was separated from her when she stumbled into a widening crack. Marjie and her brother pulled her mother out of the crack just as four people rushed up from the other side. Then they couldn't go on. There they were, seven people stuck on a piece of ground standing ten feet above all the ground around them and a hundred yards from solid ground. A crack split in half the spot on which they were huddled, but never widened. Half an hour passed before firemen came and helped them down from their perilous perch. Marjie's father was waiting and crying with joy because he had seen the hole where their house had stood before he learned of their position on the upheaved earth.

Dr. Caughran said, "My cold storage plant at Valdez went into the bay; my house went off the bluff into the Inlet. In those five minutes I lost a quarter of a million dollars but that meant nothing compared to seeing my kids and then my wife come up out of the crushed house onto that little toadstool of land beside it. I felt peaceful and slept well that night just knowing my family was safe."

Dr. Royce Morgan reported that an attorney friend was taking a steam bath at the time of the quake. The nameless friend said,

"I was in the nude on Main Street for two minutes, then someone handed me a towel; another man took off his shirt and handed it to me; then another gave me his coat."

Virginia Cutshall remembered that during the time of intense silence just after the quake, while she lay as one whose legs were without bones, she kept hearing the weights of the cuckoo clock hitting the wall with an erratic, irregular rhythm.

Far out in the agitated ocean a wave grew higher as it rushed toward the shaken land. At Seward, one hundred thirty miles south of Anchorage, it had to pass through a narrow passage. There it gathered momentum and raced forward like a wall of water. In eight days, Seward, a town of 1,900, was to celebrate its selection as an "All-American City" because of its economic self-improvement. At 5:44 P.M. the forty-foot wall of water rushed through Resurrection Bay, smashing over the new port, ripping boats loose from the dock, and sending everything in its path tumbling forward, including a sixty-ton locomotive which landed six blocks away.

Big fuel tanks near the dock crumbled in the onslaught, spreading oil over the waters. Suddenly, the water caught fire and a wave of flame rushed inland. Just ahead of the flames small boats, riding the crest of the tidal wave, sailed over trees thirty feet high and ended up in a pasture on the other side of the woods. Cars, dogs, and debris swept past on the waves and the whole town seemed to be afire. When the water and fire receded, families were rescued from rooftops.

In Kodiak, Bill Cuthbert, skipper of the SELIEF, was just sitting down to supper when he felt a jolt that made him think a drunken sailor had rammed into his boat. Storming out on deck, he saw masts waving madly all over the bay. Realizing at once that it was an earthquake, he turned on his radio to the emergency band. The alarm soon came: expect a tidal wave; get to high ground. But Bill Cuthbert couldn't; he had a lame engine. So leaving his boat tied to the dock, he went to the galley and waited.

The first wave wasn't bad, but the second hit with a roar and in an instant every line, every anchor, every pier, snapped and broke and the harbor became a wild maelstrom of swirling boats and debris.

Cuthbert waited for the next wave and fifty-five minutes later it hit, this time with less force but more height. Again his heavy scow was whirled around and battered its way through buildings, finally coming to rest on top of a crushed store.

State trooper Don Church, who had sounded the alarm over the marine radio, was trying to contact each of the remote villages on the island. Family by family, village by village, he called. The Martins were missing; no trace of their cattle ranch. In days to come he would fly out to check on each family. But on Good Friday he could not reach two of the villages by radio: Afognak and Ouzinkie. He dispatched fishing boats to see about them. Then he began calling fishing boats. Most replied; ominously, others didn't. The SELIEF did.

"SELIEF, SELIEF, where are you?"

"It looks," answered Cuthbert, "as though I'm in the back of the Kodiak schoolhouse five blocks from the shoreline."

Because of Church's warning, most of the village families escaped. But at Afognak, Ouzinkie, Old Harbor and Kaguyak the destruction was almost complete.

The First Baptist Church of Valdez was the only Southern Baptist church to suffer severe damage. The Home Mission Board of the Southern Baptist Convention marked "paid" on a loan it held on the church. "We are also cancelling a $10,000 gift lien contract the board has held since 1954 so the church can exchange its present site for a new one in the proposed new town site," said G. Frank Garrison of Atlanta, director of the loans division.

After the sea again became serene, the land quiet, and the roar of the wall of water receded, Alaskans began picking through the wreckage in search of the missing. The figure of known and presumed dead was astonishingly low. Perhaps it can be explained in terms of Alaska's sparse population, small towns, and low buildings. Most Alaskans think the answer was found on their knees.

RESIDENTS FLEE AS FLOOD WATERS SWEEP FAIRBANKS

Dazed disbelief was the first reaction to the rising waters of the Chena River as rains fell relentlessly in August 1967. SBC leaders in town for the Alaska Baptist Convention kept fearful vigil with fellow Fairbanksans the night of August 14. The convention, scheduled for August 14-17, did not convene.

Early in the morning of August 15 the Chena crested at nineteen feet, causing immediate evacuation of half the city's residents. Many tried to escape by car, only to stall and have to be rescued from car tops. "If we had been told the water would cover our houses, we couldn't have believed it."

Hundreds stacked tables, chests, and chairs and climbed to rooftops to await rescue. Above, blankets, dog, baby, and Grandma have been lifted up; now Mama scrambles up as ABC executive secretary E. W. Hunke, Jr., watches from where he is stranded.

All Eielson AFB helicopters aided in rescue operations. They provided transportation between evacuation centers and the airport. Because bridges washed out and highways were cut off, the only way out of Fairbanks was by air.

BAPTISTS JOIN OTHER EVACUEES AT REFUGEE CENTERS

River boats, canoes, airboats, and amphibious cars worked around the clock as all of Fairbanks became navigable. Oil spills caused fires to blaze in many places, but fire trucks were unable to respond to alarms. Separation of family members caused great concern.

Propeller boat boards passengers—the lame, children, adults—all needed help. Everyone lost possessions. Only those living in upstairs apartments saved household goods. Many had to be moved twice as waters continued rising. Calvary Baptist Church stands in background.

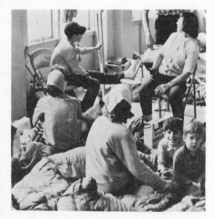

At the Lathrop High School refugee center togetherness reached the saturation point with 70 persons crowding into classrooms built to contain 35. A baby was born and a couple married during the days spent at this center.

SBC personalities at Lathrop refugee center include Glendon McCullough (1), Dr. Donald Ackland and Mrs. Porter Routh in front, Howard Alexander behind Dr. Ackland, Dr. E. H. Westmoreland, and Dr. Porter Routh. Baptist leaders aided in organization of rescue activities.

FAIRBANKS' NEEDS AND FRUSTRATIONS MOUNT

Most pets had to be left behind. Fear, hunger, then viciousness sounded in the frantic howling of stranded and starving dogs. Poignant words were, "My dog got drowned." This lucky child did not lose his pet.

Throughout the nightmarish hours rescue demanded immediate attention. Then the hordes began to feel hunger pangs; food quickly became a concern. By the time the first meal was served eager anticipation showed in every face. One day's meat included 1200 hams and 700 pounds of wieners.

Although nearby Fort Wainwright suffered $15 million loss in heating, power, and communication facilities, their personnel and vehicles continued to provide needed transportation for evacuees. Baptist leaders were moved twice before being flown out to Anchorage.

Howard Alexander (l) and Dallas Lee, HMB photographer, inspect collapsed wall of Alexander's basement. E. W. Hunke, Allen Meeks, Felton Griffin, and E. H. Westmoreland had to be rescued from their convention sleeping quarters here when the wall gave way.

RECEDING WATERS REVEAL SHAMBLES
THROUGHOUT CITY

Subsiding flood waters left unsightly heaps of rubbish starkly reflected in turbid puddles as evidence of the widespread devastation. Piles of debris littered the city. Moldering remains of food clung to ceilings. Buckled concrete, cracked walls, and jammed doors characterized all kinds of structures.

Hunke with Ross Covington, Fairbanks layman. Scheduled to move soon to Madagascar, Covington had corresponded with the FMB concerning beginning work there. "Operation Dryout" delayed his move. Sorting, stacking, washing, soaking, drying—"Getting everything done seems to take forever."

Although rugs lay stretched out on rooftops, the smell of stagnation lingered in the air long after the sun succeeded the rain. Irreplaceables—valued stamp collections, rare books, photographs—were ruined. J. T. Burdine, pastor of University Church, lost his entire library.

Becky Burdine's room at University Church's parsonage. Packed and ready to leave for her freshman year at OBU when the waters rose, Becky returned home from the evacuation center to find everything ruined, her home declared a total loss.

WATER DEVASTATION FAILS
TO QUENCH OPTIMISTIC SPIRIT

Funeral service held at First Baptist Church for Mrs. Josephine Newlan was attended by Pastor Marson, the funeral director, E. W. Hunke, and the woman's son. The son, seeking help, returned home to find his mother drowned in her kitchen with her dog and cat.

C. O. Dunkin's souvenir shop. Dunkin began Fairbanks' first Southern Baptist church and also the first native mission organized in Alaska by Southern Baptists. Often supporting himself as a sign-painter, Dunkin lost no time in putting up new signs which captured the Fairbanks spirit.

Open-air construction of A-67 Centennial Exposition Baptist Booth allowed surging flood waters to flow through, leaving little damage. Futile sandbags lie in foreground. Churches were not so fortunate; University Church was hardest hit. Student work team from Tennessee left the day before the flood struck.

Though Friendship Mission reflects beautifully in the receding waters, church basements and pastors' homes still had from 32 to 55 inches of water standing ten days after flood crested. Kerosene blowers flown in from Anchorage helped speed up drying process.

NEW FAIRBANKS PASTOR
ARRIVES ON FIELD DURING CLEANUP

Bill Duncan (c), arriving to pastor Fairbanks' Hamilton Acres Church, at airport with E. C. Chron (l) and state legislator Frank Getman of Sitka (r). Coming from Las Vegas, Nevada, Duncan arrived at height of cleanup. He is ABC president for 1969-70.

Duncan's first view of his new parsonage revealed a shambles left by 68 inches of water. The inside was bare except for studs; cabinets, appliances, floor tiles, wallboard, trim, insulation and electrical outlets had been destroyed, pulled out, and discarded.

In order to take a look at his new church building, Duncan had to clamber over remains of kitchen and educational materials blocking the entrance. The basement was still being pumped. A crying Siamese kitten had been rescued from atop floating ceiling tiles.

Every church lost pianos; University Church lost both a grand piano and Baldwin organ. Duncan found unglued piano; soggy hymnals and literature matted with mud, pieces of equipment from children's departments—record players and broken dolls—made heartbreaking spectacle.

"WAITING TO REBUILD WAS THE HARDEST PART OF ALL"

The state executive committee met in Anchorage early on August 16 to decide on priorities. They decided the greatest immediate need was help with church buildings. Volunteer workers found rubbish already cleared out and stacked in front of St. Johns when they arrived. One wall was caving in.

Paul Adkins of the HMB had caught a 5 A.M. flight to Alaska, carrying $10,000 in emergency relief funds to be used immediately. Tickets for evacuation of families took most of this. Pastors and laymen were freed to begin pushing trash into piles with snow shovels or help church families face problems.

Completion of eight years' work with Fairbanks natives found John and Lillian Isaacs fighting tetanus shot reaction and working to clear out rubbish. Wallboard and insulation had to be stripped from church walls, floor tiles removed, then parts of walls knocked out to make it possible to remove rubble.

Grabbing sandwiches and coffee on the run, church members spent long hours getting their buildings cleared out so rebuilding could begin. The HMB guaranteed pastors' salaries for at least three months, declared a three-month moratorium on interest and loan payments, and appealed for 100 construction specialists.

SOUTHERN BAPTISTS RESPOND QUICKLY
TO FLOOD VICTIMS' NEEDS

Within 24 hours this clothes dispensary was set up and diapers, shoes, or whole wardrobes made available at Anchorage Faith Baptist Church. The Baptist Building was open around the clock to meet emergencies. The state mission offering designation was changed to "Fairbanks Flood Fund."

The Sunday School Board contacted architectural consultant Ernie Myers, then traveling in Canada, assigning him to check the church buildings for damages. Because waters receded only an inch every 2 hours, boat transportation was necessary when Myers arrived for his survey.

Seven airlines carried the specialists free of charge. Carpenters, electricians, pipefitters, dry wall men, painters, tile layers, brick masons, cement finishers, plumbers, pilots—102 in all—came to help. The HMB was flooded with calls and telegrams from volunteers.

Preparing electrical fittings for the log cabin Salcha parsonage proved to be a new experience for this Lower 48 worker. A place to hold the wiring had to be gouged out of solid logs before work could continue. Specialists helped pull nails and cut and fit wallboard—did many jobs.

BAPTIST WORK BECOMES
"BIGGER, BETTER, AND STRONGER"

Pastorless Eielson Park Church was delayed in building by 32" of water. Electrician Joe Fallon (r) had preached in Alaska during 1967 spring revivals, became interested in work here, came as a volunteer flood worker, then later accepted a call to pastor Eielson Park Church.

Lumber from Fairbanks yards floated downriver, creating critical shortage. Dick Evans of Anchorage United Builders coordinated boxcar loads of materials for Baptist churches before trainloads of supplies were frozen. Hunke (l) stands with Clarence Epps, Anchorage city building inspector for 12 years, who directed work.

Thousands of dollars worth of materials were needed for rebuilding. One load of wallboard was lost when a boat coming from Seattle sank, creating a shortage for suppliers. Nailing up proceeded so rapidly that what had seemed an inexhaustible supply of sheetrock soon became only a dwindling stack.

B. L. Williams (l), 72, from Kentucky and his son, B. L. Williams, Jr., (r) from South Carolina, insulate exterior walls at Friendship Mission. They were one of two father-son teams. Forty workers came from Tennessee—the "Volunteer State." The men were recruited through HMB and Brotherhood services.

BAPTISTS WILL ALWAYS REMEMBER
FAIRBANKS' CENTENNIAL SUMMER

E. C. Shettles (1), First Baptist Church, Memphis, volunteered to serve as head cook. He set up his "cafe" in the basement of Fairbanks First Baptist. Hard work and big appetites can cause complaints, but among these flood workers the consensus was that every meal was the "best ever."

Men from 17 states formed friendships as they consumed food and shared the day's experiences. Progress was rapid at the 8 damaged Fairbanks churches. After supper the men worked on private homes of church members. Ladies from all the churches helped serve dinner at First Baptist.

To help feed workers Civil Defense donated surplus "C" rations. Oliver Marson, Jr., doesn't seem to be worried about winter's imminent approach. With a warm parka and all that food, why should he? Haste was urgent, however. Labor Day brought the season's first freeze.

Many of the men testified that they understood the concepts of Christian vocation and vocational witness for the first time. At 7 P.M. they met for a devotional period. Their demonstration of concern did not go unnoticed—the Fairbanks *Daily News Miner* carried two accounts and commendations of their work.

10

". . . A Good Report Through Faith . . ."

Hebrews 11:39

From *Report of the Executive Board of the Alaska Baptist Convention, Twenty-first Annual Session,* Muldoon Road Baptist Church, August 16-18, 1966.

Elected E. W. Hunke, Jr., as Executive Secretary of the Convention.

From *Minutes of the Executive Board of the Alaska Baptist Convention,* November 11, 1966.

A motion was made that the Organizational Manual be approved by the board as a basis for work. . . .
Message of the Executive Secretary, E. W. Hunke, Jr., contained the following information regarding some personal suggestions for board consideration:
Development of a Loan Fund
Update the bookkeeping procedures and provide for machine operation
Plant a Southern Baptist church in every churchless town in Alaska
Clarify responsibility regarding Baptist work in Canada. . . .

From *Minutes of the Executive Board of the Alaska Baptist Convention,* June 30, 1967.

The twenty acre Seward Highway property has been deeded by the Home Mission Board to the Alaska Baptist Convention and has been recorded.
Discussion is underway with Broadway bonds for the establishment of a loan fund for the convention.
The Executive Secretary met with a committee in Clear regarding a pastoral missionary for that area.
Foy Rogers, mission secretary for Mississippi, visited our state and initiated plans for a group of men from Mississippi to come to Alaska during the 1968 state convention in the interest of starting new work.

From *Report of the Executive Board of the Alaska Baptist Convention, Twenty-Third Annual Session,* Calvary Baptist Church, Fairbanks, August 13-15, 1968.

Responded to the need of flood stricken Tanana churches by organizing the reconstruction of buildings and supplying human need.

Reactivated the Pioneer 2000 Club to enlist gifts for new work and voted to provide complimentary subscriptions of the *Alaska Baptist Messenger* to its members. The first call was approved for purchase of a new church site on North Kenai Road.

Alaska's landscape is a vast canvas on which God's masterpieces are brushed with vivid hues. Soon after Bill Hunke arrived in Alaska, he wrote in the *Messenger:* "I have seen a snowflake. Elsewhere the snow melts together in a slush, but the extreme coldness here preserves the shape of the flakes. Sunday morning as I journeyed to Eagle River to preach, the sky was a brilliant blue; the sun was warm and bright; and the ice fog frozen on the trees sparkled like a thousand diamonds."

Before many months Hunke journeyed to the Arctic to meet at Kiana with missionaries Harley and Martha Shield, Shirley Korte, Valeria Sherard, and Norman and Gunita Harrell to plan the next year's work. He reported:

> We had conferences in the morning and services at night, but all during the afternoons we rolled fuel oil barrels up the hill. We tried to sleep in crowded quarters with the dogs howling all night like coyotes on the Texas prairies. I kept hearing some kind of animal breathing heavily outside the door and was confident I would be eaten alive before the night ended.
>
> After the conclusion of the Kiana conference, we all went to Kobuk by bush plane. By this time I understood Valeria's strategy. The conference part had been in Kiana so she could get her barrels rolled up the hill. I had not read the small print on the Alaska Baptist Convention Executive Secretary's job description.
>
> In Kobuk the accommodations were more crowded than at Kiana. The women took the small log room along the backside of the log chapel and the men slept on the floor in the chapel. We drew the curtains when dozens of little faces began to peer through the windows. Because the door had no lock, for a while the chapel was as busy as Grand Central Station.
>
> On September 22, my birthday, I was not forgotten. Gunita cooked me a cake complete with candles, the missionaries sang "Happy Birthday," and we had a good time. By this time a red

stocking hat I had been given to cover my ears had earned me the title of "Red Baron." To further complement this wardrobe, my birthday present, which looked like a small hat made of fur, was actually a nose cover to prevent my nose from freezing off. The motor boat trip down the Kobuk River to Shungnak to dedicate the new building was a frightening experience. We had no trouble going. The people responded when they heard the call to worship, accomplished by beating on a pan with a spoon. During the service they sat on the bare plywood floor because they had no pews. But the trip home was difficult. We left too late and the dense darkness of the Arctic settled on us enroute. Even in daylight, finding one's way in the Kobuk River with its hundreds of snake bends and merging streams is a chore. The small lantern, shielded to cast light on the river before us, did little good. Time after time the motor propeller ground into the gravel to spin us around and send us down river again with the current. In spite of being bundled up tightly, we were very cold. I heard Valeria crying softly. The Northern Lights were not nearly so beautiful to us that night as were the lights of Kobuk. Dozens of lanterns dotted the river's edge to show us the way home. The Eskimo people were concerned about our being out on the river so late.

Because E. W. Hunke had met with the Alaska Baptist Convention Executive board in June 1966 and again in August before his responsibilities began with the convention on September 1, he gained an insight into ways of streamlining the operations and improving the effectiveness of the board. In Arizona he had studied the Booz, Allen, and Hamilton plans for setting up convention boards and had led the Utah-Idaho missions committee to adopt and use the principles outlined in the firm's reports. He applied the same operational procedure to Alaska's constitution, by-laws, and policies, and when he first met with the board officially, he had an Organizational Manual ready to present to them. The manual recommended an internal board restructuring which would provide for long range planning, establishment of priorities, structured communication, coordination of effort, and efficiency.

The state board had operated unilaterially with administrative, missions, education, and Christian service committees. No committee job descriptions or policies had been written and time was devoted to immediate operational concerns, with board meetings often lasting beyond midnight hours just trying to assign areas of responsibility. The new structure allowed for the convention president and the chairman of each of four board committees to compose the executive committee. The new committees were: administrative, finance, operations, and program. Objectives, responsibilities, organization, and convention authority were all spelled out in the manual.

Also included in the Organizational Manual adopted by the board were Articles of Incorporation for convention institutions and agencies, Policies and Procedures for convention institutions and committees, and Contracts and Agreements with other agencies, such as the Annuity Board and Home Mission Board of the Southern Baptist Convention.

Because the Home Mission Board had periodically audited the Alaska convention's books, Hunke felt a careful examination of the accounting system was in order. The accounting firm of Peat, Marwick and Mitchell studied the accounting set-up and recommended a new chart of accounts and unified state budget instead of the sixty-four different accounts then carried on the books. Surplus Home Mission Board funds were returned or spent as designated. Alaska Baptist funds have always been carefully handled by employees, and the books are no longer audited by an outside agency.

When Foy Rogers graduated from Southwestern Seminary, Hunke invited him to come to Arizona as missionary. Instead, he became director of missions for Mississippi, but one year he led Mississippi Baptists to send thirty-eight laymen to Arizona on a mission crusade. They began nineteen new churches in two weeks.

At a Southern Baptist Convention after Hunke came to Alaska, Foy Rogers asked him what he could do for missions up there. The greatest need was for associational missionaries, since Alaska had none, so Hunke figured that if twenty Mississippi missionaries were to give two weeks service, it would be the equivalent of having an associational missionary on the field for a year. Rogers went back home and set about enlisting his state's associations and churches to send their missionaries to Alaska; seventeen came.

One of them remained in Anchorage to survey; the others went out two-by-two into churchless communities. When they reassembled for a debriefing session, vitally needed information about Baptist families all across the state was shared and priorities and guidelines for future mission implementation were developed. Some of these new works have come into existence: King Salmon, North Kenai, Montana Creek, and Haines home Bible fellowship, for example. One missionary, Hollis Bryant, returned to Alaska to pastor the Juneau First Baptist Church.

❈   ❈   ❈

Every Alaskan community is unique in some way, but in the case of King Salmon, it was a difference with a sadness, for never in its history had there been a church in town. Through the years people with the park service, in the air force, working for the Federal Aviation Administration or the weather bureau had come and gone, but no spiritual ministry existed. Opposition and pressure prevented the establishing of churches; petitions were circulated to keep them out. Nevertheless, beyond the facade of hearty laughter and rough language at the town tavern were hungry souls waiting, waiting like the old derelict boats I saw dying at the dock.

When the Bob Johnsons arrived in King Salmon in 1959, they were astonished when their efforts to find a place to worship proved futile. They organized a Sunday school which met regularly in their home until they rotated in 1964. Several air force boys volunteered to help continue the Sunday school, but the work went on for only a short while. Back in the Lower 48 the Johnsons continued to be burdened for the need of the people of King Salmon, and prayed that they might return. They were able to come back in January 1969 and rejoiced to find that others had been helping bridge the spiritual abyss during their absence.

In late 1964 Dennis Mabee, a Catholic boy in the air force, became concerned for the children he saw playing in the streets on Sunday mornings. Through his efforts the Katmai Club building of the FAA was secured for Sunday school. Thirteen children came the first Sunday. When Dennis rotated, Bill Duke, a trained musician, and Dan Brooks, who was in charge of base chapel services, continued the witness begun by the Johnsons and Mabee.

In 1966 Hershel and Joy Rinker moved to King Salmon, and when Bill and Dan rotated, the Rinkers took over the responsibility for Sunday school. There were twenty-four enrolled at that time, none over fifteen years old. They enlisted a Sgt. Curry to begin an adult class and at one time had eighteen adults attending regularly. As the enrollment climbed to the eighties, the Rinkers began to plan activities for the many teenagers who had been enlisted, and soon had sixteen young people coming from Naknek, a neighboring town, to join with their own group for Bible study and fellowship. Feeling the need for a pastor's leadership as never before, the Rinkers began to pray earnestly. Instead of a pastor being provided immediately in answer to their prayer, Hershel began to have to work six days a week, further increasing the need for help. They contacted the leaders of their denomination, the Nazarenes, with no results. Next they tried an interdenominational group, but they had no financial means to offer aid. Consequently, when the Rinkers went Outside on vacation in 1968, they presented the need to every group who would listen to them, thinking surely that as churches heard of their victories—even to drawing the largest crowd ever assembled in the town of 800 for their Christmas drama in 1967, someone would respond, but no one did.

While traveling through Anchorage on their way back home, the Rinkers decided to look up a former member of the King Salmon group. He invited them to attend church with him, so they found themselves sitting in the congregation of Muldoon Road Baptist Church, listening in amazement as Pastor Virgil Chron announced from the pulpit that his brother, E. C., was in the King Salmon-Dillingham area seeking housing for two men who were arriving to survey in anticipation of beginning a Baptist mission.

In August 1968 the two area missionaries from Mississippi came to King Salmon to survey and report on the needs. They found that most of the families had no religious preference at all, but more had a preference for Baptists than for any other denomination. They cautioned that a pastor serving there would have to be able to minister to people of many denominations and cope with constant rotation of leaders and members; he would have to lease land from the state, for all land was state-owned, and should build as soon as possible for the Katnai Club, FAA-owned, was a barrier to those not involved in FAA, and also it was not in good condition for services after Saturday night activities there. One Sunday a drunken man, left over from the night before, stayed for Sunday school, though he was in no condition to do so.

With the consent of the group at King Salmon, Muldoon Road Baptist Church began supplying a preacher twice a month; the first service was October 6, 1968, with forty in attendance and E. C. Chron bringing the message and reading a letter from the sponsoring church assuring them of support.

The mission's first pastor, Don Rollins, arrived and conducted his first service on June 8, 1969. After great difficulty in purchasing property, the mission building was begun on July 19, 1969. James Boney, a builder from Texas, came to give his time to lead the building program. On three occasions plane loads of people from Muldoon Road came to help. The first service in the new building was on October 25, 1969, with 94 present, including 36 from out of town.

Though the Rollins live in King Salmon, they hope to reach out to the other villages in the southwestern part of Alaska and provide a witness. In order to help make this possible, the North Central Baptist Church, Gainesville, Florida, and the Second Baptist Church, Little Rock, Arkansas, provided money for a small plane which was purchased late in 1969.

A Pioneer 2000 Club call and one-half the 1969 state mission offering helped make the new building a reality. Sgt. Paul Nichols was the first one baptized in the new baptistry, but a small girl was saved in the baptistry while cleaning it out in preparation for dedication day.

When the Rollins need medical services, they have to jet in to Anchorage. In May 1970, Donna, their six-year-old daughter, had to undergo a number of tests. Mrs. Rollins had taken on the care of a two-year-old boy, and since they couldn't afford a plane ticket for him too, Don had to stay home and play mother. The "Muldoon Moosecall" ran this unpaid advertisement: "The Rollins have sled dogs that they brought from Fort Yukon to King Salmon. They don't need them there and buying dog food by the ton is expensive, so they are trying to give them away. If you need a good dog, already trained to a sled, all you have to do is pay their plane fare down. Let us hear." Not many people who read the announcement could realize the grief involved. I have seen how much the Rollins children care for their dogs, which are pets and not just sled dogs trained to win races. June Chron commented, "Missionaries are people the likes of whom most of us cannot imagine. The heartaches, loneliness, physical discomforts, are all hidden by big smiles that are genuine. They are living proof that the Lord is sufficient."

Kodiak conjures up pictures of king crab and brown bear for the gourmet or the hunter. To historians, Kodiak means Shielikof and Baronof, *Lord of Alaska* and *Cry of the Wild Ram,* and an annual outdoor dramatic pageant attended by thousands of visitors. To the rest of Alaska, Kodiak is the "Banana Belt," warmer in winter and cooler in summer than other parts of the state.

Families living on Kodiak Island find the number of miles they can travel limited by the lack of roads. One Baptist called the existing roads "early twentieth century cowpaths." Though they are unpaved and narrow with sharp rocks and deep holes, they are crowded with Detroit's latest models.

During the summer of 1967, Kodiak became a burden on the hearts of two Southern Baptist families living there because they missed the familiar organizations and warm evangelistic preaching they were accustomed to. Eight daughters in the two families had been in G.A.'s and Y.W.A.'s and missed the mission education and fellowship. One girl was concerned about completing her Queen Regent step. The families began to discuss the possibility of having the mission organizations even though they had no church, and made inquiries at the Alaska Baptist Convention for materials. They invited Miss Louise Yarbrough to come from Anchorage to help them organize. Ten girls met with Miss Yarbrough on September 18, 1967.

Other families were contacted and on September 19, 1967, twenty-one people met in the Ottis Williams home to hear about Southern Baptist work in Alaska. As the group met and prayed, they felt impressed to form a Southern Baptist fellowship and set a date for a second meeting. Some confessed that they had been praying for years for such a group; they were further challenged by a $100 check from the Calvary Baptist Church in Anchorage which Miss Yarbrough presented to them.

When Mrs. Robert Fling, "Mrs. W.M.U." herself, made an unscheduled stop in Kodiak because of bad weather, thirty-one people gathered at the William Perry home to hear her talk on missions.

A combination fellowship dinner and organizational meeting was held on October 28, 1967, at the Buskin Beach House. Allen Meeks came from Anchorage and assisted as the group of thirty-eight elected their moderator, vice-moderator, clerk, and treasurer.

The Kodiak Electric Association auditorium was used by Latter Day Saints on Sunday mornings, but was made available to the Baptists on Sunday afternoons, so on November 5, 1967, the group met at 1:30 P.M., and voted to form a Southern Baptist church. A name was chosen and date set, and on December 3, 1967, the Frontier Southern Baptist Church was constituted with thirty-four members. Executive secretary E. W. Hunke led in the organizational service and agreed to serve as interim pastor until the group could secure their own pastor. A Sunday school program began in January 1968, meeting after the worship service.

The first mission offering given by the church was an $80.25 check given by the G.A.'s and Y.W.A.'s. The girls continue to have a mission study and project each month and assist in the nursery every Sunday.

The church called Ray Hustead as pastor. He accepted and moved on the field to preach his first sermon on July 21, 1968. Mr. Hustead had served a tour in the air force in Anchorage, and had surrendered to preach while a member of First Baptist there. He pastored the Fairview Baptist Church in Anchorage from January to September 1957. After release from the service, he returned to his home in Texas, completed college and seminary, married Trudy Rackley, and pastored Fairview Baptist Church of Evant, Texas. In July 1964, the Fairview Baptist Church of Anchorage called him again, and he returned to Alaska, pastoring that church until accepting the Kodiak call. The Husteads have three daughters.

Most visitors who land at the Anchorage International Airport at night are intrigued by the sight of brightly lighted structures strung along Cook Inlet all the way down the Kenai Peninsula. These out-of-season, Christmas-tree-looking, offshore drilling rigs introduce them to Alaska's vast oil wealth and the black gold rush which began in 1957 when a wildcat well was brought in near Kenai, about one hundred and seventy highway miles south of Anchorage. These rugged iron islands, which in daylight look like fragile spiders standing on tiptoe, are built to withstand minus forty degree temperatures, ice floes up to six feet thick, the crash of ice cakes rushed along by thirty foot tides, winds up to one hundred miles per hour, and continual earthquakes. Hundreds of new residents have been brought to the North Kenai area by the oil industry and construction work. Many of them had been members of Southern Baptist churches before moving to Alaska.

On the closing night of a revival in 1967 at Anchorage Faith Baptist Church, E. W. Hunke gave a unique invitation. He asked if the church would agree to sponsor a mission in North Kenai. The church called for a business session, voted to sponsor the mission and to investigate the possibility of purchasing two burned out trailers to serve as a temporary chapel and parsonage for the mission. The immediate action was sparked by Ed Johnson, an Anchorage pharmacist and chairman of the missions committee of the church. Mr. Johnson had moved to Alaska because he wanted to help in mission work. Later, he and his family drove the long road every Sunday to help the people in North Kenai get the mission started.

After church on the night the revival ended, several men of Faith church went to look over the trailers by flashlight. They reported back to a group gathered at the home of W. O. Johnson that they thought the trailers would do. That week the trailers were bought and moved to Faith church, and the men and women of the church went to work cleaning, repaneling, painting, and carpeting the first trailer. When they finished, the chapel trailer had one long room for services, a rest room, and a small room with cabinets at the back.

In 1962 Jimmy Rose, who was pastor of Kenai First Baptist Church, had seen the need for services on North Kenai Road and had conducted home Bible studies in the area for a time. During E. W. Hunke's first trip to North Kenai in 1966, bumping over the unpaved road in Kelly Dickson's Scout, he and Kelly had discussed the growing need and expressed hope that services might soon be reinitiated. On May 9, 1967, thirteen people met with Hunke and Ed Wolfe, pastor of Faith church, indicating that they wanted to belong to the new mission. A group of them had already begun meeting in homes for prayer and Bible study, anticipating the beginning of the mission. Maurice Murdock from Soldotna agreed to preach for them until they could secure a pastor.

In June 1967 the chapel trailer was hauled to Kenai and parked in the Otto Schneiders' front yard until land could be purchased. The August 4, 1967, *Minutes of the Executive Committee of the Executive Board of the Alaska Baptist Convention* recorded the following action:

> Motion was made by Felton Griffin, seconded by Dyke Brandon, (1) that $200 earnest money be made available from undesignated State Mission funds to Spenard Faith Baptist Church to negotiate for a 2½ acre site on North Kenai Road; (2) that the HMB be encouraged to make site funds available for the site; and (3) the Executive Secretary be authorized to work with the church in providing a means for financing in event the HMB does not have funds available for the purchase; motion carried.

Before the month was over, Roy Moore, with his wife Barbara and their four children, came to serve as mission pastor. In July the other trailer, renovated by then, joined the chapel trailer, serving as a home for the Moores. The large room of the chapel continued to be the meeting place for all church activities, including a picnic on Labor Day. They had planned to go to the beach, but it rained, just as it had been doing all that summer.

By Halloween both intermediate and junior G.A.'s had been organized. They planned a party which was announced several weeks in advance by someone getting up in service and saying "the viper is coming." While the party was in progress, the viper did come—Frances Johansson, the Swedish "vindow viper." A memorable experience for the girls was presenting a skit for an associational W.M.U. meeting when Mrs. Fling, W.M.U. president for the S.B.C. was the guest speaker.

Problems developed as the work went on; the water well pump filled with silt from the newly drilled well. The Moores had to carry water for three weeks, then Leo Johansson took several days of his Christmas vacation, after being out on an oil platform for two months, to lift the pump, clean, and put it back together. Don Myers from Anchorage, who was working in Kenai that month, came out to the mission every night and worked late. The temperature was not going above zero even during the daytime, so the men could only work a short time before having to go to the parsonage to warm up.

In December 1967 Faith Baptist Mission of North Kenai was officially recognized as a Project 500 church.

The first week in January a lean-to of three bedrooms arrived at the mission property, giving the Moore family some welcomed living space.

During the spring revival in 1968, the chapel was full every night. The evangelist, James Watson, from Mississippi, stacked his bed on top of the song leader's bed to make more room for people to sit in the back room. The middle Sunday there were two worship services with seventy-four attending.

The October 10, 1968, *Minutes of the Executive Committee of the Executive Board of the Alaska Baptist Convention* reported the following action:

> W. E. Midkiff reported that Tustumena Association pastors met at Sportsman Lodge on Monday, September 30, and after detailed discussion wished to go on record as favoring the establishment of another Baptist mission in the North Kenai area.
> The Executive Committee entered a period of discussion on the

proposed project. President Wolfe indicated that the initial plan was to move the Faith Chapel as soon as possible to start another mission. He indicated that Spenard Faith Baptist leaders, and Roy Moore, would lend every possible assistance to the new project.

A motion was made by Felton Griffin and seconded that ABC leaders obtain the best possible option on North Kenai land with a view to purchasing property in the name of the Alaska Baptist Convention, and that the Glennallen Chapel be moved on the new property. Motion carried.

A motion by Felton Griffin and seconded that the Alaska Baptist Convention leaders issue a call to 2,000 Club members requesting $5 from each to assist in securing the new property.

When suitable property was located at Mile 15, a call went out to members of the revitalized Pioneer 2000 Club to send their $5 to help buy the land. About a thousand dollars came in, enough to take care of closing costs and the first few payments. The down payment money came from Darrel Hearth who had once lived in Alaska and belonged to Calvary Baptist Church. He sent the money to the church and asked that it be put into a new mission. The mission also obtained a loan from the Home Mission Board Site Fund, and the work of getting the Glennallen trailer moved and set up began.

When the day for dedication arrived on January 12, 1969, the electricity was still not connected and the chapel had to be heated by small propane heaters. The service was held in the afternoon by candlelight with E. W. Hunke bringing the message.

Faith Mission is unique because it has two meeting places. After the expando chapel trailer which had been used at Glennallen was moved to the area, services were held on Sunday at both Mile 8 and Mile 15 in order to reach more people. Members of the mission have shared the following testimonies:

Mrs. Gene Damron:
I thought I was at the end of the world when I came to Alaska. I am thankful for friends who have prayed with and for me and stood by in times of special need. I feel that Jesus has used my circumstances for his good and to work out his will in my life. I realize anew that places I worship—trailer or sure enough church building—are not important, but that I worship in Spirit and in Truth.

Mrs. Jerry Harris:
The first Sunday my little Beginner girl attended Sunday school,

she said the teacher didn't share any of the food. I found out later the Beginners meet in the kitchen of the parsonage, and she thought the teacher was going to serve some of the food that she saw in the cupboards.

Mrs. Roy Moore:
It is thrilling to see people willing to serve the Lord in a new mission and to do without many of the things they would find in a large church. Faith Baptist Church has been so helpful and concerned about the work here. I am happy I can serve the Lord even with the use of my home.

Mr. and Mrs. Amol Hilger:
Being members of the Faith Baptist Church, Anchorage, from the time we arrived in Anchorage, we had heard much about the little mission church down in Kenai. We had never attended a mission, so when we learned we were moving to Kenai, we were eagerly looking forward to being a part of this mission, but we didn't quite know what to expect. We were overwhelmed at the warmth, friendliness, and the Christian spirit that greeted us the first Sunday we attended church at the mission. We knew then that our lives were going to be enriched and take on a special meaning from the opportunity of being a small part of the mission. Already we have been blessed with a much clearer awareness of the many ways we can better serve the Lord.

Up and down the Alaska rail belt are many small communities without churches. Road construction crews are working to complete the new Anchorage to Fairbanks highway by 1971. E. W. Hunke felt these communities should be reached with the gospel. The solution seemed to lie in placing a missionary in the Matanuska Valley to work the rail belt north, and another in the Fairbanks area to work south. When this approach was discussed with the Home Mission Board, state convention board, and University Baptist Church, the groups responded by uniting their efforts and placing James Akin at Palmer and Gene Mockerman at Clear.

The Clear work had begun in 1962 with one ministry at Rex, the rail stop, and the other at the new town of Anderson, about fifteen miles away. In October 1967, these Clear Site missions constituted into the North Star Baptist Church.

After the first pastor, Billy Caine, resigned, Hunke met with a missions committee of the church to find out what qualifications they would require in a new pastor. They listed four: first, he would have to love the out-of-doors, because that was about all there was around Clear, Alaska. Second, he would have to be married because it would be too lonely for a single man. Third, the man and his wife would have to be able to get along with the mosquitoes. Fourth, the man's wife would have to be the kind who would not panic when she looked out the window in the morning and found a bear eating out of the garbage can.

Gene Mockerman came to Fairbanks as a flood worker. He had been saved in Las Vegas, Nevada, when pastor M. K. Wilder led his church to pray for God to send them an electrician. As they prayed, God converted Mockerman. After the flood hit, Hunke prayed for construction workers, especially for electricians, plumbers, and a contractor; Mockerman, Don Myers, and Clarence Epps came in answer to the prayer. University Baptist Church interviewed Mockerman about pastoring the work at Clear, so shortly after the workers left Fairbanks, Mockerman came back, bringing his wife Maxine and their two children.

Maxine said when they finally reached Clear Site, she understood where it got its name. "It was really Clear outa' Sight." For many months after they arrived at Clear, the Mockermans' water was polluted from the flood. During a visit with us, Maxine wrote in the Guest Book, "Oh, how nice to have clean, beautiful water and take baths." She was always bubbling over with wonder at the marvels of Alaska. She told us that they had passed a little town up the road (Eklutna) where an old Russian church had dog houses out in front of the building. "I think that is the most considerate thing I've ever seen," she gushed, "for them to provide a shelter for their sled dogs while they have their church services." However great the idea may have been, what she thought were dog houses were really the houses for departed spirits; she had seen an old cemetery left over from days when the custom was to place the body on top of the ground with its belongings around it, and in some cases to construct a small house over it.

In September 1967 Moderator Leo Josey and Missions Chairman Mike McKay of the Chugach Association met with several families interested in beginning a church in the Sand Lake area. The group met for several months at the Allen Meeks home. Every Sunday afternoon during the first month of services, a rainbow arched across the Chugach Range, making the promises of God seem very real to those seeking his will for the new work. On

October 1 the church closed its charter membership with twenty-eight members and constituted as the Jewel Lake Baptist Church.

The church purchased a home in the neighborhood and met in it while a first unit basement was being constructed on property nearby. The Alaska Baptist Convention had already made a down payment and the association had made several years' payments on the property, which was given to the church. During August 1968 tents were erected on the property and, with the help of two Mississippi missionaries, a Vacation Bible School was conducted which enrolled more than one hundred children. E. W. Hunke served as interim pastor of the church until they called Glenn Huisinga in July 1968.

The first service in the completed basement was in December 1968. A second Home Mission Board loan was obtained in 1970 in order to complete the upper portion of the building. Mr. Huisinga resigned in May 1970. The Allen Meeks, Frank McKinney, and Lt. Col. William Chambless families have been leaders in the church from the beginning.

While James E. Akin was attending Howard Payne College, Brownwood, Texas, Odell Lene, who was then serving in Alaska, spoke at a ministerial fellowship meeting about the mission opportunities. It was Akin's first impression of Alaska as a mission field, but from that time in 1948 he felt the Lord wanted him to serve in Alaska.

While my husband and I were students at Golden Gate Seminary, we met James Akin. Our church initiated a mission at Brentwood, California, and called him to pastor it. He remained there during his four years in seminary. In the meantime we went to serve the First Baptist Church at Vernal, Utah. When we left that church to become Home Mission Board employees, the Vernal church called James and his wife Fern to serve them. He remained with them for two years before coming to Alaska in October 1956.

The Akins came first to pastor the Trinity church of Anchorage for four years. Then he pastored the church at Seward, at Big Delta, and the Tok Baptist Mission. The Clearwater Baptist Mission was begun by the First Baptist Church of Big Delta while Akin was there in 1962. He held services at Northway and Scotty Creek (near the Canadian border) in conjunction with the work at Tok. While at Tok, Akin was engaged in building the church building, building his home, maintaining the church program, driving a school bus and working in a grocery store to finance his family needs, and at the same time carrying on the two mission programs which required trips of up to 170 miles twice a week over an icy road in temperatures of minus sixty degrees during the winter.

The Akins came to serve as missionaries in the Matanuska and Susitna Valleys under the sponsorship of the Grandview Baptist Church, Anchorage, in April 1968. Mike McKay, chairman of the Missions Committee of the Chugach Baptist Association, contacted them about coming to the new work. The first services of the Montana Creek Mission were held in the old school building, located at Mile 95½ of the Anchorage–Fairbanks Highway. This was the meeting place until the owner's residence across the highway was sold in September 1968. The mission met in the home of Tom Covington in the Willow area until they were offered the Kennerson homestead dwelling (early model house trailer with a log leanto), located at Mile 1 on the Talkeetna Cut-off. The mission met there from October 20, 1968, until April 1969, when the place was sold. Again they met in the Covington home for one Sunday, then were able to secure a tent from the Camp Committee of the Chugach association. The tent was erected in a gravel pit at Mile 98 on the highway. They met in the tent from April until October. With money given for mission work in the Mat-Su Valley area, contributions of the 2000 Club, gifts of individuals, and much voluntary labor, they were able to move into their new mission building on October 12, 1969. The mission continues to meet in this building at Mile 98½ on the Anchorage-Fairbanks Highway, near the Talkeetna Cut-off.

Besides the Montana Creek Mission, the Matanuska-Susitna Mission work includes the Palmer Bible Study Fellowship meetings, which the Akins started in April 1968, just after arriving on the field, and the Big Lake Bible Study Fellowship, which began in August 1969. There had been work in both Big Lake and Palmer prior to this time, but they had ceased having regular services.

In 1967 the state convention executive board elected Don Wright as pastoral missionary for the Tongass Association. The five year missions pilot project is jointly sponsored by the First Baptist Church of Ketchikan, Tongass Association, the Home Mission Board, and the Alaska Baptist Convention. Wright lived first at Ketchikan and served as pastor of the Annette Mission.

When Bob Day, Southeastern lumberman and road builder, joined the Ketchikan First Baptist Church, he became a contact man for starting a mission in Petersburg, which according to E. W. Hunke, "lies cradled like a jewel in a majestic setting of mountains and waterways which surpasses description." Mr. Wright initiated weekly services in Petersburg, and a mission was begun there in March 1968. It was one of the Project 500 missions, sponsored jointly by the denomination and the Ketchikan church.

Don Wright and his family moved from Ketchikan to Petersburg in September and live in a trailer purchased by the mission. They conduct worship services in the Episcopal church building.

The name "Tustumena" was chosen as the name of a new association organized in May 1968. The word means "crossing over." One of the Alaska ferries bears the name, and because Kodiak Island is a part of the new association, the idea of crossing over carries that relationship, as well as having the significance of crossing over into a new endeavor for Baptist work.

Sometimes the crossing over isn't so easy, however. Sudden winds come up and small boats become lessons in faith for those caught out at such times, as E. W. Hunke testifies below:

> The turbulent tides of Tuxedni Bay driven by twenty mile per hour winds tossed the tiny outboard boat for an hour before we sighted the fishing boat *Dixie Lynn*. Docking two boats in the midst of raging waters is not an easy task. Anticipation of anchoring in a protected bay helped the four of us, drenched to the skin, to tie things down for the trip. Roy Self pointed the thirty-five foot fishing boat toward Kasilof across Cook Inlet and Kelly Dickson, Howard Halsell, and I braced ourselves as the ship battled six foot waves on rip tides for our journey home. Later we learned that the storm sank the fishing boat *Skelak* and downed two planes. I gained a deeper appreciation for hymns of the sea, for sailors, for commercial fishermen, and for the price of salmon.

The organizational meeting of the Tustumena Association was held at First Baptist Church, Kenai, with Kelly Dickson and his church acting as hosts. Much advance preparation had been done by the pastors and leaders on the Kenai Peninsula. The organizational meeting moved along without any problems. The first officers elected were: moderator, Maurice Murdock; assistant moderator, Frank Bullock; clerk, Connie Miller; assistant clerk, Elizabeth Mize; treasurer, Martyn Bacheler; assistant treasurer, Troy White; song leader, Herman Gladden; educational leader, Bill Gay; historian, Ann Gay; youth rally president, Dewey Halsey. Trustees were James Bennett, Warren Colvin, Otis Williams, and Carl Fisher. Four churches and one mission sent messengers to the organizational meeting.

Meanwhile, the work beyond the Arctic Circle was strengthened when Harley and Martha Shield went as missionaries to Kotzebue in the summer of 1966. Several converts had been awaiting the coming of good weather, open water, and the missionary so they could be baptized. On August 7, the members of the Kotzebue Baptist Church gathered on the beach in front of the church with song books sang to the accompaniment of an accordian. Since the street is the main one in town, the occasion was observed by almost everyone in the village. Mrs. Lulu, a young Eskimo mother, gave a clear testimony of her faith to onlookers before being baptized.

In September, members of the mission at Kiana walked down the bluff behind the building to the edge of the Kobuk River where Missionary Shield baptized two junior girls, Jennie Westlake and Sophie Stoney. A third service was held before freezeup, this time back at Kotzebue; the weather was decidedly cool with a stiff wind whipping the sound into choppy wavelets. The attendance was small and the service shorter than before, but two happy candidates, Velnita Tickett, an Eskimo, and Tim Shield, the missionary's youngest son, were immersed. Recently, as I visited the Shield family, we prayed sentence prayers of thanks at family devotions and when Tim's time came, he said, "Thank you, God, that I can live in Kotzebue and don't have to live down in some big, old, crowded city. Amen."

The Home Mission Board sent Alaska's first US-2 couple, Norman and Gunita Harrell, to serve in the Arctic villages in 1966. They lived in Kobuk, population sixty-four, and went once a week by dog sled, boat, or bush plane to Shungnak where they helped build a mission building. The month before they returned to Ft. Worth to resume their seminary studies, they baptized twelve Eskimos at Shungnak and eight at Kobuk. In the August 1966

Ambassador Life, Norman told what living conditions in an Eskimo village was like for them:

> What is it like to live in Kobuk, Alaska? . . . There are no telephones, no TV's, no drugstores or shopping centers or street lights or running water (we get it from the river), no movie houses or cars or hospitals, dentists, doctors, or city garbage collectors, no cleaners, no laundromats, and no dozens of other things you take for granted even in the smallest towns in the Lower 48.
>
> As you can see, we soon discovered that we had been spoiled by city life. At first it was a shock, changing to this rugged sort of life.
>
> For example, I had never chopped wood before; suddenly I found myself driving a dog team into the timber to chop down a tree or two (get that!) for the church stove—and in 40° below zero weather too.
>
> But the more we packed water, cooked on a Coleman stove, and washed clothes on a rubboard, the less we "hated" doing these things. Now—and this seems amazing, I'm sure—we take these things for granted. . . .
>
> What has happened, how we have changed personally, has been the most important thing about coming to Alaska. It seems as if we, here in the cold, hard Alaskan wilderness, have been forced to live closer to God. We have had to depend more and more upon him. . . . We wish everyone had a opportunity to serve in Alaska, especially in the bush areas.[18]

Once while hunting for the water hole he had cut in the ice, Norman slipped into the icy river water. Another time after he had fired up the wood stove in the apartment at the back of the log mission building, he noticed butter dripping from the shelves above the stove and freezing on the floor like a weird, upside down icicle. Eskimo friends explained to him that he should have insulated the floor as well as the walls and ceiling of the house. When the Harrells left Kobuk to enroll at Southwestern Seminary, they said, "We haven't been to Jerusalem or Judea or Samaria, but we feel as if we have been to the uttermost part of the earth. We'd like to go back."

*   *   *

On July 27, 1969, the North Star Baptist Church of Clear, Alaska, voted to sponsor the Point Barrow Baptist mission. A fellowship representing fifteen families met in the Barrow home of Joe Upickson, an Eskimo layman, for the first service. Gene

Mockerman traveled to the historic trading center, located five hundred and fifty miles north of Fairbanks, for the service. The 1,600 residents of the community experience three months without sun in winter, and eighty-two days in summer when it doesn't set. The community is without water, sewers, or sidewalks, but a hospital, schools, and the Arctic Research Laboratory are located there. Guest preachers have flown in to preach for the mission. Point Barrow became well-known when Will Rogers and Wiley Post died in a plane crash nearby.

"The vise-like grip of winter gradually tightens her tenacious hold on the Alaska interior during November. While temperatures plunge below zero in Fairbanks, the city of Ketchikan, known as the gateway to Alaska, still enjoys a mild Pacific Coast forty-seven degrees. Eerie fog lightly glazes the bending birch; green spruce trees, heavily laden with fresh fallen snow, sparkle with full Christmas-like splendor; a bright red sun reluctantly yields her brief winter journey over Alaska to the billowing clouds with a blazing raspberry sunset. Though its glory is sometimes marred by bended bumpers and folded fenders, Alaska is still a challenging place of service for the young at heart," thus E. W. Hunke philosophized during his first winter in Alaska.

Allen Meeks is one of the youngest-hearted persons I know. Allen became secretary of religious education for the Alaska convention in 1964. He had already spent three years in Alaska as educational director at Anchorage First Baptist Church before coming again from Arkansas to serve in the new position. He is always interested in new promotional ideas, but says he has never beaten what Aubrey Halsell came up with down in Arkansas.

Back in Aubrey's early college years at Ouachita, he pastored a small church in Rison, Arkansas. One summer he had a tent meeting. Even back then Aubrey had a reputation for getting things going, and sometimes his methods wouldn't have gotten the Nashville seal of approval. The highlight of this particular revival was his publicity. He mounted a loud speaker on top of his car and drove up and down the streets of Rison, that quiet little rural town, hollering, "Fire, fire!" All the people rushed out on their porches to see what the commotion was about, and when he had a big enough crowd gathered, Aubrey would bellow, "Hell's a-burning! Come to the tent meeting and hear all about it."

Allen and his wife Ruth are well loved over the state. They lead conferences of all kinds constantly, and always make people feel glad they came because of their jolly laughter and radiant personalities.

At the state convention in 1967, which was rescheduled for November 7-8 in Anchorage after the Fairbanks flood, the convention accepted the Orton Ranch property given by Marion Dunham and the deed to the twenty acre plot on Seward Highway from the Home Mission Board.

Other important action at that time included providing for the employment of a state missions secretary in the 1968 budget and increasing the state mission offering goal fifteen percent annually above receipts of the year before. The convention adopted an agreement between the state convention and Broadway Bonds, Inc., and set aside $10,000 as a guaranty fund for the Broadway Plan.

E. C. Chron surrendered to preach one Sunday, sold his used car business that week, and preached at Seward the next Sunday. After pastoring three churches and helping to initiate two others, Chron accepted the position of missions director for the Alaska convention in 1968. He serves also as missionary for the Chugach association. His decision to enter the ministry came while he served as Sunday school superintendent of Anchorage First Baptist Church. His Cessna 180 has greatly aided the mission program throughout the state. Last fall when I accompanied him and my husband on a survey trip, I got a new perspective of Alaska. We flew over towns that testified to a century's neglect, through canyons where the light was sharp enough to give their ragged borders outlines, over autumn foliage with colors rich enough to taste, and going toward the Arctic, we saw the first black blasts of winter poised over the mountains waiting for the right mood to sweep down.

Judy Rice was elected W.M.U. secretary late in 1968. Judy served twice as summer missionary in the Northwest, then as a US-2 worker in Portland, Oregon, where she participated in teaching kindergarten, and assisted in all the W.M.U. work of the state. Judy can eat more ice cream at one sitting than anybody else. She has become proficient at riding the runners of dog sleds in the Arctic, and even managed to stay on the runners behind a snow-machine when it was a matter of stay on or perish. Once she and

Valeria Sherard were the only passengers on an Arctic flight, except for a load of frozen caribou carcasses which were stacked tightly in every available spot. Soon after the plane took off, the caribou began to thaw and drip. The girls were kept busy trying to dodge the trickles of blood that began etching the floor. Judy said the worst thing was that the eyeballs thawed and began rolling around in the sockets, staring at her from all directions.

Baptists in Alaska soon learn to accept conditions as they find them. If we go to Southeastern or bush out to the interior, we don't necessarily expect to get back on schedule. Jerry Craig from Anchorage Calvary took Dr. A. B. Rutledge, Home Mission Board executive secretary, to the airport to catch a plane to Kodiak during our World Missions Conferences in 1968. Jerry's size is exceeded only by his sense of humor, so on the way out he told Dr. Rutledge that during that time of year he was sure to get fogged in for weeks at Kodiak. He also told him about the outdated planes and the motors which were always going out. Dr. Rutledge found the information somewhat disquieting.

Sure enough, the next day we got a phone call from Dr. Rutledge. He announced that he was fogged in, and was calling Fred Mosely to conduct the next Home Mission Board meeting. The fog lifted, however, making it possible for Rutledge to return to Anchorage the next day in time to make the board meeting. But when his plane landed, we were startled to see all the firetrucks speeding out to the runway. It seems both Jerry's predictions had come true. An engine just outside Rutledge's window had sputtered out while they were flying over the Pacific Ocean. The plane missed its scheduled Homer stop and came on to Anchorage where emergency equipment was available.

Down in Southeastern Alaska where the rainfall is fourteen feet a year, they accuse us in Anchorage of having to sprinkle, especially since we are facing our second summer of drought. One pastor said he visited a Methodist service and saw them baptizing by passing around a moist washcloth; another said he visited a Presbyterian church and they just gave their candidates a promisory note. Our Seward pastor was accused of announcing on the bulletin board outside the church that the next Sunday's sermon would be "Skiing on the Sabbath," or "Are our young women backsliding on their weekends?"

Everyone in Alaska has stories to tell. Probably the most often heard stories are hunting sagas.

Visitors to Alaska always want to hunt or, at least, photograph black, brown, grizzly and polar bears; mountain sheep and goats; and see Siberian husky dogs, which are favorites all over the state. Fishing in rivers, lakes, and offshore waters for an abundance of trout and salmon remains on the "must" list for all who come. Observers have reported that twenty-eight thousand salmon per hour pass a given point on the Susitna River, and the annual run of silvers, kings, reds, and humpies is so regular, the fishing derbies are scheduled months in advance. At one of the very first annual state convention sessions an entry in the *Minutes* states: "Discussion relative to changing the time of the Convention the coming year so that the fishing season would not conflict with the dates of the Convention was carried on." The date was set to fall on the week following the second Sunday in August, just preceeding moose season and after good fishing was over.

Humorous experiences occur during hunting and fishing seasons. One Fairbanks officer was questioned at great length by a man as to the legal way to kill a grizzly bear. The man asked what to do after he shot the bear, how to take care of the hide, etc. The officer asked, "Where are you planning to hunt this bear?"

The man replied, "Well, I've got one in my cabin right now."

Another officer appeared in court one day after arresting one of the local go-go's for fishing without a license. She retorted that she hadn't been fishing—she was just washing her spinner. The judge fined her $50 for washing her spinner.

Hunting can be dangerous. One guide was helping a Hollywood cameraman, who wanted pictures of a bear tumbling over a cliff. He shot a female—by mistake—and they dragged her to a cliff. While the cameraman set up, the guide propped his rifle against a tree and sat on the old bear.

The cameraman got ready and looked up. But he didn't say anything—just stared. The guide turned just in time to see the female's mate not 15 feet away.

He dived for his gun and fired, hitting the bear just below the eye as it lunged. The bear fell, hit the female, and they both tumbled down the cliff. The photographer kept on staring. He never shot a frame.

Mrs. Aubrey Short has shared the following bear story that her husband liked to tell. Aubrey and Seth Moore left Fairbanks headed for big game country just at dark and drove for two hundred miles before setting up camp. They only met two cars and knew that the nearest habitation was the trapper cabin of an Indian forty miles away. Two moose and a white caribou appeared in their headlight, but the season for them was closed. When the sun came up at 3:25 A.M., they continued on another 120 miles along a chain of lakes to their destination. They hunted muskrats that day and did some exploring, finding that the snow was still knee-deep in places, causing some concern that perhaps they were too early for bear.

They headed for the upper lakes the next morning and saw moose and wolf tracks but no bear signs. After walking about four hours, they started down a mountain slope and in a place where the snow had melted away, they saw where something had scratched up the ground. Aubrey thought it had been a bear looking for grubs and tender roots, but they couldn't see a track plain enough to tell for sure. About forty feet away they found a mound about the size of a grave.

"I think that's where a wolf has buried a rabbit," Seth observed. Aubrey walked up on the mound and started kicking at it. A deep, vicious growl rolled out from almost directly underneath him. Both men levered a shell into their 30.06 rifles and waited. Nothing moved. After taking off their packs to be sure they had both hands free at all times, they began a cautious search of the area. Just about three feet to his right, Aubrey found a hole the size of a big barrel. The growl had come from the hole; they were standing right on top of a bear's den. The mound was the dirt she had piled up to keep the north wind out of the opening.

They had no way of knowing whether it was a black, a grizzly, or a Kodiak, or how many were in the hole. What if they missed a vital spot in their excitement? Never a year passes in Alaska without someone being killed by a bear. They walked off about a hundred yards to talk it over. If one man were crippled, the other would face the impossible task of carrying him four miles back to camp over the roughest terrain imaginable. To leave a crippled man while one went back would mean abandoning him to the wolves. They considered leaving it alone, but couldn't see doing that because they hadn't meant to just hunt until they found a bear, and then walk away and leave it.

They finally decided to move up close to the hole and stare straight into it until their eyes got used to the change from the glare of the snow to the darkness of the den to see if they could tell what was in it. After about two minutes in this position, Seth said, "It's a black wolverine. I can see its foot."

He was about to shoot when Aubrey saw something move down that seemed to come from above the animal that was visible. "Wait, Seth," he hissed. "I see a nose the size of a cow's. That bear must be as big as a mule."

Not more than three inches of the nose came into sight. It soon became apparent that they would have to shoot down through the nose, which wouldn't be a killing shot. Aubrey decided that Seth should be the one to shoot her through the nose. "Don't worry," he promised. "When she comes out, I'll let her have it."

Seth raised his gun. It seemed as though he aimed for ten minutes. At last he squeezed off the trigger. Simultaneously with the report of the gun came a tremendous growl and sticks and leaves came flying out of the hole. The old she-bear was coming out with her mouth wide open. He had hit her in the top of the nose; the bullet had broken her lower jaw and killed the cub, lodging in its left front paw. Without further ado, Aubrey shot the sow in the mouth with a 30.06 Silvertip with 220 grains of powder behind it. She quivered a bit, then relaxed and fell over dead.

After some minutes of pulling and hauling, they succeeded in dragging her out of the den and began skinning her out. It took them two hours to finish the job. Aubrey's bullet had gone all the way through her length-wise and lodged under the skin in her hip. Putting the skin in Aubrey's pack, they started back to camp, loaded up and were back in Fairbanks just after midnight.

The bear was a black that would weigh about 400 pounds, probably having lost some 150 pounds since holing up for the winter. The taxidermist said it was the prettiest coat he had gotten that year. That was because they got her before she had time to rub off any of it. The cub was the size of a house cat. Aubrey hoped to be able to get a grizzly and a Kodiak, but hoped for no more excitement than this hunt had provided.

L.A. Watson got his black bear, whose skin adorns one dining room wall of his home, during a revival in Valdez. Watson reported, "The revival did not turn out so well, but the bear hunting was fine." He and Mr. Hardesty decided to go out on Monday and just look around since bears were reported to be thick in the area. Watson took his hunting clothes and gun and skinning knife along, "just in case." They saw a bear beside the road and the decision was that Watson should get out of the car and shoot it. He said, "I got him the first time, but when I started shooting, I got trigger happy and unloaded my gun before stopping. If someone had come along and seen me in my preaching clothes—tie, pocket handkerchief, and all, dragging that bear out to the car, he would have thought I was crazy. To me, the clothes mattered little; the bear was the main object."

Mrs. Max Hively, a member of Ketchikan Baptist Church, told this bear story. Loud, persistent barks from the family dog, which she had just let out of the house about 7:00 A.M., caused her to go outside her apartment to try to prevent the dog's disturbing sleeping neighbors. Just as she started around the corner of the house, she saw a black bear about three feet from the back door, sniffing at the garbage can. She reported, "My return to the front of the house was somewhat swifter than my exit had been." As to what became of the bear, she couldn't say. Everyone was afraid to look out the window for fear of seeing it.

Everyone has a bear story; the following was related by E. W. Hunke: "We couldn't understand why the cow moose didn't run. She appeared to be a statue beside the road. A vicious look, stomping feet, and a snort rewarded my effort to step out of the car to take her picture. A tiny calf lay at her feet. We thought it was newly born until a patiently waiting huge black bear moved slowly back into dense, shadowed forest. A ring of blood and saliva on the back of the baby moose marked its wound from the bear's teeth. As mother moose trotted nervously a few steps, a second calf that had been concealed in the bushes joined her. When they crossed over to the other side of the road, another would-be good Samaritan who had stopped, helped me lift the wounded calf into his campwagon. We hoped that a game warden might be able to save its life."

Felton Griffin can tell hunting stories for hours on end. The following are two of his favorites.

No one likes to talk about his plane accidents; they usually come about because the pilot does the wrong thing or is in the wrong mood, and it's a bit embarrassing. One plane I tore up was just that. I was out hunting moose with a friend of mine. I had put him out on four or five moose already, but every time he walked into the woods, he got lost and never could find his way to the moose. I'd circle over the moose so he could go up and shoot it, but he couldn't seem to make it.

Finally, I put him out on three big old bull moose and told him again, "Friend, I'll fly straight to them after you get out. Come to where I'm circling and you can't miss them." I flew and I circled, flew and circled for nearly an hour, and when I spotted him, he had walked past one of those bull moose. He wasn't more than a hundred feet from it; the moose was looking straight at him, shaking its head. He had his back to the moose and was standing up on a little knoll with his gun lying on the ground at his feet. He was waving me off, giving the signal we had agreed on, "I can't find the moose."

I thought, "Great heavenly days, man, you can smell him from there." I decided to show him the moose was really there, so I wheeled my little plane around, dipped the tip of the wing right over the moose, pulled it in a tight circle—and that's where I made my mistake. I pulled it too tight. Any pilot knows what happened then. When a plane stalls out in a turn like that, it goes over on its back and heads straight for the ground—which that one did. I was pulling and heaving on the stick, and by the grace of God, it straightened out just before I went into a big alder thicket that cushioned my fall and probably saved my life. The plane was totaled out, but I wasn't even dazed. The only damage was that I broke my glasses and cut my cheek a little. When the plane stopped, it was on fire; the cap of the gas tank had jarred off and fire was shooting out into the cabin and out from under the cowling. If I had been even a little addled, I would have burned. I kicked the door open and grabbed for my little fire extinguisher, but it had broken loose. I looked around, got my gun and my friend's camera, then found the fire extinguisher and was able to get the fire out and save all our camping gear. I guess God had a few more sermons he wanted me to preach, and that's the only reason I'm still alive.

Everywhere I go, people want to know if I ever shot a bear. Well, I've seen bears, I've shot bears, I've heard a lot of bear stories, but the best one I ever heard didn't happen to me. It happened to two lawyer friends of mine, who one summer day were out at a lake in their cabin. One of them was lying on a bunk and at his side was a thirty caliber automatic carbine. The other was at a table by a small window, sitting with his shirt off because the cabin was warm and stuffy. A garbage can was sitting right by the open door of the cabin. The one who was sitting by the table was a hairy man; he looked almost like a bear himself in the semi-darkness of the cabin.

My friend on the bunk related that the first thing he knew he was awakened by hearing the other man talking. He said he looked up and there was a bear eating out of the garbage can.

"Go ahead and help yourself; we didn't want any of that stuff anyway. It's just garbage," went the one-sided conversation his friend was carrying on with the bear.

The man on the bunk was a little startled by the situation, but the bear wasn't. Soon the bear looked in the door. Up in the middle of the table was a big bowl of meat balls and spaghetti they had prepared for their supper. The other, hairy chested man was sitting across the table from the bear. It walked on into the cabin, up to the table, and reared up on its hind legs.

"Don't you put your dirty old paw in that. That's our supper, and if you reach out there to take that, you're going to pull back a nub," the man in the chair warned the bear. And the bear backed off. But he came back up and reared up again. A big jungle knife was hanging on the wall, so the fellow reached up and grabbed it down.

"I'm not kidding you. If you reach out for our supper, I'm going to hack your paw right off." The old bear dropped back down on the floor, walked back to the garbage can and on outside the door.

Meanwhile, the man on the bunk had eased up the carbine, which had a full magazine in it, just in case the bear jumped his friend. He said when the bear went on outside, he jumped up and ran to the door, and there the bear stood about ten feet away. His friend yelled, "Now don't you come back again!"

The bear looked around and made a lunge for the man standing in the door. He emptied the carbine into the bear and dropped him right on the threshold.

I have every reason to believe the story is true because the man who was talking to the bear has served as the chief justice of the state supreme court for many years now, and the other man is a lawyer who wouldn't dare perjure himself in the presence of a Baptist preacher.

According to Marion Dunham, the greatest need Baptists have now in southeastern Alaska is a boat ministry. "There is no possible way to get into these villages, camps, or beachhomes other than by boat," he stated. Flying is too expensive, and when a preacher goes out by himself, he can't take anything along. A boat could float in and tie up for several days and have a conference-type ministry during the daytime and worship and evangelistic services at night. After three to five years, the loggers finish cutting the timber and move on thirty or forty miles up the channel. The ministry would need to be able to move with them; a chapel would not be practical, but a boat would.

When I visited the Ketchikan church one night in May 1969, two of the families I met talked about the need for the boat ministry. The Aikins, Allen and Ann, both graduates of Baylor University, had lived in Ketchikan about four months before he was sent out to the boondocks as a forest ranger. They were at the Davidson Logging Camp at North Whale Pass. While they were there, Marion Dunham flew up many times to have services for them. They located another Baptist family and were able to get others to come to their home for a home Bible fellowship meeting. They had just moved back to Ketchikan, and though they were happy about coming back to town, they were concerned for the families out of the reach of the gospel.

I overheard another couple asking E. C. Chron for some home Bible fellowship materials. I introduced myself to them, the Harold Newmans, and found that they had bought a place in Elfin Cove across from Glacier Bay. Last winter they put in a foundation and oil tanks and hope to have a comfortable home by next winter. All summer they live on their boat and make their living as commercial fishermen. They had been Methodists, but began coming to the Baptist church in Ketchikan and liked the way the gospel was preached there. They asked Pastor Dunham about joining, and he told them not to be in a hurry, but when they couldn't stay out any longer, to come on. About a year later they came forward for baptism. They are eager to witness to the isolated community where they make their winter home. On the floor of the Dunham's living room lies "Mr. Brown," a brown bear skin given by Mr. Newman to his pastor.

We traveled down to Ketchikan on the *Malaspina*, one of the beautiful ferries that plies the Inland Passage. Ken Florian, captain of the *Malaspina*, is a dedicated Christian. He holds services in the lounge where our state board met while we were passengers on his boat. Another Ketchikan Christian who owns a big boat is Leland Daniel. It took some hard praying to get Leland started to church, but finally he began to come once in a while when he was home. He was a good man, a rugged individualist, but not a Christian. The first serious conversation Leland engaged in at the church had to do with tithing. He felt that if he accepted the Lord, he would have to start tithing, and he seemed to be fighting that even more than becoming a Christian. For several Sundays he stayed after church and argued with Mrs. Dunham about it.

A few weeks afterwards, Leland was towing a barge with his big ship, named *The Christian* after his conversion, when a storm came up with about a forty mile per hour wind. The barge went between two reefs into a little bay. He got into the bay, got a line on the barge, and tried to bring it back through, but his ship got caught on the reef. The propeller and gear box locked. Because he couldn't steer the boat at all, he got quite excited, but remembered to throw it out of gear immediately. He fell down on his knees and prayed, "Lord, if you'll save me and my ship, I'll accept Jesus as my Savior and start tithing."

When he went back to try again to steer the ship off the reef, the wheel was loose, the ship was floating free, and he was able to put it in gear and get the barge out unhurt. He knew something had been damaged, so came back into town instead of proceeding on to Prince Wales Island. When he put the ship on the ways and looked it over, it didn't seem to be in bad shape, but when he opened the gear box, he found that several teeth had been sheared off. If he hadn't thrown it out of gear the instant he had, he would have lost everything. There were just enough teeth left to catch and allow him to get back. He made a profession of faith before the church and was baptized, but it was a long time afterwards that he told the whole story to Pastor Dunham.

Another boat ministry that has been carried on in Southeastern Alaska is that of Captain Stabbert and the *Willis Shank*. Stabbert grew up in Texas and his wife in Oregon; both had been active members of Baptist churches. Following the war they moved out to the west coast where they met a devoted Christian man who felt called to do mission work in Alaska. His name was Willis Shank; his desire was to have a great boat and to visit and minister to the islands and villages in southeastern Alaska.

The night before Willis Shank left the Seattle area to come to Alaska to begin his work, he stayed in the Stabbert home. The next day before his plane reached Annette Island, it crashed into the big mountain near there and Shank was killed. Stabbert was not a preacher. He was a construction worker, but the next few months after his friend's death, he had such a compelling burden on his heart to carry on the work that Willis Shank had dreamed of that he finally began trying to find a big boat to buy himself. He located an old minesweeper left over from the war and rebuilt it into a hospital ship. He interested a group of Christian businessmen in providing some financial help for the venture. Then he picked up a load of dentists and doctors who volunteered their services for the chance to go to Alaska, and brought them up to the Indian villages and lumber camps to meet the physical needs of people.

About three years later the government began sending health services up into that part of the territory, more or less eliminating the need for Stabbert's hospital ship. He decided to revamp his ship and his program. He began to appeal to the colleges across the country to send him their best young people. He said that if any one of these Christian young people could raise $150 for his food, he would take him aboard for the summer and carry him to work on mission projects along the coast of Alaska. The young people responded to the opportunity. Stabbert would first bring the whole group to Ketchikan with orientation all the way up from Seattle. Then he'd drop off half a dozen of them at Metlakatla and another group at Klawok and take some more on to Craig, and so on. They'd have Vacation Bible Schools and do visitation, then he'd pick them all up and take them on to new areas. They spent the whole summer that way.

Marion Dunham tells of his contact with Captain Stabbert and the boat he called the *Willis Shank:*

> It was during the summer of 1961 when we had just gotten Orton Ranch and were back in there cleaning it up that Captain Stabbert brought in that big 140 foot ship. His young people were hiking around the trail. I'd met Stabbert the summer before, just in passing, but this time he stopped to talk quite a long while. He asked us what our program was at the ranch and what we had planned all summer. He wanted to know if he could bring his entire crew in the next weekend to help clean up the ranch. We were happy to have them offer to help us, of course.
>
> But the following weekend, instead of bringing them, he called us from Annette Island and asked, "How would you like to have a ninety-six foot building on Orton Ranch? There's one available, and it won't cost you a thing."
>
> I told him we wanted it, but how about getting it out there and putting it up? He said, "You want it; we'll put it up for you." That building was up before the week was over. Those young people took that eighteen by sixty foot barge through the tide race at midnight when it crested at seventeen feet and the barge was high enough off the rocks to keep from dragging. The young people were lining the bank with long poles guiding it through while the tide was going in. The next day they took sections of it and ferried them up to the ranch in small boats.

As the years passed, Captain made a few more trips up in the summertime. He felt his heart and home were in Alaska. He wrote me that he was coming back on one more trip then taking his ship south, but he wanted to talk. When he arrived in town, I went down to meet him. I stayed so long that Mrs. Dunham got worried about me, but Captain Stabbert and his wife were really burdened and seeking God's will. He said, "We've been working in this inter-denominational work for so long; we wonder what good we've really done. The only thing we can point to is Orton Ranch and the building we put up out there. We've been thinking seriously about our church relationship and whether we ought to sail under a banner or stay inter-denominational."

I said, "You sound as if you're feeling a little guilty and condemned because you've just sort of freelanced it." They admitted that it was so, and they wanted to come back home again to a Baptist church.

"You shouldn't be ashamed of your banner; Baptists don't have a thing to be ashamed of. Whatever you do should be through churches instead of being outside," I went on.

They agreed and asked if they would be accepted as part of our church. I told them to try it and see. The next day Captain Stabbert and his students were to have charge of our worship service, and after the service ended, the two of them came forward on promise of letter from the Baptist church they had neglected so long. Following the service I talked to their youngest son Danny out in the vestibule. I asked him if he were a Christian. He said that he was, so I asked him if he had ever followed the Lord in baptism. He said no, but that he wanted to. I presented him to the church that night and asked them if they would authorize me to baptize him in the Naha River that Tuesday night because his parents had already gone out there to the ranch. Just before dark as the mist was coming down on the river, we had the group gather out under the old woodshed and I led Danny out and baptized him in the river in front of Orton Ranch. The Stabberts are still in that ministry and still members of our church. He's looking forward to being up this summer. He says he's ever so much happier to be identified with a local church. It makes it seem just like coming back home every time the *Willis Shank* docks in Ketchikan.

When Bill Hunke first arrived in Alaska, he felt limited in promoting a program of mission advance because the convention did not have a loan fund. Several months after he had shared his feeling about this need with the state executive board, Pastor Joe Patterson of the Juneau First Baptist Church reported that a woman had a small amount of money she wished to give to Baptist work. The gift was given to start the loan fund.

Dr. Noel Taylor of the Broadway Bond Corporation of Houston
came to present the convention-backed bond program to the state
board in August 1968. As soon as the convention approved and
entered the plan, an appropriation of $8,000 was made from un-
designated funds and added to the Juneau gift and the memorial
funds of Chuck Lollis, a serviceman from Anchorage Calvary
church killed in Southeast Asia. This became the Alaska Baptist
Loan Fund and also serves as the guarantee fund for the bond
plan.

The Kenai First Baptist Church has made two issues of the
convention-backed Broadway bonds. A portion of the issues was
added to the loan fund, with accrued interest. The fund was operated
by a committee of seven members named by the convention. The
executive board has recommended that the responsibility be assigned back to the board's finance committee because this committee meets regularly and can better administer these trust funds.

The work of Southern Baptists in Canada has long been on the
heart of executive secretary Hunke. A deacon from the White
Horse Baptist church has corresponded with the Alaska Baptist
state office each year requesting that Alaska Baptist pastors stop
by to visit in the church there during the summer months. One
year this deacon made a trip to Alaska and stopped by the convention office to seek to establish closer ties with Alaska Baptists.

During the annual secretaries' meetings in Nashville in December 1969, Dr. T. A. Patterson of Texas stopped Mr. Hunke in the
hotel lobby and asked if he had any interest in Baptist work in
Canada, then invited him to attend a meeting with a group of
other interested Baptists in a hotel room that night. Besides Hunke
and Patterson, the group included Dr. H. D. Bruce of Texas, William Eugene Grubbs, W. A. Carpenter, the associational missionary
working in Canada from the Oregon-Washington convention, the
director of the Fleming Foundation, and Ray Roberts of Ohio.

The needs of the Baptist work in Canada, the losses reported
by the two regular Canadian Baptists conventions, the burdens of
those present and others for the work in Canada, and the progress
of Southern Baptist work there were discussed.

The period of prayer, asking to be allowed to take Canada for
Christ, that ended the first meeting seemed like a haystack prayer
meeting experience to those involved. Because Alaska parallels

Canada along the Pacific Ocean, her responsibility for that great mission field is becoming a felt need among many Alaskan Baptists. The boundaries of Alaska Baptists may stretch even further in future years than they have in the past.

* * *

The greatest challenge of Alaska to Southern Baptists is not its wealth, but rather its poverty of spiritual things as reflected in the sweet faces of children, lonely faces of soldiers, rugged faces of old sourdoughs, determined faces of homesteaders, stoic faces of natives, despondent faces of women in wintertime—for these we pray.

Thousands of military personnel come here; separated from friends and far from home, they either indulge more freely in sin or serve the Savior more devotedly. The *Anchorage Daily News* for February 12, 1970, quoted chief of detectives Lt. Earl Hibpschman, "Last Tuesday night there were eighteen known prostitutes in plain sight on Fourth Avenue, Wednesday there were twenty, and Thursday there were forty-six." Anchorage has come a long way since the Alaska Railroad started a tent camp on Ship Creek mud in 1912 and since it boasted only one traffic light on Main Street in 1952. Now the original log cabins downtown squat at the base of tall office buildings, and the Eskimos loitering on Fourth Avenue mingle with wealthy socialites shopping for mink coats at exclusive furriers, but most of its people are here in a struggle for gold instead of God, just as were those who came to the Klondike in the last century.

Plans for Alaska's future sound fantastic. Tandy Industries have leased land across Knik Arm from the Matanuska-Susitna Borough for the development of a new city—Seward's Success—right across the bay from Anchorage. Construction is to begin this summer on the twenty-first century city, which will be climate controlled with shopping and other facilities within an enclosed mall-type area having a constant temperature of sixty-eight degrees. Seward's Success dwellers will be moved to and from their city by aerial tram in eight minutes to a parking garage on the Anchorage side of Cook Inlet. Tandy representatives say that these city dwellers will never be more than a third of a mile from where they want to be, and will be "the healthiest people in Alaska because they'll walk a lot." Southern Baptists have already been given a church site.

No one who visits Alaska can forget the series of soul-stirring experiences it provides. Even the streets, alive with whirling yellow leaves one day and white with a crisp crunching cover of new snow the next, speak more to the listening heart than just the crackling of the leaves or the squeaking of the snow. Crumpled slabs of thawing sea ice, valleys smothered by wintry clouds waiting for the young, thawing spring, teenagers in distant villages riding Hondas and wearing buttons which read "Eskimo Power" sound forth their message.

My most exciting moment watching Alaska's natural phenomena came when I first saw icebergs being calved by Columbia Glacier and hurled out to sea. Our ferry had gone in very close to the glacier's face, and the sea around us was a churning smother of emerald green milky froth and splintering ice. Suddenly an enormous jagged crack gaped across the face of weathered ice, widening into a black chasm as we stared. Then a section of the glacier, as huge and rough surfaced as a mountain craig, split slowly away, wavered, hung suspended, then plunged into the sea before us, leaving exposed a cavern of beautiful blue-green ice. Seconds later a thunderous roar reached our ears. Where the mass of ice plunged down, the water rose up in a towering wall, then spread outward with the speed of a tidal wave. Ice floes bobbed on the racing water, spinning, shattering, tossing at its crest as they hurtled forward. When the swelling wave hit our boat, it was lifted upward as by the hand of a mighty giant. Before we regained our balance, a roar like a salvo of cannon-fire let us know that another chunk of ice had broken away.

As I thought of the tremendous power at work releasing whole ridges of ice from the face of that palisade of glistening whiteness standing seamed and veined with its fissures and crevasses, faces with lines of sin etched deeply flashed into my consciousness. Southern Baptists must claim and grasp and harness the dynamo of God's almighty power and create a new kind of history for Alaska.

Appendix A

June 1879   Baptist mission work begun in Alaska by Mr. and Mrs. W. H. R. Corlies of Philadelphia. Emily Corlies was the daughter of the Josiah Goddards, missionaries of the Tri-ennial convention, who was born in Siam while her parents waited to enter China. In 1882 Mrs. Corlies opened the first school in Juneau; later they built a church at Taku Harbor where they worked with the Taku Indians.

1886   Two Baptist couples, the W. E. Roscoes of California, and the James Wirths of Washington, went to Kodiak and Afognak as teachers.

1893   Woman's Home Mission Society of the Northern Baptist Convention built an orphanage on Wood Island, two miles from Kodiak village.

1896   The Wood Island Baptist Church organized on June 26, the first Baptist church in Alaska. Led by Mr. C. P. Coe, Superintendent of the Wood Island Mission, the church began with five members.

1897   First Baptist chapel erected.

1938   Hilda Krause opened Baptist Nursing Home for tubercular children in Juneau.

1940   New church and parsonage begun at Kodiak after a navy base was developed there and the village of 500 grew to a town of 2,500 in one year.

1941   Miss Frances Black, first Southern Baptist worker, arrived in Juneau.

1941   Baptist services begun in their home on Gastineau Avenue, Juneau, by Mr. and Mrs. W. P. Griffin, Missionary Baptists from Arkansas.

Jan. 1943   First Baptist Goodwill Center begun in Juneau by Miss Black.

Sept. 19, 1943   First Baptist Church, Anchorage, organized—first Southern Baptist Church in Alaska.

Sept. 17, 1944   First Southern Baptist service in Fairbanks conducted by C. O. Dunkin.

Nov. 24, 1944   First issue of *Alaska Baptist Messenger*, William Petty, editor.

March 27, 1946   Organizational meeting of Alaska Baptist Convention.

Aug. 22-23, 1946	First Annual Session of Alaska Baptist Convention.
July 12, 1947	C. O. Dunkin opened first Native Baptist Mission in Fairbanks.
August 1947	First employee of Alaska Baptist Convention, Odell Lene, appointed to raise funds from Texas churches.
August 1947	B. I. Carpenter first missionary appointed to Alaska, supported first by New Mexico convention, then in Dec. 2, 1948, by Home Mission Board, SBC.
August 1949	Organizational meeting of Alaska Baptist W.M.U. with Mrs. Felton Griffin first president.
1949	First children cared for by Mr. and Mrs. B. C. Evans in the Turnagain Children's Home.
1949	First simultaneous revival crusade in Alaska.
1949	First student summer mission program in Alaska.
Nov. 1949	Home Mission Board made its first gift to erect a Baptist church building in Alaska.
Sept. 10, 1950	Organization of first association in Alaska, Chugach Baptist Association.
Oct. 1950	First Territorial Week of Prayer for Missions observed.
1951	Southern Baptist Convention officially recognized Alaska Baptist Convention as an affiliate.
1951	Greater Friendship Baptist Church, Anchorage, first Negro congregation in Alaska and first to join ABC.
April 1953	First direct work with native people in Anchorage with the opening of the Native Mission.
1953	First Southern Baptist work in Arctic opened when Dick Miller went to Kotzebue.
Feb. 1955	First Evangelistic Conference and semi-annual executive board meeting at Calvary Baptist, Anchorage.
Jan. 11, 1956	L. A. Watson arrived as first full-time executive secretary. State Baptist office opened on Sixteenth Avenue.
1956	Charlie Sheldon of Kobuk first Eskimo to baptize converts.
1956	First Tentmaker Regular, J. Keith Blalock, arrived in Alaska.
1956	First Baptist Student Union work begun at University of Alaska.
1957	First Direct Missions Conference.
1957	First state W.M.U. executive secretary, Louise Yarbrough, employed.
1957	First Sunday School Convention.
1958	Willie and Martha Johnson first graduates of Native Training School; first Eskimo couple appointed by Home Mission Board.

1958	Mr. and Mrs. George Abdouch first donors to the Alaska Baptist Foundation.
1958	First Native Missions Conference.
1959	First organization of Pioneer 2000 Club.
1960	First Arctic Bible Conference at Kotzebue.
1960	Jerrie Bushnell received first Y.W.A. Citation.
1960	First Standard Sunday school in Alaska, Calvary Baptist, Anchorage.
1961	First graduation of the Alaska Baptist College Seminary Center with Ed Strunk, Horace Hall, and Marcella McClure receiving certificates.
1961	First Stewardship Conference.
1961	Irene Kalerak of Anchorage first Eskimo crowned G. A. Queen.
1965	Mr. and Mrs. Ted Twinley first persons in Alaska to receive special citation diploma in church study course.
1965	Leo Josey first Negro pastor whose church received Home Mission Board supplement.
March 20, 1967	Don Wright first missionary pastor pilot project.
Aug. 16, 1967	First use of Home Mission Board Disaster Fund for Fairbanks flood relief.
Nov. 1967	First rescheduled state convention.
1968	First convention-backed Broadway Bond issue by Kenai First Baptist Church.
May 20, 1969	First Special Session of the state convention for purpose of revising constitution.
1969	First state Y.W.A. retreat.

Appendix B

HISTORICAL TABLE I

Session	Date	Place	Annual Sermon
Org.	Mar. 27-28, 1946	Anchorage, 1st	J. T. Spurlin
1st	Aug. 22-23, 1946	Fairbanks, 1st	Felton Griffin
2nd	Aug. 30-31, 1947	Juneau, 1st	Orland R. Cary
3rd	Sept. 8-9, 1948	Anchorage, 1st	Orland R. Cary
4th	Aug. 24-25, 1949	Fairbanks, 1st	Horace F. Burns
5th	Aug. 15-17, 1950	Anchorage, Calvary	Odell Lene
6th	Aug. 14-16, 1951	Kodiak, Community	B. I. Carpenter
7th	Jul. 29-31, 1952	Ketchikan, 1st	Orland R. Cary
8th	Sept. 22-24, 1953	Fairbanks, 1st	Dan Tyson
9th	Aug. 17-19, 1954	Juneau, 1st	John C. Denton
10th	Aug. 23-25, 1955	Valdez, 1st	Michael L. McKay
11th	Aug. 7-8, 1956	Spenard, Faith	James H. Rose
12th	Aug. 13-15, 1957	Anchorage, 1st	Richard A. Miller
13th	Aug. 12-14, 1958	Anchorage, Calvary	Felton Griffin
14th	Aug. 11-13, 1959	Sitka, First	Carl Elder
15th	Oct. 23-27, 1960	Fairbanks, 1st	John Jeffcoat
16th	Oct. 24-26, 1961	Spenard, Faith	James E. Akin
17th	Aug. 14-16, 1962	Valdez, 1st	S. W. Driggers
18th	Aug. 13-15, 1963	Anchorage, 1st	Felton Griffin
19th	Aug. 13-14, 1964	Ketchikan, 1st	Michael L. McKay
20th	Aug. 10-12, 1965	College, University	John Canning
21st	Aug. 16-18, 1966	Anch., Muldoon Rd.	Edward E. Wolfe
22nd	Nov. 7-8, 1967	Anchorage, 1st	Virgil A. Chron
23rd	Aug. 13-15, 1968	Fairbanks, 1st	Harley Shield
24th	Aug. 12-14, 1969	Sitka, First	James E. Akin
25th	Aug. 11-13, 1970	Anchorage, 1st	Felton Griffin

HISTORICAL TABLE II

Year	President	Vice-Pres.	Recording Sect.	Executive Sect.
1946	Felton Griffin	Odell Lene	C. O. Dunkin	Felton Griffin
1946	J. T. Spurlin	Odell Lene	C. O. Dunkin	Felton Griffin
1947	J. T. Spurlin	Odell Lene	Orland Cary	Felton Griffin
1948	J. T. Spurlin	Felton Griffin	Helen Carpenter	B. Clarence Evans
1949	Felton Griffin	Orland Cary	W. A. Petty	B. Clarence Evans
1950	Jimmy Bolton	Orland Cary	Jane Chandler	W. F. Lewis
1951	Jimmy Bolton	Felton Griffin	Ruth Woods	Russell Simmons
1952	Felton Griffin	Orland Cary	John DeFoore	Russell Simmons
1953	Orland Cary	Velton Walker	Avery Richey	Russell Simmons
1954	Dan P. Tyson	Avery Richey	Georgia Simmons	Russell Simmons
1955	John DeFoore	John Dickerson	Georgia Simmons	Russell Simmons
1956	B. I. Carpenter	John Dickerson	Georgia Simmons	L. A. Watson
1957	B. I. Carpenter	James H. Rose	Georgia Simmons	L. A. Watson
1958	E. E. Evans	Harry Borah	Georgia Simmons	L. A. Watson
1959	Felton Griffin	O. W. Marson	Beth Davis	L. A. Watson
1960	Carl Elder	Jack Turner	Beth Davis	L. A. Watson
1961	Bill Parson	James Dotson	Beth Davis	L. A. Watson
1962	James Dotson	John Jeffcoat	James Henderson	L. A. Watson
1963	John Jeffcoat	W. H. Hansen	Francis Sutherlin	W. H. Hansen
1964	Aubrey Short	James Whisenhant	John Camp	W. H. Hansen
1965	James Whisenhant	John Canning	Bernice Gillespie	W. H. Hansen
1966	John Canning	O. W. Marson	Bernice Gillespie	E. W. Hunke, Jr.
1967	O. W. Marson	Edward Wolfe	Bernice Gillespie	E. W. Hunke, Jr.
1968	Edward Wolfe	Roy Moore	Milly McConnell	E. W. Hunke, Jr.
1969	Edward Wolfe	Bill Duncan	Milly McConnell	E. W. Hunke, Jr.
1970	Bill Duncan	Richard Miller	Milly McConnell	E. W. Hunke, Jr.

Appendix C

CHUGACH BAPTIST ASSOCIATION

neal + navey attend

CALVARY BAPTIST CHURCH, Anchorage: Odell Lene, Arthur Hinson, John N. DeFoore, Jack Turner, John Canning, William H. Hansen.

EAST THIRD BAPTIST MISSION, Anchorage: Thomas H. Miller, Michael L. McKay.

FAIRVIEW BAPTIST CHURCH, Anchorage: Velton Walker, J. C. Denton, Ray Hustead°, Ed Thompson°, Robert Gingrich, Lee Hillon, Robert Branson, Ray Hustead, Frank Bullock.   *Bell + Battair Paston once*

FAITH BAPTIST CHURCH, Anchorage: B. Clarence Evans, H. E. Allison, Fred Chapman, Marvin Lytle, James B. Dotson, J. Aubrey Short, Ben D. Windham, J. Richard Perkins, Edward E. Wolfe, Roy O. Young°.

FIRST BAPTIST CHURCH, Anchorage: Aubrey Halsell, Carl C. DeMott°, William A. Petty, Felton H. Griffin.

FIRST BAPTIST CHURCH, Birchwood: Frank L. Miller, C. E. Stites, George W. Kesterman, Robert L. Chadwick.

FIRST BAPTIST CHURCH, Butte: John L. Booth, Delbert Burnett, Tommy Pitman, Charles Crutchfield.

FIRST BAPTIST CHURCH, Eagle River: James Vanderford, Marcus F. Price, E. C. Chron, James A. Henderson, John P. Camp, Jr., E. C. Chron, E. W. Hunke, Jr.°, Rawls Pierce.

FIRST BAPTIST CHURCH, Palmer: E. N. Sullivan, Michael L. McKay, Charles LeClair, Avery Richey, John T. Dickerson, Clifford S. Mc-Connell, John T. Dickerson, Lee Hillon, Don Smith, James E. Akin.

FIRST BAPTIST CHURCH, Valdez: James H. Rose, J. W. T. Stewart, William H. Hansen, James H. Rose, Frank C. Sisson, Lester Bonner, Leonard Everman.

GRANDVIEW BAPTIST CHURCH, Anchorage: Forest W. Carter, Edward Evans, C. H. Terwilliger, Richard C. Copeland, W. T. Carlson, Roy L. Grove, Clifford S. McConnell.

GREATER FRIENDSHIP BAPTIST CHURCH, Anchorage: Charles Kennedy, Clarence Belton, M. L. Lewis, O. R. Pigford, Leo A. Josey, Sr., H. K. Griffin.

IMMANUEL BAPTIST CHURCH, Anchorage: Charles H. Thurmond, James H. Rose, Charles H. Thurmond, Samuel Ganaway, Frank R. Burger, Johnny Newton, Wesley Pruitt.

JEWEL LAKE BAPTIST CHURCH, Anchorage: E. W. Hunke, Jr.*, Glenn Huisinga, R. J. McMillan.

KING SALMON BAPTIST MISSION, King Salmon: Donald J. Rollins.

MULDOON ROAD BAPTIST CHURCH, Anchorage: Virgil A. Chron.

NEW HOPE BAPTIST CHURCH, Anchorage: Ernest Smith, Boyd L. Rodgers, William B. Lyons.

SUNSET HILLS BAPTIST CHURCH, Anchorage: Roy O. Young, E. W. Hunke, Jr.*, Thomas Kilpatrick.

TRINITY BAPTIST CHURCH, Anchorage: Wyatt Flowers, James E. Akin, John O. Jeffcoat, Donald E. Wright, E. C. Chron, Tommy Pitman*, Dupre Gowan.

UNIVERSITY BAPTIST CHURCH, Anchorage: Ernest A. Ragland, A. C. Maxwell, Richard Lunsford, Gus Hayworth, George Wilkinson, E. W. Hunke, Jr.*, Keith Foster.

TANANA VALLEY BAPTIST ASSOCIATION

CALVARY BAPTIST CHURCH, Fairbanks: John T. Thomas, Bill Parsons, Alfred Richards, John O. Jeffcoat, Eldridge L. Miller, I. V. Walker.

EIELSON PARK BAPTIST CHURCH, Eielson Park: George Wilkinson, John T. Dickerson, Joe Fallon, Billy Caine, *Keith + Rachel Were members there*

FIRST BAPTIST CHURCH, Delta Junction: Paul Hilty, Richard A. Miller*, Donald R. Davis*, Lloyd Elder*, William Kuykendall, James Samples, James E. Akin, Louis M. Belcher, Harold H. Rhodes, Huel L. Waddell. *their Pastor*

FIRST BAPTIST CHURCH, Fairbanks: C. O. Dunkin, O. R. Cary, Donald R. Davis, Oliver Marson, Donald R. Davis.

FIRST BAPTIST CHURCH, North Pole: Hunter Rentz, Al Wendt, Carl A. Smith, Philip Tilden, Carl Elder, H. A. Zimmerman, William W. Phymes, Larry Ragland, Charles Brown, Jerry Lloyd Brown, Mack L. Roye, Donald E. Blankenship, O. L. Hibpshman, Frank Miller, Bill G. Duncan.

FORT YUKON BAPTIST MISSION, Ft. Yukon: Robert Craun, Oliver Marson, Donald J. Rollins, Brad Hughes*, Shirley Korte, J. D. Back.

FRIENDSHIP BAPTIST MISSION, Fairbanks: C. O. Dunkin, O. R. Cary*, Richard A. Miller*, John T. Dickerson, John O. Jeffcoat, John Isaacs.

HAMILTON ACRES BAPTIST CHURCH, Fairbanks: Carl A. Smith, John Smith, Carl Elder, J. Aubrey Short, William H. Hansen, Robert Buchanan, Edward E. Wolfe, Bill G. Duncan, Hugh Hamilton.

NORTH STAR BAPTIST CHURCH, Clear: Jerry Jarrell*, Billy Caine, Eugene Mockerman.

SALCHA BAPTIST CHURCH, Salcha: Bill Wyser*, Robert W. Paquette, Ray E. Penfield, Rayburn P. Moore, John T. Thomas, Keith Foster, Rayburn P. Moore.

ST. JOHN BAPTIST CHURCH, Fairbanks: Robert Jackson, Charles Alston, S. L. Banks, H. M. McCowen, James A. Hill, Robert J. Seals, David Thomas.

TOK BAPTIST MISSION, Tok: James E. Akin, John Dillman*, Bill Baxter.

Keith Pastor

University Baptist Church, College: John T. Dickerson, J. T. Burdine, E. L. Baker.

TONGASS BAPTIST ASSOCIATION

Annette Baptist Mission, Annette: Charles Boyer, Donald E. Wright, James Dan Hill.

First Baptist Church, Juneau: J. T. Spurlin, L. L. Richardson, Jimmy Bolton, Oliver Marson, Bryant Osborn, A. A. Palmer, S. W. Driggers, Richard H. Moore, Joe H. Patterson, E. W. Hunke, Jr.°, Hollis V. Bryant.

First Baptist Church, Ketchikan: B. I. Carpenter, Dan Tyson, Harry Borah, Marion B. Dunham.

First Baptist Mission, Petersburg: Donald E. Wright.

First Baptist Church, Sitka: Leroy Stringfield, Dale Proctor, James Samples, Richard A. Miller, William Neal Baker.

Glacier Valley Baptist Church, Juneau: Frank Lescallette, Robert Edward Owens, Stanley A. File, Olyn F. Roberts.

TUSTUMENA BAPTIST ASSOCIATION

Faith Baptist Mission, North Kenai: Roy L. Moore.

First Baptist Church, Kenai: George Johnson, James H. Rose, Tommy Kelly Dickson.

First Baptist Church, Seward: B. I. Carpenter, A. C. Maxwell, James E. Akin, T. W. Craighead, Frank Bullock, E. W. Hunke, Jr.°, James H. Rose, Joe Fallon.

First Baptist Church, Soldotna: Maurice Murdock, W. E. Midkiff.

Frontier Southern Baptist Church, Kodiak: E. W. Hunke, Jr.°, Ray Hustead.

ARCTIC BAPTIST MISSION (ESKIMO)

Emmonak Baptist Mission, Emmonak: Richard A. Miller, Harry Wilde, Willie Johnson.

Kiana Baptist Mission, Kiana: Richard A. Miller, Roy Brentlinger, John T. Thomas, Valeria Sherard.

Kobuk Baptist Mission, Kobuk: Richard A. Miller, Charlie Sheldon, Roy Brentlinger, Norman Harrell, Mike Brown.

Kotzebue First Baptist Church, Kotzebue: Richard A. Miller, John T. Thomas, Roy Brentlinger, John Klepac, Harley D. Shield.

Selawik Baptist Mission, Selawik: Richard A. Miller, Valeria Sherard, Willie Johnson, Shirley Korte.

Shungnak Baptist Mission, Shungnak: Norman Harrell, Mike Brown.

ARCTIC BAPTIST MISSION (INDIAN)

Chalkyitsik Baptist Mission, Chalkyitsik: Don Rollins, Brad Hughes°, Shirley Korte, J. D. Back.

Venetie Baptist Mission, Venetie: Don Rollins, Brad Hughes°, Shirley Korte, J. D. Back.

° Interim pastor.

Appendix D

CATEGORY	1949	1959	1969
Number of Churches	5	23	37
Additions by Baptism	181	452	788
Additions by Letter	276	991	1,455
Total Membership	857	4,860	10,479
Total Church Giving	$42,500	$272,130	$1,047,591
Total Gifts to Missions	$6,746	$40,700	$119,998
Church Property Value	$180,000	$1,526,525	$6,212,465
Sunday School Enrolment	638	4,133	7,773
Vacation Bible School	554	2,367	4,355
Training Union Enrolment	220	1,748	3,489
W. M. U. Enrolment	95	968	1,355
Brotherhood Enrolment	0	202	304

State Missions in Alaska. Pg. 310.

James Eastland appointed as missionary or Chaplain to the Pipeline ministry summer '7x this former air-force Chaplain had served in Alaska for 3 yrs.

References

1. C. Y. Dossey, "Crusading in Alaska," *Home Missions*, January, 1951, p. 8.
2. Mrs. J. B. Lawrence, "Alaska, a Land of Surprise," *Home Missions*, December, 1951, p. 11.
3. Dr. Courts Redford, "Baptists Are 'Flying High' in Alaska," *Home Missions*, August, 1953, p. 8.
4. Mrs. B. I. Carpenter, "Progress Is Keynote of Alaska Baptist Convention," *Home Missions*, December, 1953, pp. 11-13.
5. C. Y. Dossey, "Fifth Alaska Crusade," *Home Missions*, January, 1955, p. 26.
6. Dr. Wade H. Bryant, *Home Missions*, January, 1955.
7. Dr. J. T. Burdine, "Motorcycle Missionary," *Home Missions*, June, 1963.
8. Valeria Sherard, "We Get Letters," *Royal Service*, February, 1965, p. 13. Used by permission of Woman's Missionary Union, SBC.
9. Valeria Sherard, "We Get Letters," *Royal Service*, December, 1965, p. 11. Used by permission of Woman's Missionary Union, SBC.
10. Mrs. Helen Carpenter, "Meteorology—Religion Alaska," *Home Missions*, June, 1952, pp. 20-21.
11. Irene Berryman, "No Longer Average," *Home Missions*, March, 1953, pp. 8, 23.
12. Dallas M. Lee, "Grandma Tucker: Living a New Faith at 108," *Home Missions*, January, 1968.
13. Mrs. John Isaacs, "Uncle Tom Willock—Eskimo," *Home Missions*, August, 1961.
14. Kelvin Coventry, "The Man Who Bought Alaska," *Upward*, March 6, 1960. © Copyright 1960, The Sunday School Board of the Southern Baptist Convention. All rights reserved. Used by permission.
15. Mrs. B. I. Carpenter, "Bob Found Christ in Alaska," *Home Missions*, December, 1954, pp. 10-11.
16. *Home Missions*, May, 1964, p. 2.
17. *Denver Post*, April 5, 1964, p. 29A.
18. Norman Harrell, "On the Edge of the Arctic," *Ambassador Life*, August, 1966, pp. 14-15. Used by permission.